Administrative Reorganization of Mississippi Government/A Study in Politics

Thomas E. Kynerd

UNIVERSITY PRESS OF MISSISSIPPI / Jackson
1 9 7 8

This volume is authorized
and sponsored by the
University of Southern Mississippi
Hattiesburg, Mississippi

Library of Congress Cataloging in Publication Data

Kynerd, Thomas E
    Administrative reorganization of Mississippi
Government.

    Bibliography: p.
    Includes index.
    1. Mississippi—Politics and government.   I. Title.
JK4636.K96   353.9′762   77-8799
ISBN 0-87805-038-8

To Mom and Dad

Contents

List of Tables

List of Charts and Figures

CHARTS

Acknowledgments

This study could not have been completed without the assistance of many people. I am particularly indebted to Dr. Leon A. Wilber, former chairman of the Political Science Department at the University of Southern Mississippi, for providing many helpful suggestions and often needed encouragement. I am also grateful to Dr. Robert E. McArthur of the University of Mississippi, to Dr. Wilbur Devereux Jones of the University of Georgia, and to Dr. Pat McRaven of Memphis State University for reading the manuscript and for their suggestions. Special recognition and deepest appreciation go to my wife, Nancy, who was a faithful critic of the project and who cheerfully typed drafts of the manuscript.

Much of the information for this study was gathered from interviews. The author expresses his sincere appreciation for the cooperation of the many people listed in Appendix F who gave their time for personal interviews.

Introduction

In 1915, the *American Political Science Review* published the following letter from a Minnesota hotel owner to the state fire marshal:

> Dear Sir:
> The state hotel inspector has ordered me to put in a new floor. One of your deputies has ordered me to tear down the building. Which shall I do first?

Although this letter dramatized the need for more coordination among state agencies in Minnesota, such problems were by no means unique to that state. The publicity received by the letter helped focus attention on the organization of state governments which, in 1912, had been described as "deplorably bad." In the wake of the growing criticism and adverse publicity, a number of states undertook efforts to reorganize. The first successful reorganization occurred in 1917, and since that time nearly every state has reorganized at least once and some have reorganized two or more times.

In 1930, Mississippi began its first effort to reorganize. Although the study made in that effort described the state's administrative organization as "chaotic," the attempt to reorganize failed. In 1950 a second study was prepared. This time the state organization was described as "confusion compounded." In spite of this second very critical indictment, reorganization failed again.

A third reorganization effort—with a study estimated to have cost in excess of $250,000—was begun in 1970, but so far the results have been no better than in previous attempts. Interest in reorganization in Mississippi generated by that effort has not died out, however, and it is still possible the latest try will be more successful than its predecessors. Only time will tell, of course, whether this latest endeavor, or any reorganization effort for that matter, will ever be successful in Mississippi.

Since Mississippi practically stands alone as the only state in the nation unable to reorganize its administrative structure, and since so much time and money have gone into its unsuccessful efforts, it seems natural to ask why these efforts have failed. This study is an attempt to answer that question.

For purposes of the study, an unsuccessful reorganization effort is defined as one which was unable to produce a significant reduction in the overall number of state agencies, boards, and commissions. Historically, such a reduction has been one of the most prominent objectives of reorganization attempts. This objective has been based on the management principle which says that no one person in executive authority can supervise, coordinate, or otherwise manage the activities of 200, 150, 100, or even 50 separate agencies, boards, and commissions.

In the course of this study it was convenient to view each reorganization effort in the four stages depicted below.

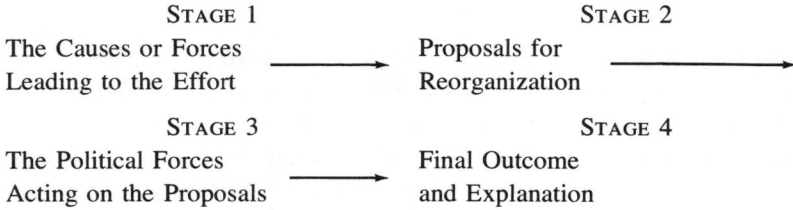

STAGE 1	STAGE 2
The Causes or Forces Leading to the Effort ⟶	Proposals for Reorganization ⟶

STAGE 3	STAGE 4
The Political Forces Acting on the Proposals ⟶	Final Outcome and Explanation

The explanation of each unsuccessful try at reorganization follows an investigation of the causes and forces leading to the effort, a description and analysis of the actual proposals for reorganization, and a thorough consideration of the political forces acting on the proposals.

Tracing each of the four described stages involved a systematic ''reading'' of newspapers of the 1930s, 1950s, and 1970s. Another important source of information was the more than 65 personal interviews conducted with people who were directly involved both pro and con in the reorganization efforts or who otherwise had firsthand knowledge of pertinent events. Official documents of legislative and administrative activities served as the third major source of information.

The analysis of the Mississippi reorganization efforts is preceded by a review of the reorganization movement in the other American states. Since the reorganization movement is not unique to Mississippi, a much fuller understanding of the state's efforts is gained from a review of the experiences of other states. By seeing what approaches have succeeded and which have failed in other states, one can feel more confident in offering explanations for the outcome of reorganization efforts in Mississippi. More importantly, a knowledge of the experiences of other states coupled with an analysis of the unsuccessful Mississippi efforts can provide a base for judging what conditions and approaches would be most conducive to success with future reorganization efforts. The conclusions to this study will summarize relevant findings and offer such a judgment on the prospects for reorganization in Mississippi.

It should be noted that this study does not endorse any of the reorganization proposals that have been made and it does not attempt to discover any alternative proposals.

This book went to press during the 1977 legislative session. At the end of that session the legislature established a joint legislative committee to study the organization of the executive branch of state government and directed it to report its findings and recommendations to the legislature by December 1, 1977. It will not be possible to review the work of that committee in this book.

Administrative Reorganization of Mississippi Government

1 / The Movement for Administrative Reorganization of State Government

By the beginning of the twentieth century, industrial development was producing notable changes in the economic and social life of the nation. One aspect of these changes was the increasing demand for more services from government. The general pattern of response was to provide the new services by creating new administrative agencies. This was done in such an unplanned and haphazard fashion that by 1900 many states had 100 or more boards and agencies. As government simultaneously became larger and more complex, ways were sought to make it more efficient and at the same time to make it more accountable to the people. The result was a broad movement for the administrative reorganization of state government.

The year 1912 is often noted as the beginning of this movement because of the stimulus provided by President William Howard Taft's Commission on Economy and Efficiency in the National Government. Acting on his belief that economy would result from efficient organization, President Taft directed the commission to study the administrative machinery of the executive department "with a view to the assignment of each activity to the agency best fitted for its performance, to the avoidance of duplication of plant and work, to the integration of all administrative agencies of the government . . . into a unified organization."[1] The commission found that the organization of the national government was "deplorably bad." That finding, and the belief that the executive branches in the states were far worse, sparked the reorganization movement in the states.[2]

From that first major effort in 1912 until the present, reorganization has been a significant issue in state government in America. Throughout the entire course of the movement, however, the objectives and guiding principles of

---

[1]Message from President Taft to the Senate and House of Representatives on Economy and Efficiency in the Government Services, *Congressional Record*, 62nd Cong., 2nd Sess. 1026.
[2]Leslie Lipson, *The American Governor from Figurehead to Leader* (Chicago: University of Chicago Press, 1939), 82.

reorganization have remained basically unchanged. The classic statement of the principles of reorganization made by A. E. Buck nearly thirty years ago is still valid and should be reviewed as a point of reference. Those principles are:

1. Concentrate authority and responsibility.
2. Departmentalize related functions.
3. Avoid the use of boards for purely administrative work.
4. Coordinate staff services.
5. Provide for an independent audit.
6. Provide for a governor's cabinet.[3]

Buck noted that these standards of reorganization, developed during the first twenty years of the reorganization process, were no longer theoretical but grounded in experience and supported in practice. Countless subsequent writers have referred to the above as the guiding principles of the reorganization movement.

In the sixty-odd years of the reorganization movement there have been many peaks and valleys of interest and activity; however, three distinct phases or periods can be noted, and these will be studied in the following pages.

REORGANIZATION—PHASE I

The first phase of the reorganization movement extended from the beginning of reorganization in 1912 to the 1930s. This phase is distinctive because after the movement began, interest in reorganization showed no noticeable decline until the thirties.

In the five years (1912–17) after the Taft commission sparked the initial interest in the reorganization movement, sixteen states authorized Taft-type reorganization surveys. The interest in state government reorganization was not limited to the state houses, however. For example, at the eleventh annual meeting of the American Political Science Association six separate reports on state reorganization efforts were presented.[4] Despite this widespread interest, the first successful state reorganization was not achieved until 1917.

---

[3]Arthur E. Buck, *The Reorganization of State Governments in the United States* (New York: Columbia University Press, 1938), 14–15.

[4]*Ibid.*, 7–8; Lipson, *The American Governor*, 82; J. S. Young, "Administrative Reorganization in Minnesota," *American Political Science Review*, IX (1915), 275. This issue of the *Review* contains articles on reorganization efforts in Illinois, Iowa, Kansas, Minnesota and Oregon; See pp. 252–303.

Successful Reorganization Attempts

Illinois carries the distinction of being the first state to successfully reorganize its administrative structure. That reorganization was as broad and sweeping as those which had been attempted unsuccessfully in other states. The major difference in the Illinois reorganization plan, however, was the strategy to reorganize through the legislative process rather than by constitutional revision. Although six constitutional administrative offices remained independent of the governor after reorganization, more than 100 agencies were consolidated into nine departments.[5]

The Illinois reorganization was not easily accomplished, however. In 1913, the Illinois legislature set up a commission on economy and efficiency. The commission's report, produced under the direction of Professor John A. Fairlie, a highly respected authority on state government, was available for the 1915 legislature. No action was taken on the report, but in the election campaign of 1916, the platforms of both political parties had reorganization planks and both gubernatorial candidates were on record as favoring reorganization. While reorganization was an issue in the campaign, it is doubtful that the movement had much public support. Leslie Lipson suggests that most popular interest may have been absorbed by the presidential election of 1916 and by the approaching war. Lipson found only one editorial in the *Chicago Tribune* on the gubernatorial race, and it recognized Frank Lowden as the candidate for "more efficient government."[6]

Although both parties had endorsed reorganization in the campaign, the attitude of the Illinois legislature after the election was one of indifference. When prodded by the governor, the legislature became hostile and labeled reorganization as an executive power grab. Governor Lowden, however, was intent on pursuing reorganization and moved quickly to get legislative action. He used a combination of persuasion and coercion, realizing that his ability to do so was at its height during his "honeymoon" period. Lowden wanted to make the most of the enthusiasm that had been generated for reorganization before it could be lost on other issues. The governor's efforts paid off and Illinois became the first state to reorganize.[7]

[5]William H. Edwards, "A Factual Summary of State Administrative Reorganization," *Southwest Social Science Quarterly*, XIX (June, 1938), 53–67. This is an account of the first fifteen successful reorganizations. Buck, *The Reorganization of State Governments*, 86–93.

[6]Buck, *The Reorganization of State Governments*, 86; Lipson, *The American Governor*, 84.

[7]James Bell and Earl Darrah, *State Executive Reorganization* (Berkeley: Bureau of Public Administration, 1961), 9. Another good account of the Illinois reorganization is in Lawrence

One year later, in 1918, Massachusetts reorganized by revising its constitution to require the legislature to organize the administrative work of the state into not more than twenty departments. Massachusetts leaders used the strategy of not specifying which existing agencies were to be abolished or absorbed into which new departments. The opposition of office-holders was thereby delayed, and reorganization was discussed on its merits.

The case of reorganization in Massachusetts is striking in that the governor was largely indifferent to the movement and lent scarcely any help to those pushing reorganization.[8] The available evidence seems to indicate that the legislature took advantage of this gubernatorial apathy, with the result being an unsatisfactory reorganization. A. E. Buck offers several criticisms of this reorganization which he says, "can scarcely be called an administrative reorganization." In 1921, only three years later, a new governor asked for a commission to make a further study of the organization of state government in Massachusetts.[9]

The case of reorganization in Massachusetts seems to indicate that if the legislature reorganizes the executive branch without input or direction from the governor, the results will not meet the commonly accepted standards of an executive reorganization.

By 1937, twenty years after the success in Illinois, twenty-six states had reorganized. Representative of the states following the Illinois pattern of reorganizing without making constitutional changes were Nebraska and Idaho in 1919, Maryland in 1922, Minnesota in 1925, and Georgia in 1931.[10]

In the Georgia case it is noteworthy that the reorganization "issue" persisted and did not go away after initial defeats. In 1923, the governor recommended that the legislature take action on a recently completed reorganization study, but nothing happened. In 1927, the legislature again failed to act, even though the governor had campaigned on the issue. In 1928, the governor again campaigned on reorganization and was elected by a large majority. This time, the 1929 Georgia legislature took up the issue but effected no changes.

Herson, "Administrative Reorganization and the 1917 Reform in Illinois." (Unpublished Ph.D. dissertation, Yale, 1955.)

[8]Lipson, *The American Governor*, 100.

[9]Buck, *The Reorganization of State Governments*, 26.

[10]Arthur W. Bromage, *State Government and Administration in the United States* (New York: Harper and Brothers, 1936), 246–48; Buck, *The Reorganization of State Governments*, 8–9. Other states following the Illinois pattern were Ohio, Washington, Michigan, and California.

The third successive gubernatorial campaign in which reorganization was an issue saw Richard Russell, Jr., elected governor in 1930 on a platform endorsing the consolidation of agencies. Governor Russell followed up with "a powerful plea for reorganization in his inaugural address," and a reorganization program was finally passed in 1931. The program reduced the number of agencies from 100 to 7.[11]

Other states produced a greater degree of integration of offices and agencies under the governor than was possible in those states which, like Illinois, avoided constitutional changes. The most notable examples were Tennessee (1923), New York (1925), and Virginia (1927). In Tennessee, a high degree of centralization was possible because there were few constitutional restrictions. A. E. Buck reports that a series of budget deficits made reorganization an important issue in Tennessee in the gubernatorial campaign of 1922. Governor-elect Austin Peay fell heir to a reorganization plan arranged by a private interest group. Before the first legislative session, the new governor canvassed legislators, securing pledges of support for reorganization. Peay followed up at the beginning of the session by sending a package of reorganization bills to the legislature where they were promptly approved.

Meanwhile, New York was having difficulty getting through the most extensive reorganization undertaken by any state up to that time. In 1920, Governor Al Smith sought action on a reorganization plan, but the legislature refused to cooperate. Smith became governor again in 1923 and, despite legislative opposition, immediately began to work for reorganization. In 1925, one of three reorganization amendments was adopted, clearing the way for the consolidation of more than 180 agencies into 20 departments. The amendment also provided for the appointment of three elected officials.[12]

Again, one of the primary factors in the success of the reorganization was the leadership of the governor.[13] Popular support for the reorganization was also evident. Lipson notes that the people of New York had been concerned to a far greater degree than the people in other states. He points out that reorganization had been a major issue in New York campaigns for more than ten

[11]Buck, *The Reorganization of State Governments,* 77–79.
[12]*Ibid.,* 219–21.
[13]See Frederick C. Mosher (ed.), *Governmental Reorganizations: Cases and Commentary* (New York: The Bobbs-Merrill Company, Inc., 1967). In an analysis of the cases presented in the book, the editor finds that the most frequent "spark" setting off the reorganization process was a change in the top leadership; see pp. 502–503.

years, and that from press, radio, and platform the attention of the average citizen had been drawn to the problem of organizing and administering the state government.[14]

Virginia presents another classic case of reorganization. A state commission on economy and efficiency was set up in 1916. The commission's recommendation for a biennial budget was adopted in 1918. In 1922, another study was made but the legislature of 1924 took no action on the report and, as Lipson said, "the initiative had to come from elsewhere." Harry F. Byrd, a gubernatorial candidate in 1925, took the initiative and made a "vigorous" plea for reorganization. Byrd was elected and made reorganization and tax reform the keynotes of his inaugural address. Governor Byrd then offered the legislature specific objectives for reorganization. The legislature responded with a resolution to adopt a short ballot amendment and also provided for another study of the state administration. This study report, delivered in 1927, was called "one of the outstanding surveys of a state administration." Byrd enlisted the aid of a group of businessmen to form a citizens' committee for reorganization and the plan was passed during a special legislative session in March of 1927. The short ballot amendment was prepared by that session and it won ratification in June of 1928.[15] One student of the situation, George W. Spicer, commented that the amendment would have failed by a wide margin had it not been for the "vigorous and intelligent leadership of Governor Byrd."[16]

Unsuccessful Reorganization Attempts

A comparison of the foregoing cases of successful reorganizations with others that fared badly may help isolate some of the factors that bear on the success or failure of reorganization.

Perhaps the first unsuccessful effort associated with the state reorganization movement was the one made in Oregon in 1909. That effort proposed the consolidation of 46 state agencies into 7 departments. It failed, according to one account, because the proposed changes were too "radical", i.e., they proposed too much change at once.[17]

---

[14]Lipson, *The American Governor*, 91.
[15]*Ibid.*, 88–90.
[16]George W. Spicer, "The Short Ballot Safe in Virginia," *National Municipal Review*, XXI (September, 1932), 551.
[17]Bell and Darrah, *State Executive Reorganization*, 5. The Oregon reorganization is also discussed by W. F. Dodd in "State Governmental Organization, Proposed Reforms In," *American Political Science Review*, IV (1910), 243–51.

The Oregon experience and the unsuccessful reorganization effort of 1915 in New York illustrate two important factors that must be seriously considered before any reorganization effort is begun: (1) whether to reorganize by statute or by constitutional revision, and (2) whether to attempt sweeping or piecemeal reorganization.[18]

Because of the seriousness of the conditions in New York, it was decided that a sweeping reorganization was most urgent and could best be accomplished by constitutional revision. However, the revised constitution, designed to effect the needed changes, was defeated at the polls in 1915.[19] Because the reorganization effort failed, the question of whether statutory or piecemeal proposals would have been more successful is naturally raised. That question cannot be answered, but ten years later New York did have a successful reorganization. The reorganizers did not resort to piecemeal reorganization but neither did they attempt the extensive constitutional revision that had failed in 1915.[20]

While constitutional change is extremely difficult to accomplish, it is usually necessary if the most complete reorganization is sought. To reorganize by statute, however, does not mean the reorganization will be insignificant. A. E. Buck notes that 23 of the 26 state reorganizations occurring between 1917 and 1937 were statutory and that of these 23 "sixteen have adopted rather complete plans."[21]

In Arkansas, reorganization was either a subject of study or of an inaugural address or it was before the legislature in 1921, 1923, 1925, 1931, 1932, and 1933. The reorganization issue persisted for over a decade and had gubernatorial support, yet it still failed. Another important element of successful reorganization—popular support—was obviously lacking. Two prominent authors, Daniel R. Grant and H. C. Nixon, relate an account of the effort given by D. T. Herndon, secretary of the Arkansas History Commission. In Herndon's view, the Arkansas reorganization was pictured as a contrivance calculated to enable the governor to become a dictator. As a result, the people and the legislature gave the proposals a cold reception. After the failure of the reorganization attempt, a civil service law passed in 1937 was said to have

---

[18]It will be seen that the efforts to reorganize in Mississippi attempted sweeping reorganizations; the first relied heavily on constitutional revision; the second and third were largely, though not entirely, statutory.

[19]Bell and Darrah, *State Executive Reorganization,* 7.

[20]One constitutional amendment was used to effect the reorganization. See 7.

[21]Buck, *The Reorganization of State Governments,* 7–9.

been a phenomenal achievement for Arkansas where "political manipulations and pure Jacksonian democracy manifest themselves in unusual and well-nigh perfect form."[22]

Alabama's experience with reorganization in the 1930s provides an interesting comparison with Mississippi's. Both states received in-depth reports of their state administrations from the Brookings Institution in 1932. The Alabama report of five volumes and nearly 2,000 pages bore many similarities to the Mississippi report, both in defects discovered and in proposed remedies. One observer writes that the recommendations were not received favorably by the Alabama legislature or by the people, perhaps because "the report recommended too many sweeping changes for the suggestions to be adopted immediately." The report was felt to be significant, however, because it increased public interest in reorganization, paving the way for a reorganization program in Alabama seven or eight years later.[23]

A few changes were made after the Brookings report of 1932. These changes were catalyzed, in part, by the gubernatorial campaign of 1934 in which candidate Frank M. Dixon based his platform on the Brookings study. Defeated in 1934, Dixon ran again in 1938 and was elected. The day after his inauguration, he presented the Alabama legislature with a plan for reorganization that was soon adopted. The governor attributed his success to his strategy of avoiding the more controversial aspects of the 1932 report and of not attempting to go too far at once.[24]

Political Variables Affecting Reorganization

From the foregoing account of some of the more important early reorganizations or reorganization attempts, three ingredients for success in such a venture seem to be strong executive leadership, a measure of popular support, and persistence in the face of opposition or apathy. In an attempt to bring more evidence to bear on these conclusions and possibly to add another

[22]Daniel R. Grant and H. C. Nixon, *State and Local Government in America* (Boston: Allyn and Bacon, Inc., 1963), 244–45; Buck, *The Reorganization of State Governments,* 55.

[23]A good analysis of the Alabama report is by Donald S. Vaughan, *Administrative Responsibility in Alabama* (University, Miss.: University of Mississippi, 1967), 62–110. See also William V. Holloway and Charles W. Smith, Jr., *Government and Politics in Alabama* (Tuscaloosa, Alabama: Weatherford Printing Company, 1941), 62.

[24]Roscoe C. Martin, "Alabama's Administrative Reorganization of 1939," *Journal of Politics,* II (November, 1940), 436–47. This article focuses on the role of the governor in the reorganization.

dimension to them, Buck's description of the reorganization movement in each state between 1917 and 1937 is analyzed to see what factors or variables are mentioned in the description of each effort. Eight factors could be distinguished.

These factors indicate whether the initiative for reorganization came from the executive or the legislative branches, whether reorganization was an issue in the gubernatorial campaign and whether the governor made a strong follow-up to the initiative by providing specific recommendations. They also indicate whether reorganization had support from the private sector and whether a special legislative session was used in the attempt. Another factor was whether reorganization persisted as an issue after repeated setbacks.[25]

Tables 1, 2, and 3 demonstrate how the factors were distributed in the state reorganization efforts. Table 1 shows which of the eight factors mentioned above occurred in the nineteen states having successful reorganizations; Table 2 does the same for the twenty states with unsuccessful efforts. Table 3 summarizes and compares the rate at which the factors occurred in both the successful and unsuccessful reorganizations.

Table 3 indicates that there is little difference between successful and unsuccessful reorganizations insofar as the initiative for the effort is concerned. In both successful and unsuccessful efforts, the initiative came most often from the executive rather than from the legislative branches. It is important to note, however, that in the follow-up provided by the governor, a significant difference does exist between successful and unsuccessful reorganizations. In the twenty unsuccessful efforts, follow-up occurred only five times, but in the nineteen successful efforts, follow-up occurred sixteen times. Another factor showing a significant difference in its rate of occurrence is whether reorganization had been a gubernatorial campaign issue. As shown in Table 3, reorganization had been such an issue in six successful reorganizations but in none of the unsuccessful efforts.

There was no significant difference between the successful and unsuccessful efforts in the rate of occurrence of the other variables in Table 3. Further examination of Table 1, however, indicates that in the successful efforts, the variables of persistence and support from the private sector tend to occur together. On the contrary, in the unsuccessful efforts (Table 2), persistence

[25]The standard used to measure persistence was whether reorganization appeared as a major issue at least four times in a ten-year period or whether a strong plea for reorganization was made by the governor in three consecutive two-year terms or in two consecutive four-year terms.

Table 1

Political Variables Associated with the Successful Reorganizations in Nineteen States Between 1917 and 1937

	Executive Initiative	Legislative Initiative	Gubernatorial Campaign Issue	Follow-up by Governor with Specific Proposals	Executive Opposition or Non-Support	Persistence of the Issue	Support from the Private Sector	Use of Special Session
California	X			X		X	X	
Colorado	X		X	X				
Georgia	X		X	X		X	X	
Idaho		X		X		X		
Illinois	X		X	X				
Indiana	X			X		X		
Kentucky	X		X	X		X	X	X
Maryland	X							
Minnesota		*						
Nebraska		*		X		X		
Ohio	X		X	X				
Pennsylvania		*		X		X		
Rhode Island	X			X				X
Tennessee	X		X	X				
Vermont	X			X		X		
Washington	X			X				
Massachusetts		X						
New York	X			X		X	X	
Virginia	X	X		X		X	X	X

*The evidence is not clear but the initiative may have come from the legislature in these cases.
SOURCE: Adapted from Buck, *The Reorganization of State Governments*.

Table 2

Political Variables Associated with the Unsuccessful Reorganizations in Twenty States Between 1917 and 1937

	Executive Initiative	Legislative Initiative	Gubernatorial Campaign Issue	Follow-up by Governor with Specific Proposals	Executive Opposition or Non-Support	Persistence of the Issue	Support from the Private Sector	Use of Special Session
Alabama	X							X
Arizona	X	X		X	X	X		
Arkansas	X	X		X		X		
Delaware	X						X	
Florida	X						X	
Iowa	X					X		
Kansas	X	*						
Mississippi		*						
Missouri	X			X		X		
Montana	X							
Nevada		*			X			
North Dakota	X							
New Hampshire	X							
New Mexico	X						X	
Oklahoma	X							
South Carolina		X			X		X	
Texas	X	X				X		
Utah	X	*						
West Virginia	X			X				X
Wyoming		X		X				X

*The evidence is not clear but the initiative may have come from the legislature in these cases.
SOURCE: Adapted from Buck, *The Reorganization of State Governments*.

Table 3

Comparison of the Occurrence of Political Variables in Nineteen States With Successful and in Twenty States With Unsuccessful Reorganization Efforts Between 1917 and 1937

Political Variable	Occurrence in States with		Chi Square*	Was the Variable Significant?
	Successful Efforts	Unsuccessful Efforts		
Executive Initiative	14	16	.01	No
Legislative Initiative	3	5	.01	No
Follow-Up by Governor with Specific Proposals	16	5	13.75	Yes
Gubernatorial Campaign Issue	6	0	5.24	Yes
Executive Opposition or Non-Support	0	3	1.34	No
Persistence of the Issue	8	5	1.28	No
Support from the Private Sector	5	4	.01	No
Use of Special Session	3	3	.14	No

*Chi square tests the significance of the difference in the occurrence of the variables in successful and in unsuccessful reorganization efforts. The chi square tables constructed for each political variable are shown in Appendix A. The chi square values were calculated with the formulas:

$$X^2 = \frac{N(AD-BD)^2}{(A+B)(C+D)(A+C)(B+D)} \quad \text{and} \quad X^2 = \frac{N(|AD-BD|-N/2)^2}{(A+B)(C+D)(A+C)(B+D)}$$

The latter formula which incorporates Yates' correction for continuity was used when expected cell frequencies were less than five. George A. Ferguson, *Statistical Analysis in Psychology and Education* (New York: McGraw Hill Book Company, 1966), 204–207.

and support from the private sector never occur together. It can be noted also from Table 2 that support from the private sector never occurs with the variable of follow-up. Another important observation to note from the successful reorganizations (Table 1) is that executive opposition never occurs with successful reorganizations.

While the use of the special session to effect reorganization does not seem as important as had been expected, it should be noted that in the three successful efforts involving special sessions, none of them had the "support" of persistence, of private support, or of a gubernatorial campaign sponsoring reorganization.

In summary, the analysis of A. E. Buck's study of state reorganization tends to support the conclusions drawn from the preceding analysis of successful and unsuccessful reorganizations. Popular support for reorganization and the persistence of the issue, when they occur simultaneously, seem to be factors associated with successful efforts. It was also shown that in successful efforts, reorganization was often an issue in a gubernatorial campaign. The analysis of Buck's study indicates that one of the most critical variables in a reorganization effort is whether the governor follows up on the initiative for the reorganization and recommends specific actions.

REORGANIZATION—PHASE II

The first phase of the reorganization movement ended when interest began to lag during the 1930s. Although attention began to turn again to problems of state government organization from 1939 to 1947, the second distinct phase in the movement was between 1948 and 1952. During this period, more than thirty states made efforts to reorganize.[26]

This widespread state interest in reorganization came in the wake of the Hoover Commission study of the organization of the national government (Commission for Organization of the Executive Branch of Government, 1947-1949). The state reorganization studies during this phase were commonly referred to as "little Hoover commissions." A very valuable study in which Karl A. Bosworth surveyed the successes and failures of twenty-four

---

[26]John C. Bollens, *Administrative Reorganization in the States Since 1939* (Berkeley: University of California Bureau of Public Administration, 1947). Hubert R. Gallagher reports that during 1948 and 1949 alone, twenty-six states provided for reorganization surveys; see his "State Reorganization Surveys," *Public Administration Review,* IX (Autumn, 1949), 252-56.

little Hoover commissions was published in 1952. Bosworth discovered that in only two of the states, New Hampshire and New Jersey, was the legislative response to the reorganization study decidedly positive, whereas the legislative response in nine of the states was soundly negative. Limited success was achieved in the remaining thirteen states. "The spectacle of such meager accomplishment from so much effort" led Bosworth to reflect on "the politics of management improvement in the states."[27] In other words, he chose to inquire into the politics of the reorganization efforts instead of making a study of the content of the proposals and their supporting theories of organization.

Bosworth found that the motives behind a reorganization effort were extremely important and concluded that a successful reorganization effort had to be based on a sincere desire to improve the state administration. He found the economy motive to be only a slight force in effecting reorganization since state taxation was less burdensome than at national or local levels.

Bosworth then evaluated the reorganization efforts on the basis of whether the governor or the legislature sponsored the reorganization. He found that in ten of the fifteen states where some reorganization was achieved, the governor had been the chief sponsor; in five of eight states where reorganization had failed, the legislature had been the chief sponsor.

In evaluating the composition of the reorganization study groups, Bosworth found that it was of greatest importance for the members of the group to be persons of high general prestige who were also politically influential. Next in importance, he said, the members of the study group should represent more than limited elements in the political spectrum of the state.

Perhaps Bosworth's most important conclusion was that future surveys should give hard thought to the question, What are the feasible objectives of this survey? By this he meant the study should be less idealistic and more realistic as to what might actually result from the proposals. He noted that, with possibly one exception, all the state surveys that received no legislative response made proposals requiring constitutional changes. On the other hand, only six of fifteen states with significant legislative accomplishment had to consider constitutional amendments. (See Table 4.)

[27]Karl A. Bosworth, "The Politics of Management Improvement in the States," *American Political Science Review,* XLVII (March, 1953), 84–99. There was a negative response in Alabama, California, Connecticut, Delaware, Iowa, Minnesota, Mississippi, Nebraska, and Ohio. Some limited success was achieved in Colorado, Illinois, Kansas, Kentucky, Massachusetts, Maryland, Michigan, Nevada, New York, Oregon, South Carolina, Utah, and Virginia.

Table 4

Incidence of Proposed Constitutional Change in Successful and Unsuccessful* Reorganizations 1948–1952

Outcome of the Effort	Total	Proposals with Constitutional Change	Percent
Successful	15	6	40
Unsuccessful	9	8	89

*"Unsuccessful" is used here to mean a completely negative response to the entire reorganization plan. "Successful" means those states adopting from 29 to 52 percent of the plan. There is no indication that the specific parts of the successful proposals involving constitutional change were adopted.
SOURCE: Bosworth, "The Political Management Improvement in the States."

Bosworth further noted that the states had been very cautious about turning the reorganization surveys over to national consulting firms. Only two of the twenty-four states employed such firms. One of the major drawbacks in the surveys of such consultants is that they characteristically give too little consideration to feasibilities, local values, and traditions.

Bosworth also examined the manner in which the study recommendations were presented upon completion. Newspaper notices, he said, should announce the findings. Bosworth found it essential that the finished report include drafts of the legislation needed to effect the recommendations and that the study group appear before legislative committees to support and defend its proposals.

Bosworth's concluding observations were that the various legislatures exhibited some willingness to give the governor more of the tools of management, but that they were perhaps less inclined than in the 1920s and 1930s to adopt the pattern of unity-of-command—single-head for the executive organization. He concluded from this that legislatures were opposed to having the influence of the governor increased.

One year after Bosworth made his survey of the little Hoover commissions, a report by the Committee on American Legislatures of the American Political Science Association classified interest group strength in the various states as being strong, moderate, or weak.[28] Sixty-seven percent of the states with

[28]Belle Zeller (ed.), *American State Legislatures: Report of the Committee on American Legislatures of the American Political Science Association* (New York: Thomas Y. Crowell Company,

unsuccessful reorganizations in the Bosworth study were classified as having strong interest groups. On the other hand, only 29 percent of the states with successful reorganizations were classified as having strong interest groups.

On the basis of this information, it may be questioned whether there is a significant relationship between the outcome of reorganization efforts and the strength of state interest groups. The existence of such a relationship can be determined from the analysis shown in Table 5. This table compares the outcome of reorganization efforts to state interest group strength. The numbers in parentheses in the table are the results that would be expected if the outcome of reorganization were independent of interest group strength. The statistical measure derived from the analysis in Table 5 is a chi square of 1.9. This is less than the 3.8 that would be needed to indicate that interest groups had a significant bearing on the outcome of the reorganization efforts. On the basis of this analysis, using the 24 little Hoover commission reorganization efforts studied by Bosworth, interest group strength in a state does not appear to be a significant factor in the success or failure of a reorganization effort.

One of the little Hoover commission reorganization efforts not included in the Bosworth analysis was the effort in Arizona. The Arizona little Hoover commission is considered by Robert E. Riggs in an in-depth study of that state's reorganization. Although Riggs' findings proved similar to those of other studies, he cautions that there are no simple or single explanations for the unsuccessful efforts. He notes that while each case presents a unique situation never to be reproduced, it still illustrates political pitfalls that must be considered if the chances for future reorganization are to be improved.[29]

Riggs summarizes his study by recommending several "political guideposts" for consideration in future reorganization efforts:

1. Reorganization activists should fully demonstrate to the legislature the need for the proposals. Demonstrating the need to citizen groups would also help.

2. Activists must realize that certain Jacksonian principles, such as the multiplicity of elective offices, are so much a fact of political life in Arizona that they must be considered in formulating a plan of reorganization.

1954), 190–91; Lewis A. Froman, Jr., "Some Effects of Interest Group Strength in State Politics," *American Political Science Review,* LX (December, 1966), 961. Froman offers the clarification that "strength" is taken to mean strength of interest groups vis-a-vis the state legislature.

[29]Robert E. Riggs, *The Movement for Administrative Reorganization in Arizona* (Tucson: The University of Arizona Press, 1964), 43.

Table 5

Comparison of the Outcome of Reorganization Efforts to Strength of State Interest Groups

Outcome of Reorganization	Relative Strength of Interest Groups		Total States
	Strong	Moderate to Weak	
Successful	4	10	14
	(6.1)	(7.9)	
Unsuccessful	6	3	9
	(3.9)	(5.1)	
Totals	10	13	23

Chi Square $= 1.9$

Significance at .05 Level $= 3.8$

*Adapted by using the successful and unsuccessful state reorganizations identified by Bosworth (see p. 16) and the American Political Science Association classification of state interest group strength (see p. 17). The expected frequencies are calculated from the assumption that the outcome of reorganization is independent of interest group strength. The formula for calculating frequencies for the chi square is given in Ferguson's *Statistical Analysis in Psychology and Education*, 201–204, 207, 407. The chi square formula incorporates Yate's correction for continuity to compensate for the expected frequency which is less than five.

3. The plan should be advertised as a home-grown product and the political liability of having out-of-state experts prepare the plan should be avoided.

4. Reorganization will be frustrated from the outset if serious disagreement on the plan exists between the governor and the legislature based either on unusual legislative-executive rivalry, personality conflicts, or partisan maneuvering.

5. "No maxim deserves more emphasis than the necessity of compromise. The all-or-nothing philosophy . . . has reaped its natural consequence— essentially nothing." This means that "consultation and cooperation among all significant groups within the legislative and the executive branches in the formulation and sponsorship of a program are almost indispensable."[30]

In addition to the findings of the studies mentioned above, York Willbern

[30]*Ibid.*, 66–67.

has presented a list of the "forces of separatism," i.e., forces that have discouraged reorganization.[31] They are as follows:

1. Agencies prefer a maximum of autonomy.

2. A strong tradition exists for the election of many administrators rather than for their appointment.

3. Separatism is often encouraged following scandals.

4. Clientele groups prefer to have "their" agencies separate for better access and control.[32]

5. Professional groups prefer to remain individualized.

6. Federal grants often discourage agency consolidation.

7. It is felt that separate agencies can keep special programs "above politics."

8. Legislators are reluctant to increase the power of the governor.

9. Voters are often skeptical of strong administrators.

These forces may or may not apply to specific reorganization efforts; but it will be observed that some of them were factors in the Bosworth and Riggs studies above.

REORGANIZATION—PHASE III

Interest in state administrative reorganization is again at a high level, probably exceeding that of any time since the popularity of the little Hoover commissions in the late 1940s and early 1950s. For example, reorganization studies were completed in sixteen states in 1968–69 while ten other states had such studies in progress.[33] Although the number of studies continues to grow faster than the number of reorganizations, the late 1960s saw more and more states

[31]York Willbern, "Administration in State Governments," *The Forty-Eight States: Their Tasks as Policy Makers and Administrators* (Columbia University: The American Assembly, 1955), 115–18.

[32]Shortly after Willbern's work appeared, some research was done on the fear of reduced access and control resulting from proposed consolidations. The findings were that shifting a particular bureau to a larger agency was of little more significance than a change of address. It was concluded that much of the politics of administrative organization was based on myth rather than reality. Francis E. Rourke, "The Politics of Administrative Organization: A Case History," *Journal of Politics*, XIX (August, 1957), 461–78. See also similar findings by Harold Stein (ed.), "The Transfer of the Children's Bureau," *Public Administration and Policy Development* (New York: Harcourt, Brace and World, 1952), 15–29.

[33]Council of State Governments, *State Executive Reorganization, 1967–69* (Lexington, Kentucky: The Council of State Governments, 1969), 16. The Council of State Governments, *The Book of the States, 1970–71* (Lexington, Kentucky: The Council of State Governments, 1970),

act on their reorganization studies. The Council of State Governments reports that since 1965, sixteen states have had what it called major reorganizations. The council noted that this was the largest number of reorganizations for any comparable period in history.[34]

Several aspects of the state reorganization movement of the last few years should be mentioned. First, it is interesting that of the sixteen reorganization studies completed in 1968–69, not one made any reference in its title to economy and efficiency.[35] The studies carried such titles as the *Arkansas Program Planning Project,* the *Louisiana Council on Governmental Reorganization,* and the *Oregon Governor's Project '70's Task Force.* Six of the states making reorganization studies were also making economy and efficiency studies.[36] This evidence seems to suggest that a new distinction is being made between studies for reorganization and studies for economy and efficiency. Bosworth also concluded from his analysis of the "little Hoover commissions" that economy may not be the most appropriate motive for reorganization. Nevertheless, a feature article in the *New York Times* said that the motivating argument for the recent state reorganization studies was to give the taxpayers more for their money. Regarding the successes in some of the states, the writer, Joseph B. Treaster, voiced the opinion that the economy argument was overriding fears that concentrating executive power would lead to abuses.[37]

Treaster also observed that reorganizations in several states showed a trend toward more consolidation than was true of earlier reorganizations. The desire for a smaller number of departments has resulted from the growing complexity and interdependency of state programs. Another factor in the trend toward

XVIII, 137–38. The sixteen states with completed studies were Arizona, Arkansas, Colorado, Florida, Indiana, Kansas, Louisiana, Maryland, Massachusetts, Minnesota, New Mexico, North Carolina, Oregon, Utah, Vermont, and Washington. The ten states with studies in progress included Delaware, Hawaii, Louisiana, Maine, Missouri, Montana, Nebraska, New Hampshire, Pennsylvania, and Wyoming.

[34]Council of State Governments, *The Book of the States, 1974–75,* (Lexington, Kentucky: Council of State Governments, 1974), XX, 137. The sixteen reorganizations were in Arkansas, California, Colorado, Delaware, Florida, Maine, Maryland, Michigan, Massachusetts, Montana, North Carolina, Wisconsin, Georgia, Kentucky, South Dakota, and Virginia.

[35]Although the Mississippi study of 1970 was called the *Commission on Economy and Efficiency in the Executive Branch,* it can be noted that economy was not stated as an objective in the study.

[36]Council of State Governments, *The Book of the States, 1970–71,* 137–38. The six states were Colorado, Delaware, Hawaii, Louisiana, Maryland, and Indiana.

[37]Joseph B. Treaster, "States Widen Governor's Role in Effort to Benefit Taxpayers," *New York Times,* January 25, 1970, p. 49.

consolidation has been a growing interest in the systematic planning of state programs. Some of the areas in which greater degrees of consolidation are being made are welfare and health, transportation, and natural resources. For instance, Departments of Natural Resources are being structured to include fish and game, air and water resources, and all other conservation-oriented agencies; and transportation departments are encompassing aeronautics, mass transit, motor vehicles, and ports.[38]

This trend toward fewer departments may partly account for the movement to the cabinet system in some recent reorganizations. In California, for example, the reorganization provided for only four departments. The four department heads plus other of the governor's advisors formed the governor's cabinet. California's reorganization was effected by executive order. The Massachusetts legislature recently adopted a similar reorganization method, whereby the governor can make a proposal for reorganization that will become effective in sixty days if not stopped by a legislative veto. In 1968, this method of reorganizing was available to governors in seven other states. This method was extended to the Georgia governor in 1971, and in 1972 a plan was implemented to consolidate some 300 agencies into 22 departments.[39]

There is also evidence that in recent years, reorganizers are trying to be much more realistic in what they expect to achieve. A Council of State Governments report on reorganization studies of the 1967–69 period indicated that the principle of the short ballot was still being emphasized. In 1972, however, the council said the trend was to "leave undisturbed" the elective offices. This means that while some functions might be shifted from elective offices, the offices themselves would not be eliminated in an effort to shorten the ballot. The 1972 report also said most of the recent reorganization studies, in deference to the political difficulties involved, leave undisturbed the practices of using boards and commissions to head agencies.[40]

Another significant aspect of the recent reorganization movement has been the "umbrella" approach to reorganization whereby entire agencies are

---

[38]Council of State Governments, *State Executive Reorganization* (Chicago: Council of State Governments, 1969), 11–13.

[39]Council of State Governments, *The Book of the States, 1970,* 135–36, Council of State Governments, *The Book of the States, 1968–69* (Chicago: The Council of State Governments, 1968), XVII, 124; *The Book of the States 1974–75,* 137.

[40]Council of State Governments, *State Executive Reorganization, 1967–69,* 1–2; and Council of State Governments, *Reorganization in the States* (Lexington, Ky.: Council of State Governments, 1972), 14.

shifted intact to form new departments. On paper, the organization charts show this as the consolidation of a number of agencies into a single new department. Initially, however, the authority of the transferred agencies is not disturbed. The "umbrella" theory provides that each of the agencies brought into the new department will retain all of its individual powers and duties. Reorganization under this theory envisions a second phase in which the head of the new department will work to establish administrative controls over the loosely knit agencies.[41] The umbrella approach is further demonstration that states are becoming less rigid in their reorganization proposals.

A final note on recent activity in state reorganization comes from a 1967 report that said "selective" reorganization occurred in almost every state between 1962 and 1967. The report concluded that reorganization was more often piecemeal rather than sweeping.[42] Consistent with this conclusion, the current reorganization attempt in Mississippi is proceeding more as a piecemeal effort. The 1970 reorganization report also follows the recent trends discussed above in that it avoids proposing a short ballot, retains most boards and commissions, and proposes the umbrella approach to reorganization.

[41]Council of State Governments, *Reorganization in the States,* 14–15.

[42]Study Committee on Constitutional Revision and Governmental Reorganization, *Report to the National Governors' Conference,* October, 1967, p. 31.

2 / The First Major Effort to Reorganize Mississippi Administration

The Creation of the Mississippi Research Commission

The first official action on behalf of administrative reorganization of state government in Mississippi was the creation of the Mississippi Research Commission in 1930. The legislature created this commission at the insistence of the Mississippi State Board of Development, a non-profit, public-spirited agency supported by private contributions.[1] Undoubtedly the request by the development board for the research commission and the legislative response were conditioned by the serious financial problems of the state:

1. A deficit of nearly $6 million (about 20 percent of the total budget) existed for the 1930–31 biennium.

2. A net general fund deficit of over $23 million had been built up since 1900.

3. The debt maturities due in 1932–33 equaled the entire expected revenue for 1932.

4. The state could not sell its bonds.

5. Many state warrants were in circulation and in default.

6. Many teachers, pensioners, and creditors of the state had not been paid in eighteen months.[2]

The act creating the Mississippi Research Commission did not provide specifically for a reorganization study. On the contrary, the act was very sweeping, calling for a study and analysis of all phases of the agricultural, commercial, industrial, economic, social, and governmental conditions of the state affecting the health, education, employment, progress, and prosperity of

---

[1]Brookings Institution, The Institute for Government Research, *Report on a Survey of the Organization and Administration of State and County Government in Mississippi* (Washington, D.C.: The Brookings Institution, 1932), 5; hereinafter cited as Brookings Report.

[2]Mississippi *Journal of the Senate*, 1934, p. 15.

the people—a rather large order. The act further provided for a comprehensive, expert report with conclusions and recommendations to be presented to the governor and legislature before the end of the 1932 legislative session. A press report of the requirements of the act said simply that the commission was charged with "finding out what is wrong with the state."[3]

An appropriation of $150,000 was made for the work with the stipulation that the research commission secure contributions from other sources to match any funds drawn from the state allotment. The commission conducted a statewide campaign to raise matching funds, soliciting from local governments and from business. The fund-raising campaign involved meetings in most of the counties at which the proposed work and plans of the commission were explained to the people. The commission was of the opinion that the meetings were productive in that they informed the people and helped secure pledges of financial support. Many of the pledges were not honored, however, because of depressed economic conditions. Consequently, only $21,797.65 in matching funds was collected in almost a whole year's effort.[4]

Because of the time limitations and the shortage of matching funds (nearly $130,000 or 87 percent of the appropriated state funds could not be used), the ultimate scope of the work was materially restricted. As a result, the study did not consider agricultural, commercial, industrial, economic, or social problems, nor did it prepare the specific drafts of statutory and other changes that would be necessary to implement the recommendations of the survey. The survey, when finally arranged in May of 1931 with the Brookings Institution of Washington, D.C., was to cover the administrative structure of state and county government with special emphasis on financial administration and on the state's revenue system.[5] The research director offered the additional qualification that although a financial emergency existed at the time of the study, the purpose was not to formulate a program to meet the emergency but to present a program for the long-range improvement of the government of Mississippi.

As the study was getting underway in the summer of 1931, an election year,

[3]*Laws of Mississippi*, 1930, C. 69; *Jackson Daily Clarion-Ledger*, August 16, 1930, p. 1.
[4]Brookings Report, 6. The contributors to the matching fund included seventeen businesses, sixteen municipalities, and seven counties. Mississippi *Journal of the House of Representatives,* 1932, pp. 283–85.
[5]Brookings Report, 3. The commission's financial statement shows that the contract for the study was voluntarily reduced by the Brookings Institution from $35,000 to $30,000. *House Journal,* 1932, p. 283.

gubernatorial candidates were gearing up their campaigns and most of them were discussing the need for economy and efficiency in government.

The 1931 Election Campaign and Pre-Inaugural Interest in Reorganization

In the campaign of 1931, the successful candidates in the races for governor and lieutenant governor had gone on record as favoring certain economy and efficiency measures. Lieutenant Governor Dennis Murphree's platform recorded his opposition to the creation of new offices, departments, and jobs and said all unnecessary jobs should be eliminated in order to save taxpayers' money. Governor Martin Sennett Conner had also spoken out for the elimination, consolidation, and "eradication" of a large number of state departments and bureaus.[6]

Some of the unsuccessful gubernatorial candidates were also interested in efficiency and economy. Paul B. Johnson, Sr., promised that "rigid economy and judicious expenditure of public funds shall be my purpose. I am in favor of abolishing all useless offices and discharging all unnecessary employees whose salaries are draining the public treasure." George Mitchell declared himself the only really good businessman in the race and vowed to reduce the number of state employees. In response to the idea that the next administration might need to rent additional office space, Mitchell said he, as governor, would have offices to let in Jackson.[7]

A few days before the governor-elect was to take office, it was noted that the governor's mansion was in a state of disrepair. The suggestion was offered that a new mansion be built and that the overcrowding at the new capitol be relieved by moving certain departments into the old mansion. Conner replied that when he was finished in the capitol "they are going to find all the room they need there."

Such statements by Conner, coupled with the campaign rhetoric, undoubtedly contributed to the general feeling that the incoming administration would take action to economize and/or reorganize. Editorials stated that the legislature was undeniably in sympathy with the new governor and his programs and that they had complete confidence in his ability, personal integrity, and sincerity. All of this led many people to conclude that a number of state departments were certain to be abolished or combined and that the new governor would definitely make sharp changes in governmental methods.

[6]*Jackson Daily Clarion-Ledger,* July 26, 1931, p. 8, August 3, 1931, p. 9.
[7]*Ibid.,* August 3, 1931, p. 3, July 31, 1931, p. 13.

The incoming legislature was characterized as unusually non-partisan in spirit and was expected to launch into a program of economy and efficiency with promises of bringing sweeping changes in governmental structures, some of them possibly requiring constitutional change.[8] In view of subsequent difficulties experienced in the reorganization effort, it is important to note that these early discussions recognized a non-partisan attitude and the possibility that constitutional change would be needed.

Optimism for reorganization also was generated from members of the legislature. The chairman of the legislative steering committee formed to identify the major problems facing the state said, "There must be a decided elimination of duplication of efforts and every employee not absolutely necessary must be eliminated. Rigid economy must be enforced." At the beginning of the session, a bill was introduced to abolish the Agricultural Service Commission, but the bill was not immediately referred to a committee by the speaker of the house. The speaker, Thomas L. Bailey, explained that a large number of such bills were expected and that it was likely that a joint committee would be formed "to consider such matters from A to Z."[9] This early legislative activity suggested that Governor Conner's reorganization program would go forward in the legislature.

THE PROPOSALS FOR REORGANIZATION

As noted, the Brookings Institution of Washington, D.C., had been retained by the Mississippi Research Commission to study the administrative procedures and the organizational structures of both state and county government. The findings of this study and the proposals for reorganization were contained in the "Brookings Report" of 1932. The subject of the present study—the organizational structure of the state government—is examined in a separate section of the report. The introduction to that section emphasizes the importance the Brookings researchers attached to the interrelationship of the other aspects of the study, i.e., administrative procedures with emphasis on financial administration and the revenue system. Structural reorganization, however, was regarded as fundamental if the government was to be improved. Several reforms in the revenue system, including financial administration, were offered as part of the solution to the problems of the state, but the success of these reforms was

[8]*Ibid.,* January 14, 1932, p. 14, January 3, 1932, p. 6, January 4, 1932, p. 1.
[9]*Ibid.,* pp. 7, 14.

Table 6

**Primary Methods of Selecting Heads of Mississippi Government Agencies
in 1930**

Method of Selection	Number	Percent
Appointed by the Governor	23	29
Appointed by the Governor with Approval of the Senate	18	23
Ex Officio	19	24
Elected by the People	14*	18
All Other Methods	6	6
Total	80	100

*Seven of these were constitutional offices and seven were statutory.
SOURCE: Adapted from Robert B. Highsaw and Carl D. Mullican, *The Growth of State Adminis-tration in Mississippi* (University, Mississippi: Bureau of Public Administration, 1950), 38.

deemed dependent on a structural overhauling of the government. The Brook-ings Institute considered administrative reorganization so essential to the finan-cial aspects of government that there seemed "small prospect that changes in revenue laws or improvements in the system of fiscal control alone will suffice to keep the state budget in balance."[10]

The analysis that follows will make various characteristics of the state's organizational structure of 1930 clearer. For example, there were 80 agencies of state government, 10 of which were provided for by the constitution. The 70 remaining agencies had been created by the Mississippi legislature.

As Table 6 indicates, most of the agency heads were selected by appoint-ment or held their offices *ex officio*. Most of the heads of the 41 agencies appointed by the governor were made up of plural boards or commissions. Fourteen of the more important agencies were headed by elected officials.

To facilitate their analysis of the state's organization, the Brookings Institu-tion grouped all the state agencies into several functional groups. Table 7 is a summary of those groupings and indicates the number of related agencies in each functional area. Only statutory agencies are included:

[10]Brookings Report, 449. It can be noted that the budget of the state has been balanced pretty consistently since 1932 and without any substantial administrative reorganization. Some changes have been made in the fiscal system but it seems more likely that the balanced budget has been the

Table 7

Number of Related Statutory Agencies in Each Functional Area of Mississippi Government in 1930

Functional Area	Number of Related Statutory Agencies
Finance	9
Education	15
Agriculture	5
Welfare	13
Conservation	3
Business Regulation	4
Health	1
Public Works	5
Professional Examining Boards	11
Miscellaneous	4
Total Statutory Agencies	70

SOURCE: Adapted from the Brookings Report outline of all state agencies, pp. 443–44. See Appendix B for a complete list of agencies divided by functional area.

Defects in the Organization

The Brookings study reported five main defects in the state's organization in 1930:

1. The wide extent to which the elective system was used.

2. The division of power among elective officers and other agencies leading to a diffusion of responsibility and a lack of common direction and responsibility for the conduct of state administration.

3. The grouping of nonrelated functions in one office and the scattering of related functions among many offices due to the creation of numerous independent boards and departments with little reference to previously established offices.

4. The overlapping of functions and lack of coordination among state agencies.

result of the prevailing attitude that the budget must be balanced and the determination that it will be balanced. Such an attitude is probably more important than the relative wealth of the state since Representative George Payne Cossar, president of the National Conference of State Legislative Leaders, reports the surprise of legislative leaders from other states when they learn that Mississippi operates in the black. Personal interview held in Jackson, Mississippi, April 19, 1972.

5. The general complex and inflexible character of the administrative machinery which makes for inefficiency and waste.

The researchers termed the general administrative situation "chaotic," citing the election of 20 state officers as the most complicating factor.[11] The report emphasized, however, that various organizational defects interacted to produce the chaotic situation. For example, the large number of elective offices and independent agencies resulted in a division of authority and responsibility with an overlap and duplication of functions. As a consequence, no single authority operated to formulate general policy. The report noted that even if the governor was directed by the constitution to supervise the state agencies, he would be unable to do so because the nearly 80 agencies far exceeded his span-of-control.[12]

The Principles of Reorganization

The Brookings staff felt that the complicated and disorganized governmental structure could be simplified and made more manageable. The change, at the same time, would further the dual objectives of improving public service and reducing the cost to the taxpayer. Certain fundamental principles were suggested as the basis of the improvements.

The first of the three principles was that of grouping related services. The inclusion of this principle was justified in part by reference to other studies which were in "almost unanimous agreement" that improved administration required the grouping of agencies into a limited number of departments. Several advantages accrue from the grouping of agencies—the location of responsibility becomes clearer and more definite and the operation of the government organization becomes simpler and more easily understood by the voters, the legislature, and the governor.

The second principle was that of making the governor the real as well as the nominal head of the administration. According to this principle, the governor is considered a general manager having department heads as assistants and subordinates. As subordinates to the governor, the department heads would be

[11]Brookings Report, 445. Although only 14 agencies were headed by elected officials, 3 of them had three-member boards or commissions, making a total of 20 elected officials for the 14 agencies.

[12]The constitution charges that the governor shall be the chief executive officer and shall see that the laws are faithfully executed. Mississippi *Constitution* (1890), Sections 116, 123. The term "span-of-control" refers to the management principle that the number of persons any individual can effectively supervise is limited to a small number, possibly 6 to 12.

subject to his supervision, direction, and control. Implicit in this relationship would be the power of the governor to appoint and remove the department heads.[13]

The third and last principle cited in the report was that of using bureaus in place of boards in the organizational arrangement. Bureaus would have single administrative heads rather than plural heads as in boards. The major advantages of the bureau were given as: (1) the ability of the single administrator to do business with greater dispatch, and (2) definiteness in location of responsibility. The discussion of this third principle included special criticism for the *ex officio* type of board or commission.

The Proposed Reorganization Plan

Using these three principles as guides, the Brookings researchers devised a plan for the structural reorganization of Mississippi government. From their examination of the state government and the multiplicity of agencies, they decided that the state government had 13 main functions. They proposed 12 major departments to perform 12 of the 13 functions. One function, the promotion of agriculture, would not be discharged by a major state department; rather, all agricultural activities of the state government, then performed by 5 agencies, would be transferred to and be administered by the Agricultural and Mechanical College.[14]

The 12 major departments proposed in the Brookings study are listed in Table 8. To form the 12 departments, 51 existing agencies would have to be restructured and consolidated.

Of the 12 proposed departments, each of the first 7 shown in Table 8 was to be created by consolidating from 2 to 15 agencies. Four of the remaining departments were agencies or departments that existed in 1930 and were unaffected by the proposed consolidation of agencies. The only entirely new department was the proposed Department of Local Government.

In proposing the Department of Local Government, the Brookings study recognized the strongly entrenched Mississippi tradition of local self-government, but recommended a central agency to supervise, control, and assist the local governments. The department would be especially concerned with administrative reorganization and with the fiscal affairs of local units.

[13]Brookings Report, 448.
[14]*Ibid.*, 448–50.

Table 8

The Twelve Major Departments of Mississippi Government Proposed by the Brookings Study of 1932 Showing the Number of Existing Agencies Absorbed by Each Proposed Department

Proposed Major Department	Existing Agencies Absorbed by the Departments
Executive Department	9
Department of Taxation	3
Department of Treasury	2
Department of Education	15
Department of Welfare	12
Department of Conservation	3
Department of Banking and Insurance	3
Department of Justice	1
Department of Health	1
Department of Highways	1
Public Service Commission	1
Department of Local Government	0
Number of Agencies Absorbed by the Departments	51

SOURCE: Adapted from the Brookings Report, 449–618.

Local governments would also be very much interested in the proposed Department of Justice. That department would be headed by the attorney general who would be appointed by the governor. In turn, the attorney general would be given the authority to appoint local district attorneys and county prosecuting attorneys.[15]

Table 9 makes some comparisons between the organizational structure of 1930 and the proposed changes. The most notable aspect of Table 9 is that the Brookings plan would have reduced the number of elected officials from 20 to 2 and the number of *agencies* headed by elected officials from 14 to 2. The only officials to remain elective were the constitutional offices of governor and lieutenant governor. This meant that none of the 12 major proposed departments would be headed by elected officials. Only 8 of the departments,

[15]Brookings Report, 474, 615–16.

however, would be headed by single executives. Plural boards or commissions would head 4 departments—Health, Education, Welfare, and the Public Service Commission. This deviation from the general principle of substituting the single executive head for the plural head was dictated, according to the reorganization study, by conditions existing in some fields of public service in Mississippi.

The difficulty of effecting such far-reaching changes can be appreciated more fully by reviewing briefly the long tradition in Mississippi of electing the state's executive officers. Actually the state's first constitution (1817) was in harmony with the Brookings recommendations in that it provided for the election of only two officers, the governor and lieutenant governor. Other executive officials—the secretary of state, state treasurer, attorney general, and the auditor of public accounts—were appointed by the legislature. This method of selecting executive officers was changed fifteen years later when the state's second constitution (1832) provided that these officers should be elected by the people rather than appointed by the legislature. The office of

Table 9

Comparisons of Mississippi Governmental Organization in 1930 with the Changes Proposed by the Brookings Report of 1932

Factor of Comparison	Proposed	Percent of Total*	Existing	Percent of Total*
Number of Agencies	33	100	80	100
Number of Elected Officials	2	6	20	25
Agencies Headed by Elected Officials	2	6	14	18
Agencies Headed by Boards or Commissions	22	67	63	79
Agencies Headed by Single Administrators	11	33	17	21
Boards or Commissions that are Wholly or Partly *Ex Officio*	4	12	19	24

*The percentages add to more than 100 because the factors of comparison are not mutually exclusive.
SOURCE: Adapted from the Brookings Report, 437–618. Figures for *ex officio* boards are from Highsaw and Mullican, *The Growth of State Administration in Mississippi*, p. 38.

lieutenant governor was abolished by the constitution of 1832. In 1869, Mississippi's third constitution restored the office of lieutenant governor and continued as elective offices those of governor, secretary of state, attorney general, treasurer, and auditor. Another elective office, that of superintendent of public education, was added in 1869 to make a total of 7 elective state positions.

The constitution of 1869, therefore, endorsed and extended the pattern of electing state executive officers begun when the elective method was applied beyond the governor to all constitutional executive officers in 1832. The fourth and present constitution, adopted in 1890, adhered to the then established pattern of selecting public officials and again provided for the election of the 7 existing officers.[16]

While no additional constitutional offices were set up in 1890 or since, the legislature did add a number of executive offices and provided that they be filled by popular election. Between 1890 and 1932 the following elective offices were created: tax collector, land commissioner, commissioner of agriculture and commerce, a board of trustees for the state penitentiary, a railroad commission, commissioner of insurance, and a highway commission.

The Brookings proposal to reduce the number of elected officials from 20 to 2 was certainly attempting to buck a long-standing Mississippi tradition of electing public officials. Changes of the order proposed would almost certainly be difficult politically. Mechanically, most of the elected officials (13 of 18) could be eliminated by statutory action since only 5 of those to be eliminated were constitutional officers.

The Brookings Report, however, did not detail the steps nor prepare the legislation necessary to implement the proposals, although it did make recommendations of the constitutional, statutory, and administrative actions required to effect the plan. The recommended actions are shown in Table 10. Most (76 of the 98 recommendations) could have been effected through legislative actions. Thirteen of the recommendations were for constitutional changes that would have affected 5 of the 12 proposed departments. Only 9 of the recommendations (less than 10 percent) could have been accomplished by administrative action. It should be noted that the changes in Table 10 are only the basic changes involved in setting up the 12 major departments. Two other constitutional changes would have been required to have the auditor appointed

---

[16]William N. Ethridge, Jr., *Modernizing Mississippi's Constitution* (University of Mississippi: Bureau of Public Administration, 1950), 55–57.

Table 10

**Types and Extent of Action Recommended by the 1932 Brookings Report
to Set Up the Twelve Major Departments of Mississippi Government**

Department	Actions Required			
	Constitutional	Statutory	Administrative	Total
Executive (Dept. of Adm.)	1	7	—	8
Taxation	—	7	2	9
Treasury	3	2	—	5
Justice	4	6	—	10
Education	4	13	3	20
Health	—	2	—	2
Welfare	—	13	—	13
Highways	1	14	2	17
Conservation	—	5	—	5
Banking and Insurance	—	2	2	4
Public Service Commission	—	1	—	1
Local Government	—	4	—	4
	13	76	9	98

SOURCE: Adapted from the Brookings Report, 291, 355, 356, 914–24.

by the legislature rather than elected by the people. Many other constitutional and statutory changes were suggested in parts of the report dealing more specifically with problems of the revenue system and with financial administration.

To summarize, the Brookings Report of 1932 proposed changes in the state government that can only be described as drastic. The theory underlying these changes was that related services should be provided through a single department, the governor should be the real head of the administration, and the departments of government should not be headed by plural boards or commissions. In the main, the Brookings Report proposed to put this theory into practice: (1) by grouping the important functions of state government into 12 major departments headed mostly by single department heads to be appointed by and to serve at the pleasure of the governor; and (2) by making the governor the head of all administration by eliminating all other elected officials except the lieutenant governor. Additionally, the report proposed that a new

Department of Local Government be established to supervise and assist local governments.

THE STRUGGLE FOR REORGANIZATION

The Governor's Commitment to Reorganization and His Plan of Implementation

As indicated earlier, reorganization was a subject of discussion in the 1932 Mississippi legislature as it awaited the inauguration of the new governor. In his inaugural address, Mike Conner made his first direct appeal to the legislature for action on reorganization. Although the governor would address the legislature several more times on behalf of reorganization, his inaugural message was important because it (1) showed his commitment to reorganization;[17] (2) offered a plan for proceeding with reorganization; and (3) brought up the matter of priorities and the possibility of additional taxes. Over a dozen issues were covered in Conner's address, but the greatest emphasis was reserved for the questions of finances and reorganization.[18]

The immediate problem facing the state in 1932 was how to meet its financial obligations.[19] The solution to the problem apparently lay in some combinations of additional taxes and more economy and efficiency in government. For example, it was suggested that any increase in the tax burden should be preceded by administrative reform, thereby "rendering governmental operations more efficient and less burdensome."[20] While it was probably good politics to combine a tax increase with a call for more economy and efficiency, it seems evident that Conner's interest in economy and reorganization was not politically motivated.[21] The following quotation from Conner's inaugural address helps illustrate his position:

> To restore the state's credit to a sound basis, it is not sufficient to balance the budget by reducing expenditures or by increasing revenues or both. It is essential that we adopt certain administrative reforms, to protect the state against a recurrence

---

[17]This point must be considered in light of the suggestion in the previous chapter that the role and leadership of the governor are vital to the success of a reorganization effort.

[18]*Senate Journal,* 1932, p. 77.

[19]Prior to the inauguration, a legislative steering committee listed revenues and appropriations the number one problems of the state. *House Journal,* 1932, pp. 71–72.

[20]*Senate Journal,* 1932, p. 68.

[21]In addition to documentary evidence, interviews with people who knew and opposed Conner support the conclusion that he was not playing politics with the issue of reorganization.

of present conditions, to assure economy and to eliminate waste and inefficiency. To this end, I submit the following definite recommendations.[22]

The governor's discussion of administrative reorganization emphasized the need for such a movement and offered a plan for achieving positive results. The 80 state agencies, Conner said, created confusion and waste because of overlapping functions, conflicts of jurisdictions, and duplication of services. He cited Georgia's reorganization of 1931 which reduced 102 departments to 18 with expected savings of $1 million a year. He gave similar examples from reorganizations in Tennessee, New York, Virginia, and North Carolina.

Governor Conner felt that Mississippi could achieve economy and efficiency by following the lead of these states, adding, "I recommend and earnestly urge upon you a complete reorganization of the administrative machinery of the state government in all its phases, along practical, business-like and economical lines." Conner counseled the legislators against the piecemeal approach to reorganization.[23] He also said that his own legislative experience[24] convinced him of the difficulty of preparing reorganization legislation in the face of the demands already requiring legislative attention. Another possibility he rejected was that of having an interim committee prepare the legislation. This would have meant an unacceptable delay of at least two and possibly four years if constitutional changes were involved.

The governor believed the quickest and most efficient way to deal with the problem was to create immediately a special legislative committee to consider administrative and organizational changes. The legislature would then proceed to speedily enact the usual biennial revenue and appropriation measures. When that business was completed (expected to take about one month), the legislature would recess so the reorganization committee could make its study and prepare the necessary reorganization legislation. The legislature would then reconvene to consider the proposals. There was some reason to believe the recess plan would be considered since a recess had been discussed two weeks before by those not connected with the governor.[25]

Conner's inaugural message also mentioned what he called an awakened

[22]*Senate Journal*, 1932, p. 74.

[23]*Ibid.*, 75. In a later discussion, Conner warned legislators that if they took up reorganization piecemeal, they would become "tired and worried with more lobbyists than this capitol ever saw." *Jackson Daily Clarion-Ledger*, February 19, 1932, p. 3.

[24]Mike Conner had served eight years in the legislature. He was speaker of the house at the age of twenty-four.

[25]*Senate Journal*, 1932, pp. 75–76; *Jackson Daily Clarion-Ledger*, January 4, 1932, p. 1.

and aroused citizenry that was ready to offer its "wholehearted and sympathetic cooperation." Nevertheless, Governor Conner felt inclined to make a most earnest appeal to the press and public for their cooperation and support. In a concluding remark, the governor sought to establish rapport with the legislature by citing again his legislative experience and asking to be considered "as one of you."[26]

Although the recess plan had the possibility of getting the promptest consideration for reorganization, another motive was involved. Conner wished to avoid the expense of paying the legislators the extra money required for a special session. (The thrifty governor had earlier been opposed to the participation of the National Guard in the inaugural parade because of the expense to the state.) Conner's concern over the added expense of a special session would be mentioned again in a later attempt to reorganize. Compared only to the purported benefits of reorganization, this concern over the "cost" in retrospect seems like false economy. It must be remembered, however, that, at the time, some public employees were not being paid. Even when employees received their regular paychecks they could not cash them at face value. The financial plight of the state is further illustrated in a request from the Board of Supervisors of one county for Governor Conner to suspend the sentence of a woman for slashing her husband because the county had no money for feeding the prisoner.[27]

Action on the Governor's Plan

Three days after Governor Conner's inaugural address, House Concurrent Resolution No. 7 was introduced to set up a joint legislative committee to study the state's organizational problems. This resolution was not considered but in its place another one was introduced by thirty-eight members endorsing: (1) the *principle* of a recess, and (2) the policy of balancing the state's budget. While the measure passed by vote of 87 to 46, it did not seem to bind the house to any definite course of action.[28]

The resolution received little or no attention in the senate and the legislature seemed to be following its tradition of avoiding substantive issues early in the session.[29] In a short time, however, this foot-dragging on the reorganization

---

[26]*Senate Journal,* 1932, pp. 67, 96.

[27]*Jackson Daily Clarion-Ledger,* January 19, 1932, p. 8, April 8, 1932, p. 6.

[28]*House Journal,* 1932, pp. 141–42.

[29]Three months later the Senate Rules Committee reported the resolutions "Do Not Pass," but by then it was really a moot point. *Senate Journal,* 1932, pp. 141, 794.

issue would play into the hands of those opposed to any efforts to balance the budget by increasing taxes.

The matter of increasing revenues from taxation was complicated by the belief that existing taxes, primarily property taxes, could not be raised without bringing them to near destructive levels. New sources of revenue therefore had to be considered. About two weeks after the inauguration, it became obvious that the proposal for a general sales tax would be given serious consideration.[30] In the first week of February, the House Ways and Means Committee was reportedly studying a 1 percent sales tax and the Senate Finance Committee a somewhat larger rate for the same tax. Governor Conner was not drawn into this early debate and had not officially endorsed the idea of a sales tax. Questioned further, he said he was not disturbed by the early differences and voiced optimism that the legislature would "work out the program in a few days."

But the revenue program was not worked out in a few days. And, as the opposition to the program grew, the reorganization issue became entangled with the finance debate and the prospects for reorganization were materially diminished. A resolution was introduced in the House of Representatives to make it the policy of the house not to consider any proposal for additional taxes until all possible expenses had been cut through the consolidation and elimination of departments and institutions (including hospitals and colleges).[31] The resolution was referred to the Appropriations Committee from which its backers realized it would never emerge. Their motion to suspend the rules to allow immediate consideration of the resolution lost by vote of 43 to 86. What looked like a decisive defeat, though, was a demonstration that the anti-sales tax forces had nearly the two-fifths vote necessary to defeat a revenue proposal.[32]

This resolution was the first show of strength by the opposition and it came on the heels of a report that the businessmen of the state were planning a mass protest against the sales tax.

The governor's optimism of the previous week rapidly diminished. His difficulties were further complicated by the distribution of a circular in the legislature which asked: "Shall the Legislature follow the Governor's rec-

---

[30]It should be emphasized that no other state had adopted a general sales tax as a major source of revenue at this time, although the national government was also debating such a tax as a source of revenue.

[31]*Jackson Daily Clarion-Ledger*, February 5, 1932, February 7, 1932, p. 17.

[32]*House Journal*, 1932, pp. 229–31; *Jackson Daily Clarion-Ledger*, February 11, 1932, p. 1.

ommendation relative to the creation of a Reorganization Committee?'' The pamphlet reminded readers of the governor's request for the immediate creation of a reorganization committee and questioned, ''Why the delay?'' The purpose of the circular was not to advance reorganization but to serve the ends of the ''anti's'' by confusing the issue. It was true that Conner had asked for the immediate creation of a reorganization committee, but according to the approach he outlined, the legislature was to devote its energies to revenues and appropriations and then recess. The recess would have given the committee time to study the reorganization problem and prepare the appropriate reform legislation. Further, it was generally understood that to achieve the objective of a balanced budget, additional revenues would be required even with a budget reduction of 33 percent.[33]

No one said reorganization could accomplish such reductions, but it was hoped that the determination to cut the budget to around $20 million would appease the ''anti's'' who now sought to delay any consideration of the sales tax until a tentative budget had been submitted showing the necessary cutbacks. In response, the House Appropriations Committee chairman made it plain that his committee would set a budget not exceeding $20 million, a 33 percent reduction from the previous biennium. The Fees and Salaries Committee chairman added that all salaries would be cut at least 25 percent.[34]

When it became evident that the revenue program would meet with determined opposition, Governor Conner responded that he would ''take the program to the stump if necessary.'' Then, by invitation, he addressed a joint meeting of the two finance committees and took a determined stand for a 3 percent sales tax. Conner also appeared before a mass meeting of merchants, explaining to the protestors that while appropriations would be slashed by one-third, the state would still need an additional $4.5 million to balance its budget.[35]

Shortly after the governor began speaking out, the sales tax proposals cleared the committee and went to the floor for debate. Repeated defeats followed, however, and on March 8, 1932, Conner felt compelled to deliver another special message to the legislature endorsing and defending the sales

[33]*Jackson Daily Clarion-Ledger*, February 12, 1932, p. 8, February 14, 1932, p. 4; *Senate Journal*, 1932, p. 286.
[34]*House Journal*, 1932, pp. 298–99; *Jackson Daily Clarion-Ledger*, February 16, 1932, p. 10, February 24, 1932, p. 10, February 28, 1932, pp. 1–2.
[35]*Jackson Daily Clarion-Ledger*, February 13, 1932, p. 1; *Jackson Daily News*, February 12, 1932, pp. 1, 12.

tax.[36] He noted that every elected state official had also publicly supported the tax and reminded the legislators that they had been in session ten weeks with the major problems of taxes and reorganization unsolved.[37]

Two days after this message the house passed a 3 percent sales tax.[38] Before it was approved in the senate, however, a considerable amount of money and energy was expended in protesting the tax. In one instance, special trains brought thousands of protestors to the state capitol in Jackson. One radio station ran a newspaper advertisement asking listeners to tune in and hear E. B. Livingston, the "Will Rogers of the Mississippi Legislature," speak against the sales tax; this was quite possibly the first political message ever aired over radio in Mississippi.[39] A number of full-page newspaper advertisements also voiced opposition to the sales tax. One such ad, which ran on the eve of the largest anti-sales tax rally, featured a list of Jackson merchants who would close their businesses in order to participate in what was called a "mighty demonstration."[40]

The "mighty demonstration" turned out to be an all-day affair in which an estimated 10,000 people participated.[41] No violence was reported although armed guards were posted at the governor's mansion at the end of the day— probably a precautionary measure resulting from a near incident when a group of protestors attempted to visit the governor's office. The incident was reported as follows:

> Representative Sam Lumpkin of Lee County who held an unfinished walking stick in his hand on which he had been whittling with a pocket knife spoke challengingly to the group pressing nearest the entrance with a warning not to attempt a forced entrance, and an unidentified man (a protestor) drew a pistol, levelling it across the shoulder of a bystanding newspaper representative.[42]

[36]That Governor Conner provided strong leadership is confirmed from discussion with Dr. R. A. McLemore, director of the State Department of Archives and History, Jackson, Miss., August 9, 1971, and with former representative and anti-sales-tax leader E. B. Livingston, Pulaski, Miss., March 13, 1972.

[37]*Senate Journal*, 1932, pp. 284–93.

[38]*House Journal*, 1932, p. 408. See House Bill 328 entitled "The Emergency Revenue Act of 1932."

[39]*Jackson Daily Clarion-Ledger*, March 14, 1932, p. 7; personal interview, Pulaski, Miss., March 13, 1972.

[40]*Jackson Daily Clarion-Ledger*, March 15, 1932, p. 11. Every Jackson business reportedly closed for the demonstration. The *Pascagoula Chronicle Star* (March 18, 1932) described it as a "monster demonstration" in an article entitled "Monster Crowd Stages Protest."

[41]*Jackson Daily News*, March 16, 1932, p. 1.

[42]*Jackson Daily Clarion-Ledger*, March 17, 1932, p. 1. Governor Conner's wife recalls that Representative Lumpkin used his walking stick to knock the pistol from the man's hand. Telephone conversation with Mrs. Mike Conner, February 27, 1973.

Although the sales tax was still being opposed in the streets and in the senate, passage of the tax program in the house was enough of a break in the sales tax log-jam that legislative attention turned to reorganization. Four days after the house passed the tax bill, a concurrent resolution was adopted providing for the immediate appointment of a joint legislative reorganization committee to consider and report speedily on the reorganization of state and county government. The committee was directed to make a study and draft the legislation necessary not only to reorganize state and county government but also to make them more efficient and economical.[43]

The Reorganization Committee was made up of 15 house members appointed by the house speaker and 10 senate members appointed by the lieutenant governor. As soon as the members were named to the committee, 11 reorganization-type bills that had received no action because of the sales tax fight were referred to the committee.[44]

The committee approached its task with much enthusiasm and dedication, believing they had been given "a very great responsibility" to consider the important subject of reorganization. The 25-member committee divided into 11 subcommittees to study the arrangement of departments proposed in the Brookings Report. The committee had been directed to report in one week on the necessity and advisability of having the legislature recess so the recommendations could be prepared. Governor Conner felt that the work of the committee could only be done during a recess or a special session. He appeared before the committee and asked them to save the taxpayer the expense of a special session by recommending a recess. The committee reasoned that a "complete and coordinated plan" of reorganization would require a recess, since its members were also members of important standing committees and were exceedingly busy with pending matters.[45]

At the beginning of the fourth month of the legislative session, the proposed recess and the unsettled tax question were considered the two major issues facing the legislature.[46] All hopes for the recess ended rather abruptly in the house with the adoption (by vote of 83 to 45) of a resolution that no recess be taken for the purpose of planning reorganization. The recess proposal was

[43]*House Journal*, 1932, p. 422. The senate passed the resolution four days later. *Senate Journal*, 1932, p. 472.

[44]*House Journal*, 1932, p. 505; *The Daily Clarion-Ledger*, March 24, 1932, p. 10.

[45]*Senate Journal*, 1932, pp. 562–64; *Jackson Daily Clarion-Ledger*, March 29, 1932, p. 1.

[46]*Jackson Daily Clarion-Ledger*, April 4, 1932, pp. 1,7. Both houses agreed on April 7, 1932, to go to conference on the tax bill. *House Journal*, 1932, p. 612; *Senate Journal*, 1932, p. 637.

highly unpopular among legislators because it meant they would be asked to return for additional deliberations but with no additional pay. The legislature also seemed to be weary of the thought of returning for a session on reorganization that might equal that of the sales tax for longevity.[47]

A newspaper editorial said that a comprehensive reorganization effort and the split session it would entail would run well into the summer and that this would hardly be fair to the lawmakers, especially since they had already been meeting as long as for an average session. One legislator reported that many members were eating at the Coney Island Hamburger Stand because the session was becoming so drawn out over the sales tax. Also, a half-dozen senators, reportedly in jest, introduced a bill to have an appropriation of public funds to pay board and lodging for the legislators. (The bill was withdrawn when the lieutenant governor ordered it referred to the Committee on Charitable Institutions).[48] Other expressions of sentiment in the legislature against extending the session for reorganization came in the form of resolutions for final adjournment. The defeat of the recess proposal also led to speculation that the governor would accept an ''early'' adjournment and call the legislature back into special session for reorganization.[49]

After the rejection of the recess, the Reorganization Committee attempted to proceed with its work, but because of the usual rush of business preceding final adjournment, the group decided unanimously that it could not do justice to the reorganization problem. All bills previously referred to the committee were returned and further work was suspended. Although this was construed as the abandonment of reorganization in the regular session, the committee stated that it had been impressed with the desirability and ''pressing necessity for a thorough reorganization.''[50]

Governor Conner, therefore, remained as convinced as ever of the need for reorganization, and about ten days later delivered another special message to the legislature. Conner reviewed parts of his inaugural plea for reorganization and noted that the vast majority of the legislators made campaign pledges to

[47]House Concurrent Resolution No. 30, *House Journal,* 1932, p. 612. (The Senate also rejected the recess proposal; see *Senate Journal,* 1932, p. 649.) Personal interview with former representative E. B. Livingston, Pulaski, Miss., March 13, 1972; *Jackson Daily Clarion-Ledger,* April 8, 1932, p. 12, April 9, 1932, p. 1. At this time, the sales tax had not yet passed.
[48]*Jackson Daily Clarion-Ledger,* April 13, 1932, p. 6, April 19, 1932, p. 7.
[49]*House Journal,* 1932, pp. 330, 490, 572; *Jackson Daily Clarion-Ledger,* April 12, 1932, p. 7.
[50]*Jackson Daily Clarion-Ledger,* April 13, 1932, pp. 6-7.

reform and reorganize the government.[51] "I feel," said the governor, "that I would be derelict in the discharge of my pledge to the people and of my official responsibility if I did not again most earnestly urge and implore you to undertake this constructive work . . . without further delay."[52]

Conner reviewed four courses of action open to the legislators: 1. do nothing; 2. remain in session for the study and preparation of the legislation; 3. take a recess until summer or fall; 4. wait until the next regular session or have a special session. Governor Conner felt the best alternative was the recess. The legislature had other ideas, however, and on May 9, both houses adopted a resolution directing the Reorganization Committee to make recommendations to the next session of the legislature. In little more than a week, the legislature adjourned despite the governor's dissatisfaction over the prospects of waiting until the next regular session for a report from the Reorganization Committee. A few days after adjournment, the chairman of the committee, Senator William B. Roberts, said the group soon might urge Conner to call the legislature into special session for reorganization. More than a year elapsed, however, before the governor began an active and open campaign to get legislative action on reorganization in advance of the 1934 regular session.[53]

Before considering that campaign, the various attempts at piecemeal reorganization during the 1932 session should be reviewed.

Ongoing Attempts at Piecemeal Reorganization

Despite Governor Conner's admonition against a piecemeal approach to reorganization, from the first day of the 1932 session and continuing into the 1934 session, measures were introduced to rearrange and consolidate individual agencies or groups of related agencies in piecemeal fashion. Many of the bills would have improved the overall administration, and some no doubt would have abolished and eliminated unnecessary agencies. A few of these piecemeal measures illustrate the seriousness of the financial condition of the state and suggest that reorganization was not so much the point of some of the bills as was retrenchment. For example, at one of the public meetings held to

[51]An editorial appearing the same day said reorganization had been a constant theme since the summer campaign of 1931. *Jackson Daily Clarion-Ledger,* April 26, 1932, p. 6.

[52]*Senate Journal,* 1932, p. 803. In a previous special message to the legislature on taxes and reorganization, Conner had said, "The people expect of this administration the reorganization of administrative machinery of both state and local governments." *Senate Journal,* 1932, pp. 284–93.

[53]*Jackson Daily Clarion-Ledger,* May 22, 1932, p. 6 and May 26, 1932, p. 12.

protest the proposed sales tax, a legislator told the gathering: "If we have to resort to any cutting . . . I favor the school appropriation slash." He explained that this meant to "give the primary students an education but let higher-ups rest, they probably need a little time off." A proposal was made to abolish the East Mississippi Hospital for the Insane, and another proposal would have consolidated three state institutions of higher learning—University of Mississippi, Mississippi State College, and Mississippi State College for Women. Two other institutions—Delta State College and State Teachers' College (now the University of Southern Mississippi)—would have been abolished under bills sponsored by 35 members of the house.[54]

While many bills were introduced to reorganize individual agencies, not many of them were acted on and not much of substance was passed. The governor, with reservations, signed one bill reorganizing the management of the state penitentiary and expressed hope the Reorganization Committee would go further into the question and come up with a more efficient and businesslike plan for management of that institution. The penitentiary was "reorganized" again the next session but not because of any recommendations of the Reorganization Committee.[55]

In another case of piecemeal change, the Senate Agriculture Committee was praised for rejecting a bill "designed to create a super Department of Agriculture giving a newly created official autocratic powers not enjoyed by any public official."[56]

The most significant aspect of the several piecemeal reorganization bills was the serious impact the defeat of one of them, the highway director bill, had on subsequent reorganization efforts. This defeated measure was probably the most important reorganization bill of Conner's administration. The bill was referred to by its detractors as the "Highway Dictator Bill." It would have authorized the governor to appoint a director to administer the state Highway Department, with the three-member, elected Highway Commission being retained to serve primarily as an advisory body.

The bill was introduced only sixteen days before the end of the session and was strongly opposed by Lieutenant Governor Dennis Murphree.[57] The senate

---

[54]*Ibid.*, February 25, 1932, p. 12; *House Journal,* 1932, p. 229, 1934, pp. 94, 158, 193–94. These bills were later withdrawn. Similar introductions made in the senate never emerged from committee; see *Senate Journal,* 1934, p. 223.

[55]*Senate Journal,* 1932, pp. 561–62; *Laws of Mississippi,* 1934, C. 147, p. 347.

[56]*Jackson Daily Clarion-Ledger,* April 26, 1932, p. 6.

[57]Murphree was a personal friend of one of the highway commissioners and reportedly had been assisted by the Highway Department in his election campaign. In opposing Governor Conner

resolved into a Committee of the Whole to allow Murphree to speak against the bill. Murphree referred to other efforts to create "super departments under super directors" and called the highway bill the "crowning folly." He offered the "happy suggestion" that the senate substitute the word dictator in the bill at every point the word director appeared. In spite of Murphree's efforts, the senate passed the bill 27 to 21 and sent it to the house. In a special message to the house, Governor Conner referred to the efforts of "a high government official" who had gone before both houses to speak against the bill. Such opponents, said Conner, would mislead with their charges of oligarchy so as to prejudice the people toward their viewpoints. Conner said the "real menace to free people is the unseen government steered by the hidden hand, for which the people have no opportunity to fix responsibility."[58]

In efforts to disclaim personal interest in the highway bill, Governor Conner produced a letter from a senator who said he had "supreme confidence in Conner's honesty, ability, integrity and sincerity of purpose."[59] The governor also revealed a statement signed by the 22 authors of the bill declaring they had acted on their own initiative in preparing the highway legislation. In addition, the statement noted that the authors of the bill had not been approached by lobbyists of any suppliers or contractors. It was reported, however, that one senator opposed to the bill was stirring up the "most amazing agitation that has struck the floor of the Senate in many years." The senator charged that out-of-state contractors were lobbying for the bill and had converted the committee room of the Temperance Committee into a barroom. He dramatized his point by sending an unbelieving senator and the sergeant-at-arms to the room. They returned with a wastebasket full of whiskey bottles.[60]

---

on the highway bill and on later reorganization efforts, Murphree was undoubtedly considering the possible effects of his position on his desire to be elected governor. By the time Murphree's differences developed with Conner on reorganization, he had been elected lieutenant governor twice, defeated for governor once, and served as governor for nearly a year in 1927 upon the death of the incumbent. Murphree was defeated for governor on two later occasions but was once again elected lieutenant governor. F. Glenn Abney, *Mississippi Election Statistics, 1900–1967* (University, Miss.: Bureau of Governmental Research, 1968), 88–89, 167; *Mississippi Official and Statistical Register, 1968–72*, 390–91.

[58]*Senate Journal*, 1932, pp. 875, 929, 940, 941, 1005, 1009; *Jackson Daily Clarion-Ledger*, May 10, 1932, pp. 1, 7; *House Journal*, 1932, p. 956.

[59]*House Journal*, 1932, pp. 954–56. Former speaker of the house, John Junkin, who knew Mike Conner, described him as a statesman, not a politician, and said he turned down a couple of political deals that might have secured passage of the highway bill. Personal interview, Jackson, Miss., April 24, 1972.

[60]*House Journal*, 1932, p. 955; *Jackson Daily Clarion-Ledger*, May 13, 1932, p. 13.

When the highway bill went to the house, it was referred to the Roads, Ferries, and Bridges Committee. Representative Fielding Wright, reportedly angered because the bill was not sent to his Highways and Highway Financing Committee, denounced the measure as an effort to make the governor the "czar of the highways." Wright not only denounced the bill but inquired of the attorney general as to its constitutionality. The following day, May 12, 1932, Wright received the attorney general's opinion that certain parts of the bill "clearly contravene the provisions of Section 170 of the state constitution." The attorney general reasoned that the constitution vested the control and supervision of the state highways in the Highway Commission and the proposed bill would have taken the control from the commission and placed it in a single director.[61]

The Roads, Ferries, and Bridges Committee met on May 13 to consider the bill, but by this time the opinion of its constitutionality had been rendered. The proponents of the bill, therefore, set out to correct its deficiencies so the committee could report it for action by the house. Representative Walter Sillers tried to correct the deficiencies of the bill by preparing an amendment which he also submitted for the attorney general's opinion. The opinion, however, was the same as before, except that the attorney general offered specific suggestions for making the bill constitutional. He said the bill should more clearly prescribe the power of the Highway Commission: (1) to approve the acts of the director, and (2) to control highway funds.[62]

The speaker of the house then requested the committee to meet on Saturday, May 14, to work on the bill (adjournment having been set for Wednesday, May 18). The speaker and Representatives Walter Sillers and Laurens T. Kennedy[63] appeared before the committee to help perfect the bill, but the meeting was not productive. On request of the bill's proponents, the committee met again Monday night but took no action on the legislation. With only two days remaining in the session, the last effort on behalf of the measure was a motion to have the rules suspended so the house could consider the bill as a committee of the whole. That effort also failed.

The defeat of the highway bill was considered perhaps the most decisive

[61]*Jackson Daily Clarion-Ledger*, May 12, 1932, p. 1; *The Biennial Report of the Attorney General of the State of Mississippi* (July 1, 1931–June 30, 1933), 100–102.
[62]*Biennial Report of the Attorney General*, 103–104.
[63]These three men were the most powerful men in the house. They were the surviving members of the group known as the "Big Four" in the Bilbo administration. *Jackson Daily Clarion-Ledger*, May 25, 1932, p. 6.

setback a Mississippi governor had ever experienced. The bill was called a "plan for the greatest reign of dictatorship the state has ever known."[64]

The defeat of the bill to reorganize the Highway Department is important because it was the defeat of a measure backed by both the governor and the top leadership in the House of Representatives where it failed. This unusual defeat of a forceful power bloc probably resulted from the widespread opposition of the less powerful but more numerous "common people".[65] Lieutenant Governor Murphree was the key leader and spokesman for those opposed to the plan. Murphree was very effective in stirring up the people with his accusation that Governor Conner was striving for a dictatorship.[66]

Time was undoubtedly a factor in the unsuccessful effort to get the highway bill through. Several members of the Roads, Ferries, and Bridges Committee (which did not report the bill out in time for floor action) felt compelled to make a record of their involvement in and position on the bill. They sought to show that they had engaged in no obstructive tactics and that their interest was in the constitutionality of the bill and not in its wisdom. A committee resolution was also entered expressing the committee opinion that the chairman had been fair and impartial at all times.[67]

And so the first regular session of the Conner administration ended with no reorganization of state government. The governor had enthusiastically backed reorganization but was unable to get the legislature to accept his plan of action. This was not so much a reflection on Conner's leadership as it was a matter of circumstances. The reorganization issue had come to prominence because of the state's serious financial problem. The magnitude of that problem was such that in solving it, the legislature became locked in a bitter and prolonged struggle over a new form of taxation, the sales tax. Opponents of the tax prevented its passage several times during the session but the sales tax finally won approval by a vote of 82 to 54. (This was a margin of only one vote since revenue measures require a 60 percent majority for passage.)[68] The

[64]*Ibid.*, May 17, 1932, p. 1.

[65]Former representative E. B. Livingston recalls that when going home from the capitol on weekends, he would be greeted at the train station with the question, "What are y'all doing over there, making us a dictatorship?" Personal interview, Pulaski, Miss., March 13, 1972.

[66]Personal interview with former representative Jack Ewing, Jackson, Miss., March 17, 1972.

[67]*House Journal*, 1932, pp. 1121–23.

[68]*House Journal*, 1932, p. 697. The margin of approval on the vote was reported in the press as "less than one vote." Representative Hervey Owings Hicks recalled the closeness of the vote, emphasizing that the bill passed "by only two-fifths of one vote." Personal interview, Jackson, Mississippi, April 24, 1972. (Since 82 votes were cast for the tax, that was a margin of only

legislature was exhausted and frayed after that narrow and difficult decision and was in no mood to extend the session to struggle with a controversial issue like reorganization.

The one significant piece of reorganization legislation, the highway director bill, did come up after the sales tax was passed and before the legislature adjourned. Although the highway bill passed in the senate, its backers could not get it to a vote in the house before the legislature adjourned. While time was a factor in its defeat, the highway bill also had some stiff opposition. That opposition served notice that the minority leadership could seriously challenge, if not defeat, any meaningful reorganization proposal with the emotionalism inherent in the charge of ''dictatorship.''

The close of the second longest legislative session since the 1890 constitution was called ''Mississippi's most colorful'' and ''one of the most sensational sessions in state history.''[69] Governor Conner, of course, did not abandon his hopes for reorganization at the end of that session, but the passage of the sales tax was not without its political costs and the defeat of the highway director bill carried serious implications for future reorganization efforts. The opposition to that one bill clearly illustrated an unwillingness to vest much power in non-elective officials.

The Effort to Reorganize Through Constitutional Revision

After the close of the first regular legislative session of the Conner administration in May of 1932, there was little recorded discussion of reorganization until January of 1933, when the Reorganization Committee declared by unanimous vote that no effective reorganization could be accomplished without constitutional change. A subcommittee was then formed to draft the necessary constitutional amendments. After some work on the amendments, however, the committee concluded that the proper reforms could be made only through a constitutional convention. Governor Conner later endorsed the constitutional convention as a superior alternative to a series of amendments which he said would ''make a ballot a yard wide and two or three yards long.''[70]

An effort to have a constitutional convention called began in August of 1933 when Conner wrote each member of the legislature to ''urge upon them

---

two-fifths of one vote because 60 percent of the total votes cast, 136, was eighty-one and three-fifths.)

[69]*Jackson Daily Clarion-Ledger,* May 19, 1932, p. 1.

[70]*Senate Journal,* 1934, pp. 44, 46.

the wisdom of calling a constitutional convention" and to ask for their ideas and views on the subject.[71] Conner told the legislators that he would call a special session to provide for the convention if they were sufficiently interested in the plan. This was the first of four such letters, leading one opponent of the convention to speak of the governor's "mail order convention."

The governor received ideas and opinions from several sources. The *Jackson Daily News* said Conner should not be taking a "poll" of legislators but should be leading in a strong, decisive, and definite way by calling the session. The editor of that paper also asked the people to stop writing letters to the editor to say it would be a sacrilege to alter the 1890 state constitution. The editor did not agree with such letters because he felt any part of the constitution, except maybe that pertaining to suffrage, could be changed. In the opinion of the *Jackson Daily Clarion-Ledger,* however, the proposed convention was a threat to the "wise work" of 1890.[72]

Lieutenant Governor Murphree came out strongly against the convention and was joined by the president *pro tem* of the senate, Winfred C. Adams. Governor Conner reported, however, that about one-third of the legislators had responded to his letter, and they favored the plan by three to one. He said a special session would be called as soon as a reasonable majority indicated they were in favor. About one week later, on August 22, Conner announced that a working majority was assured and he would soon issue a statement on the special session for the convention.[73]

The lieutenant governor meanwhile questioned Conner's claim of a working majority, and said he calculated that 33 of 49 senators were opposed to the convention. In reply, the governor reported that 30 senators favored the convention and declared that a special session was a certainty.[74]

Governor Conner had based his case for the convention primarily on the problems of reorganization, although he also indicated he wanted the convention to consider the revenue system and tax equalization. He did not, however, suggest any specific constitutional changes, saying that those would be left up to the convention.[75] The opponents of the convention, though, wanted

[71]*House Journal,* 1934, p. 33.

[72]*Jackson Daily News,* August 9, 1933, p. 8, August 17, p. 8; *Jackson Daily Clarion-Ledger,* August 14, 1933, p. 4.

[73]*Jackson Daily Clarion-Ledger,* August 13, 1933, p. 1, August 15, 1933, pp. 1, 7, and August 22, 1933, p. 1, and August 23, 1933, p. 1.

[74]*Ibid.,* August 29, 1933, p. 1, September 2, 1933, p. 1.

[75]*House Journal,* 1934, pp. 34, 36, 37.

to know in advance what changes would be made. The Brookings Report had been the only indication so far of what a constitutional convention might consider. Opponents therefore attacked the convention as an attempt to implement the rather drastic provisions of that study. They distributed a circular claiming that the governor had endorsed the Brookings Report and a policy of the "concentration of power and the centralization of all governmental activities in the hands of a few chosen men."[76] Thousands of copies of the circular were mailed. It went to private citizens and to every county official. Conner saw this as an attempt to frighten county officials by making them think their personal interests were in danger so they would pressure their legislators to defeat the reorganization efforts.

To answer the misrepresentations of the circular, the governor wrote his second letter to the legislators on September 2, 1933, and quoted from earlier speeches disclaiming any endorsements of the Brookings Report. Even Lieutenant Governor Murphree, already opposing the convention, felt compelled to publicly deny any link with the report. Murphree's opposition to the proposed convention was based on his belief that efforts would be made to make more public officials appointive and fewer elective. Murphree thought such changes would be attempted even if the Brookings Report had not existed. His belief was based on: (1) the sentiment exhibited for the highway bill in the 1932 session, (2) the proposals of the Reorganization Committee to replace elected officials with appointees, and (3) the fact that no one had refuted his beliefs by indicating specifically what the convention would do. Murphree expressed these views to a very receptive audience at the state convention of county supervisors and quoted an amendment prepared by the Reorganization Committee as follows: "The Legislature may abolish any office created or recognized by the constitution, in the executive department of the state or county government except the Governor and Lieutenant Governor."[77]

Murphree's reasoning had gone unchallenged, and one senator pursued the point by calling upon the governor to indicate more precisely in his next letter what changes the constitutional convention might make.[78] Conner responded with a general statement: "Nobody proposes to discard our present constitu-

[76]The circular was entitled "Mississippi—Yesterday, Today and Tomorrow." *Senate Journal,* 1934, p. 41–43.
[77]*Jackson Daily Clarion-Ledger,* September 7, 1933, pp. 1, 12, September 16, 1933, p. 5.
[78]"An Open Letter to the Governor," *Jackson Daily Clarion-Ledger,* September 6, 1933, p. 10.

tion in its entirety, or to destroy the Bill of Rights, or to set up a dictator or to violate any of the principles of Jeffersonian democracy.'' Governor Conner also addressed the convention of supervisors and indicated some desired changes related to financial administration, but gave no details of changes affecting the organization of state or county government.[79]

Conner's third letter to the Mississippi legislators went out on September 15, 1933. The main purpose of that letter was to submit a bill prepared by the Reorganization Committee providing for the calling of a constitutional convention. The governor promised to call a special session if the legislators would approve the bill. Lieutenant Governor Murphree called this ''mail order legislation.'' Murphree's protest of the preparation of the bill by the Reorganization Committee resulted in attachment of an explanation to the bill advising that the committee had neither recommended nor disapproved the constitutional convention. Murphree did not want the committee's preparation of the bill to give an authoritative stamp to the governor's convention campaign.[80]

An important aspect of the third letter was Conner's acknowledgment of his very cautious approach. His request for prior approval was not made, he said, to shirk responsibility, but was a ''sincere desire to escape the costs of an extraordinary session in the event a majority would not vote to enact the proposed legislation.'' Conner later said that the history of special sessions was neither pleasant nor beneficial and that he would not take the responsibility of calling one without advance assurances that the convention bill would pass.[81]

At a news conference on September 21, Governor Conner said he had received replies from about half the 189 legislators and their response was about two to one in favor of the convention. Conner was apparently very optimistic. He cancelled his appearance before the Chicago Century of Progress Exhibition and speculation mounted that the special session call was imminent. The governor was apparently waiting for an unmistakable majority because the call did not go out, even though on September 27 the results of the mail order vote were 87 for and 38 against, with 64 not voting. According to these results, 5 more house votes and 4 more senate votes would have given a

[79]*House Journal,* 1934, pp. 42; *Jackson Daily Clarion-Ledger,* September 15, 1933, p. 1.
[80]*Senate Journal,* 1934, pp. 44–45; *Jackson Daily Clarion-Ledger,* September 13, 1933, pp. 1, 10.
[81]*Senate Journal,* 1934, p. 45; *Jackson Daily Clarion-Ledger,* September 29, 1933, p. 1.

majority in each house. Although 3 more positive votes were reported two days later, on September 29 Governor Conner said legislators would "have to play ball soon or wait until the regular session in January."[82]

The legislators apparently did not play ball soon enough, for on October 4 Conner wrote his fourth and final letter, revealing his decision not to call the special session. He first said the plan had been sidetracked temporarily by an active and well-organized campaign of misrepresentation. He further explained that too many legislators waited too long to express their opinions and that not enough time remained to have the special session in advance of the regular session of January, 1934.[83]

From the very beginning of the governor's efforts to get a commitment for the convention by using the mails, the advantage seemed to lie with his opposition. They sent literature to private citizens and county officials who could conduct a more personal lobby against the convention. The opponents presented the convention as part of an effort to "adopt" the Brookings Report and set up a "dictator." The time Conner lost in refuting these charges was ultimately a factor in the decision not to call the special session for the convention. Governor Conner also found it difficult to answer the critics of the convention who wanted to know exactly what the convention would do.

In assessing this latest effort to set in motion the mechanisms for reform, the governor said simply that he was not discouraged by the events and that he would continue his efforts to effect reorganization.[84]

Second Legislative Session and the Last Effort to Reorganize

The convening of the legislature in January, 1934, marked the beginning of the second half of the Conner administration and the beginning of another effort to reorganize. In his biennial message to the legislature, Conner reviewed the progress that had been made in the area of state finances. He indicated that the mere cutting of state appropriations to economize was not the complete solution to the state's financial problems and reiterated the need

---

[82]*Jackson Daily Clarion-Ledger,* September 22, 1933, p. 1, September 27, 1933, p. 1, September 29, 1933, p. 1.

[83]*Senate Journal,* 1934, p. 47. The plan had been to have the constitutional convention complete the work of revision in time for the 1934 regular session to take up the matter of reorganization with a new constitution. In his biennial address, Conner indicated that he had secured a majority vote for the convention but the plan was abandoned because of the time factor; see *Ibid.,* 21.

[84]*Ibid.,* 48.

for a complete reorganization of state and county government so as to relieve the "almost intolerable burdens that result from our inefficient and inequitable administrative and tax systems."

Conner again offered a plan to meet the "great and urgent" needs for reform. He appealed to the legislators: (1) to see to the necessary governmental operations for the current period (without any enlargements); (2) to provide for a constitutional convention; and (3) to adjourn, reconvening only when the constitution had been revised so the needed reforms could be legislated based on the new constitution.[85]

After the governor outlined this course of action, a resolution was promptly introduced in the house to "provide for immediate consideration of legislation which will eliminate unnecessary boards and commissions and reorganize government so as to reduce state and county governmental expenses." The resolution was not adopted, but in the second week of the session both houses passed a resolution commending and complimenting the Reorganization Committee for its valuable findings which were deemed of vast importance. The next day a resolution was introduced and passed in the house to make it the policy of the legislature to effect economies and reforms in state and county government. The resolution did not legislate any reorganization, however, and was actually a prelude to considerable opposition to the idea of reorganization.[86]

Opposition to the Brookings Proposals for County Reform

Governor Conner, as he had done in the previous reorganization efforts, denied that the Brookings Report would be "slavishly" followed and declared firmly that "nobody wants the governor to appoint county officers." One senator told the governor that he had read and re-read the Brookings study, seeing therein steps that would lead to the appointive system. The senator was right, for the report did recommend the appointment of most county officers. Although the Brookings Report did not recommend the appointment of supervisors, the supervisors actively opposed the convention nonetheless. In addition, House Speaker Thomas Bailey reportedly possessed a copy of a letter mailed to all county sheriffs urging their opposition to the efforts to transfer county elective officers to the appointive category.[87]

---

[85]*Ibid.*, 20, 23, 35.

[86]*House Journal*, 1934, pp. 64, 99; *Laws of Mississippi*, 1934, C. 358.

[87]*Jackson Daily Clarion-Ledger*, January 15, 1934, p. 1, January 23, 1934, p. 14; personal interview with former speaker of the house John Junkin, Jackson, Miss., April 24, 1972.

While the proposals of the Brookings Report may have been cause for worry about the appointive system, the governor himself caused such worries despite his denials of the role of the Brookings study. In his biennial address, Conner spoke of the possibility that the new constitution could provide for other forms of county government besides the supervisor system.[88]

Additionally, the chairman of the Reorganization Committee gave indications that the focal point of the reform effort, after constitutional revision, might be county government. He estimated possible savings of $1 million annually from the consolidation of duties connected with the sheriff's office. But the greatest trouble with the state, he said, was the boards of supervisors, "where five men sit around a table and do nothing but divide the swag before they go home." He asked why there should be more than one supervisor.[89]

The Opposition of the Highway Department.   Another source of opposition to the constitutional convention plan was the Highway Department. This conflict was partly a carryover from the unsuccessful attempt to put the so-called "highway dictator bill" through the 1932 legislature.

The successful opposition to the "dictator bill" had charged that the bill's purpose was to give the governor control of the Highway Department. Many people likewise felt that the constitutional convention proposal was an effort by Conner to gain control over the Highway Department.[90] It was predicted that the constitutional convention proposal would fail unless the governor publicly dispelled the rumors that he was out to get control of the Highway Department. He was further advised to endorse the idea of a loan of $7.5 million for the department from the Federal Public Works Administration. A co-author of the convention bill attempted to answer the charge that Conner sought control of the Highway Department through the constitutional convention. "The Highway Department is not involved in any way," he insisted. "Certainly nobody has advocated disturbing the Highway Commission through a constitutional convention. That is all bosh."[91]

[88]*Senate Journal,* 1934, p. 23.

[89]*Jackson Daily Clarion-Ledger,* January 19, 1934, p. 4.

[90]Personal interviews with former representatives S. T. Roebuck, Newton, Miss., March 13, 1972 and E. B. Livingston, Pulaski, Miss., March 13, 1972. No personal or ulterior motives were attributed to Conner, who was consistently described as a statesman and not a politician—sometimes with the implication that he might have been more successful if he had had more of a knack for "back slapping." Personal interview with Wilburn Buckley, Jackson, Miss., May 31, 1972.

[91]*Jackson Daily News,* January 16, 1934, p. 1, January 19, 1934, p. 6; *Jackson Daily Clarion-Ledger,* January 18, 1934, p. 1.

The record does not show that the governor or any other proponent of the convention advocated changes in the Highway Department before the vote was taken on the convention proposal. Actions by Governor Conner after the vote on the proposal, however, indicate that he may have hoped for changes in that department. For example, he vetoed the loan from the Public Works Administration and in his veto message, called on the legislature to investigate the Highway Commission and to adopt legislation which would compel efficiency and economy in its operations. Conner also asked that the commission confine its activities to road work. The newspaper account of the veto message added, "in other words, make them build roads and not political machines." An employee of the Highway Department during the 1930s revealed that one month he was "assessed" $25 of his monthly $75 paycheck for use in the "political interest of the department."[92]

While Governor Conner's veto might be interpreted as an act of personal hostility toward the Highway Department, he offered substantial reasons for his action. He referred to letters he had received from the Federal Public Works administrator criticizing the Mississippi Highway Commission for making unsatisfactory progress in the expenditure of funds already granted by the federal government. The governor's veto message was even recognized as well-researched and factual by a leader of the attempt to override the veto.[93]

Another angle in the involvement of the Highway Department in the constitutional convention fight was the department's practice of putting legislators on its payroll. After the convention vote in the senate, an editorial in a Tennessee newspaper triggered heated denials of any deals between legislators and the highway people on the vote. One senator said the author should be "stigmatized as a cur" for implying that senate members sold their votes to curry favor or jobs with the Highway Department. The Memphis editorial, however, made no charge of collusion; it only referred to such allegations appearing in Mississippi newspapers.[94]

About this time, a resolution was introduced in the house "declaring it the sense of the Mississippi Legislature that no member of the Legislature during his tenure should accept employment by, with, or in, any other department of state government." Representative Walter Sillers reportedly worked on

[92]*House Journal,* 1934, p. 556; *Jackson Daily Clarion-Ledger,* March 15, 1934, p. 1; personal interview in Jackson, Miss., April, 1972.
[93]*House Journal,* 1934, p. 553; *Jackson Daily Clarion-Ledger,* March 16, 1934, pp. 12, 14.
[94]*Jackson Daily Clarion-Ledger,* January 27, 1934, p. 1; *Memphis Commercial Appeal,* January 26, 1934, p. 6.

another resolution asking the Highway Department to furnish the legislature a list showing the number of legislators and their relatives appearing on the department's payroll.[95]

Apart from any resolutions, the practice of holding jobs simultaneously in more than one branch of the government seemed to be a clear violation of the state constitution (Article 1, Section 2). The probability is high that some legislators faced a conflict of interest in this case. One senator felt that there was a connection between his vote for the constitutional convention and the firing of his brother-in-law from the department. About a year later, a Memphis paper ran a signed article stating that at least 51 legislators were either directly or indirectly on the payroll of the Highway Department, which, according to the article, had at least 50 workers in each county of the state.[96]

As far as the Highway Department was concerned, the most important issue in the convention question was whether or not the governor wanted to gain control of the department. If he did, this would mean the three elected commissioners could no longer dominate work in their more or less independent districts. Their reaction was to offer the governor certain "conditions" relative to the holding of a constitutional convention. Conner said he was informed by the department that no constitutional convention would be held unless a guarantee was included in the convention bill that the Highway Department would in no way be affected.

The convention bill, of course, contained no such guarantee. Further, it was probably never considered. The governor's purpose in seeking the convention was reorganization for economy and efficiency, and it is hardly likely that he would have agreed to make an agency the size of the Highway Department immune to any such reorganization efforts. The Highway Department had more money available to it than all other departments combined.[97]

Legislative Action on the Constitutional Convention Bill

Twenty-one senate members introduced Senate Bill 111 providing for the calling of a convention to revise the constitution or to write a new one. Although the bill passed by vote of 43 to 5, the chances for the convention

---

[95]*House Journal,* 1934, p. 175; *Jackson Daily Clarion-Ledger,* January 18, 1934, p. 10. It is interesting that Sillers was a top proponent of the constitutional convention; in 1957, as speaker of the house and in his forty-first year in the legislature, he effectively opposed Governor J. P. Coleman's plan for a constitutional convention. *Jackson Clarion-Ledger,* October 14, 1957, p. 1.

[96]*Jackson Daily Clarion-Ledger,* February 8, 1934, p. 8; *Memphis Commercial Appeal,* April 11, 1935.

[97]*Senate Journal,* 1934, pp. 215, 1001; *House Journal,* 1934, p. 559.

were virtually nil as a result of an amendment making the convention subject to the approval of the people. Lieutenant Governor Murphree cast the crucial vote for that amendment after the senate vote on the issue had tied at 23 to 23.[98]

While the senate amendment was generally regarded as debilitating, the house debate on the bill was spirited and the vote was very close. In the first direct vote on the bill, it failed by vote of 68 to 71. The bill was kept alive, however, on a motion to reconsider that passed by one vote, 68 to 67. After some amendments were adopted relating to the apportionment of delegates to the convention, the bill was reconsidered but failed again by vote of 66 to 70. Again a motion to reconsider was entered, but this time it failed by vote of 67 to 68.[99]

The bill might have been kept alive but Representative T. H. Byrd, who had twice before voted for the bill and for the earlier reconsideration motion, switched and voted against reconsideration. His vote accounted for the one-vote margin of defeat (67 to 68) on the last motion to reconsider.

According to an editorial analysis of the narrow defeat of the convention bill, the prevailing view was that the senate would not budge from its referendum requirement and that sincere advocates of the convention bill had voted against it in the house in order to prevent a prolonged and hopeless fight.[100]

Another possible factor bearing on the outcome of the convention vote was the prospect that legislative reapportionment would be considered at the proposed convention. Reapportionment was not openly discussed as a topic for consideration by the convention, but one newspaper editorial voiced the hope that a new constitution would reapportion the legislature and give southern Mississippi its proper representation. Analysis of the apportionment of the legislature in 1934, however, indicates that correcting the disparities for such areas as southern Mississippi would have meant a loss of representation for a large majority of the districts. In the view of a former member of the 1934 legislature, the proposed convention failed because of the fear that a new constitution would reapportion the legislature.[101]

---

[98]*Senate Journal,* 1934, pp. 105, 123, 136, 137, 142. A house member during the Conner administration said the convention would have carried had it not been for the opposition of Murphree. Personal interview with Jack Ewing, Jackson, Miss., March 17, 1972.

[99]*House Journal,* 1934, pp. 218, 251, 254, 269.

[100]*Jackson Daily News,* February 1, 1934, p. 6.

[101]*Hattiesburg American,* August 9, 1933, p. 2; personal interview with Mississippi Supreme Court Justice L. A. Smith, Jackson, Miss., March 17, 1972.

It is also interesting to note that when Representative Byrd voted for the bill, only one of the 65 other representatives voting similarly represented fewer people. On the conclusive vote, Byrd switched and voted against the convention. He represented only 7,523 people, while the theoretical one-man, one-vote district should have included 14,356.

Altogether, 98 of the 136 districts were over-represented since they had fewer than 14,356 people. Thirty-eight of the 136 districts were under-represented since they had more than 14,356 people. Table 11, comparing the vote on the convention to the apportionment of districts, indicates that legis-lators from under-apportioned districts were more inclined to vote for the convention (58 percent of them did). On the other hand, legislators from over-apportioned districts were more inclined to vote against the convention (55 percent so voting).

Because of this apparent relationship between legislative reapportionment and the vote on the convention, the significance of the relationship was tested by chi square analysis. The chi square was computed directly from the data in Table 11 with the formula:

$$\text{Chi Square} = \frac{N(AD-BC)^2}{(A+B)\,(C+D)\,(A+C)\,(B+D)}$$

Table 11

Vote on the Constitutional Convention Bill of 1934 Based on the Apportionment of the Legislative Districts

Nature of Vote	Nature of District Apportionment		Total
	Under-Apportioned	Over-Apportioned	
For	22	44	66
Against	16	54	70
Total	38	98	136

Chi Square = 1.85
.05 Level of Significance = 3.84

SOURCE: Adapted from U.S. Department of Commerce, Bureau of the Census, *Fifteenth Census of the United States, 1930: Population,* (Washington, D.C.: U.S. Government Printing Office), III, pt. 1, pp. 1274–80; *House Journal,* 1934, p. 263.

The obtained chi square, 1.85, is not large enough to be statistically significant at the .05 level of significance. This analysis therefore, does not support the suspicion that the outcome of the convention bill vote was significantly influenced by the prospect that legislative reapportionment would be a topic for consideration at the convention.

And so Governor Conner was defeated in another effort to get legislative action on reorganization. His plan for securing a revised constitution under which the problems of executive organization could more adequately be solved with statutory action was rejected by the legislature. As in previous efforts, Governor Conner made strong appeals to the legislature which were resisted with charges that the Brookings Report would be followed at the convention. The Brookings study was said to be a plan for the centralization of government and for the appointment of state and local officials. The most powerful groups at both state and county levels, i.e., the boards of supervisors and the Mississippi Highway Department, opposed the convention. In combination, these two groups formed an insurmountable obstacle. Either one alone would have provided formidable opposition; in fact, the Highway Department offered to permit the governor to hold the constitutional convention in exchange for a guarantee that it would not be affected by the convention. Governor Conner rejected the deal and the constitutional convention plan was defeated.

After the second unsuccessful effort to get the convention, Governor Conner still remained hopeful, but when talk emerged of a special session in the summer, he was again advised by leading newspapers to give up his "feud" with the Highway Department.[102]

There was no indication that Conner "gave up his feud" with the Highway Department, nor was any other effort made in the Conner administration to call a constitutional convention or otherwise to reorganize. In his retiring message in 1936, however, the governor reiterated his commitment to reorganization. He expressed regret that "his" legislature did not effect an extensive reorganization and expressed the hope that the new one would. Conner warned the legislature of the parasites out for selfish gain at the expense of the people. He said he was proud of his fight against the political termites who would even undertake to corrupt, coerce, and intimidate.[103]

---

[102]*Jackson Daily News*, February 9, 1934, p. 6; *Jackson Daily Clarion-Ledger*, February 10, 1934, p. 1.

[103]*Senate Journal*, 1936, pp. 31, 32, 42. See also the comments by Speaker Junkin on Page 46.

After the senate action on the convention bill, Governor Conner had said, for the "truth of the record," that the "responsibility for the disastrous results of indifference and delay will not rest upon my shoulders. I have done all that is within my province and power to do. My conscience is clear."[104]

So ended the most diligent effort of any Mississippi governor to effect a sweeping reorganization. A bill was introduced in the first month of the Hugh White administration in 1936 to provide for a constitutional convention, but the bill was never reported from committee. As a major issue in Mississippi politics, reorganization had lost its appeal. The reemergence of the issue and the second major effort to reorganize the administrative structure of state government are discussed in the following chapter.

[104]*Senate Journal*, 1934, pp. 216–17.

3 / The Second Major Effort
to Reorganize Mississippi Administration

FORCES LEADING TO THE REORGANIZATION EFFORT

The second major attempt at administrative reorganization in Mississippi began in 1950. In that year, Governor Fielding Wright delivered his biennial address and called upon the legislature to reorganize the administrative structure of state government. Governor Wright's call for reorganization came at a time when the Commission for the Organization of the Executive (National) Government, 1947–1949, popularly known as the Hoover Commission, had "stirred up no end of discussion on the vital problem of reorganization." The Hoover Commission and resulting discussion had encouraged twenty-eight states to make their own reorganization studies.[1]

While Governor Wright had not mentioned reorganization in his inaugural message of 1948, that address helps explain why the issue of reorganization came up in 1950. As he reviewed the state's financial condition in his inaugural speech, the governor showed concern over the establishment of new agencies of government. By 1950 this concern had obviously grown, for in the three legislative sessions of 1944, 1946, and 1948, over a dozen new state agencies had been created. This rapid rate of increase was questioned by government officials and by the general public as well.[2] Seven publications by the Bureau of Public Administration at the University of Mississippi between 1947 and 1950 also helped focus attention on the multiplicity of agencies. These publications either wholly or in part dealt with the administrative organization of the state and often offered plans for organizational and procedural revision.

[1]Gordon K. Bryan and Augustin Magruder, "Does Mississippi Need a Hoover Commission?: An Examination of the Reorganization Problem in Mississippi," *The Social Science Council,* III (March, 1950), 6–8.
[2]Personal interview with former representative Ben H. Walley, Jackson, Miss., March 16, 1972.

One publication, *The Growth of State Administration in Mississippi* by Robert Highsaw and Carl D. Mullican, Jr., was referred to by Governor Wright when he discussed reorganization in his biennial message of 1950.[3] The governor opened his discussion of reorganization by acknowledging the general dissatisfaction among many Mississippians with the manner in which the national government was operating. More specifically, Wright said that the federal government was becoming too centralized and too expensive and that too many bureaus, commissions, boards, and departments had been and were continuing to be created. Citing data from Highsaw and Mullican's book to compare the growth of agencies in Mississippi and in Washington, the governor concluded that Mississippi was in no better position than the national government and should begin to put its own house in order before being critical of others.

Alluding to the Mississippi Constitution of 1890 that set up the structural framework of the government, Wright noted that governmental services and functions had increased far beyond the imagination of the framers of the constitution. "We now have 103 agencies carrying on our governmental functions. . . . We have from one to ten boards, commissions, or bureaus for every letter in the alphabet except q, u, x and z. Hundreds of employees have been added to the payroll of the state, and two large capitol buildings and a new fifteen-story office building are not sufficient to house the various governmental agencies.[4]

The Governor's Recommendations and Plan for Reorganization

Following his discussion of Mississippi bureaucracy, Governor Wright made a strong plea for reorganization: "I recommend and urge a complete reorganization of the administrative machinery of the state government." He viewed this as both a challenge and a responsibility. The challenge was for the government to perform the public services needed by the people; the responsi-

[3]State Administration Series No. 10, Bureau of Public Administration (University of Mississippi, 1950). The other publications were: Robert B. Highsaw, *Mississippi's Wealth: A Study of the Public Administration of Natural Resources* (University, Miss.: Bureau of Public Administration, 1947); *A Handbook of Mississippi State Agencies,* (University, Miss.: Bureau of Public Administration, 1948); Robert B. Highsaw and Edward M. Johnson, Jr., *Aids for Governing: An Analysis of Technical Assistance in Mississippi* (University, Miss.: Bureau of Public Administration, 1948); *A Handbook of Technical Service Agencies,* (University, Miss.: Bureau of Public Administration, 1948); Robert B. Highsaw, *Administering Mississippi's Wealth* (University, Miss.: Bureau of Public Administration, 1949); Ethridge, *Modernizing Mississippi's Constitution.*
[4]*Senate Journal,* 1950, pp. 32–33.

bility was to perform these services in the most economical, efficient, and productive manner possible.

Governor Wright then presented his plan for reorganization. First, he said, efforts of individual legislators to effect their own ideas on reorganization should be abandoned in favor of a comprehensive plan which could not be prepared by a single member nor by a commission while the legislature was in session. The governor recommended the creation of a joint legislative reorganization committee to make a study and to formulate a program of reorganization. He felt this to be the quickest and best approach to the problem and indicated that he did not mean for the action on any proposed reorganization to wait for the legislature of the new administration which would take office in two years:

> It is proper that *we* carry to final completion a program of such magnitude, and one of such vital importance; therefore, as much as I dislike the responsibility of convening an extraordinary session of the legislature, should this committee work out a program of reorganization, I would feel constrained to issue the call at the committee's suggestion because, in my opinion, it would prove of such benefit to the people of our state as to be justified.[5]

In short, Governor Wright made a strong plea for reorganization even though reorganization was the twenty-third of twenty-four topics discussed in his biennial speech. A front page report of the speech in an out-of-state newspaper stated that the governor had shown solid support for reorganization.[6]

The Legislature's Response to the Governor's Plan

The legislature wasted little time in responding to Wright's request. A bill setting up a recess reorganization committee to study the state's agencies and departments was introduced in the Mississippi House of Representatives the following day. It subsequently passed both houses with votes of 77 to 46 and 30 to 10.[7] The act expressly acknowledged the governor's view that it would be impossible to undertake a reorganization study during the regular session of the legislature because of the many other matters that had to be considered.

The purpose of the act was to have the Reorganization Committee furnish the legislature with a full and detailed report on the following:

[5]*Ibid.*, 33. Italics added.
[6]*New Orleans Times-Picayune*, January 4, 1950, p. 1.
[7]*House Journal*, 1950, House Bill 22, pp. 36, 185; *Senate Journal*, 1950, p. 1027.

1. The present status of all departments, bureaus, commissions, and other agencies.

2. Existing deficiencies therein, especially as to overlapping and duplicating authority and services.

3. Recommendations as to elimination, consolidation and coordination of any and all departments and agencies of the state in an effort to bring about a more economical and efficient administration of the state government.[8]

The committee was authorized to employ any clerical and technical assistance needed to complete the study and was allotted $40,000 of state funds to defray expenses. An out-of-state consulting firm reportedly was interested in working for the Reorganization Committee, but it was decided the problem should be handled entirely by Mississippians. Subsequently, Dr. Robert B. Highsaw, director of the Bureau of Public Administration at the University of Mississippi, and two of his associates became the technical consultants for the committee.[9]

The committee was asked to submit its report to the governor by December 15, 1950, and was authorized to request and recommend therein that the governor convene a special session of the legislature to consider the report. The report was to be compiled by the Legislative Fact-Finding Committee on Reorganization of State Government, a joint committee made up of six members of each house to be appointed by the lieutenant governor and speaker of the house. An effort to have the governor appoint four committee members from the general public was defeated.[10]

Although the reorganization bill was approved by Governor Wright on April 12, 1950 (the legislature adjourning on May 6, 1950), it was not until May 31, 1950, that the members were appointed to the Reorganization Committee. Because of the delay in the appointments and the December 15 deadline, the committee was expected to go to work immediately on a task considered "one of the greatest ever assigned a legislative committee in vacation in Mississippi." Wright showed his interest in the work of the committee by attending its first meeting and reminding its members they had the opportunity to render a great service to the state.[11]

[8]*Laws of Mississippi*, 1950, C. 123, 445.

[9]Thomas Ramage Ethridge, "State Administrative Reorganization in Mississippi" (unpublished master's thesis, University of Mississippi, 1951), 56–57.

[10]*House Journal*, 1950, p. 1060; *Senate Journal*, 1950, pp. 1027, 1100.

[11]*Jackson Clarion-Ledger*, May 31, 1950, p. 1; personal interview with former committee member R. B. Meadows, Jr., Gulfport, Miss., July 14, 1972.

Organization and Procedures of the Committee. During the course of its study, the committee was to investigate the affairs and activities of all departments of state government; it was declared the duty of all state officers and employees to cooperate with the committee. The Reorganization Committee was empowered to hold public and private hearings and to subpoena and examine witnesses.[12]

At its first meeting, the committee decided to take a functional approach to the study. All the services of state government and the agencies performing them were grouped into nine functional fields. The committee then formed nine subcommittees to deal with these fields.[13]

The procedure of the study was first to have each subcommittee hold hearings and otherwise make an investigation into its area of responsibility. The technical staff would then prepare a report on the basis of the investigation. The staff's report would be considered by the subcommittee and then by the full committee. When approved by the full committee, the subcommittee report would be released to the press. The final report was assembled by the technical staff from the various subcommittee reports. It was then reviewed and approved by the full committee before being delivered to the governor.[14] (The steps in the preparation of the report are illustrated in Figure 1.)

THE PROPOSALS FOR REORGANIZATION

Unlike the Brookings Report of 1932, the reorganization study and report of 1950 dealt exclusively with state government. The major concern of the latter report was with the organizational structure of the state but, like the Brookings study, it also emphasized some financial aspects of the state's administration as well as personnel and purchasing practices.

Before examining the proposals for reorganization, we will see what the structure of administration was in 1950, note its defects, and review the principles used in the proposed reorganization. Where possible, comparisons will be made with the reorganization study of 1932.

---

[12]*Laws of Mississippi,* 1950, C. 445.

[13]The nine fields were: general government, protection to persons and property, highways and transportation, conservation and recreation, health and sanitation, hospitals and institutions, charities and correction, education, and libraries. Appendix C lists the 1950 agencies grouped into the nine functional fields.

[14]T. R. Ethridge, "State Administrative Reorganization in Mississippi;" *Jackson Clarion-Ledger,* July 14, 1950, p. 9.

Figure 1: **Actions Taken by the Full Committee, Subcommittees, and the Technical Staff in the Preparation of the 1950 Reorganization Report**

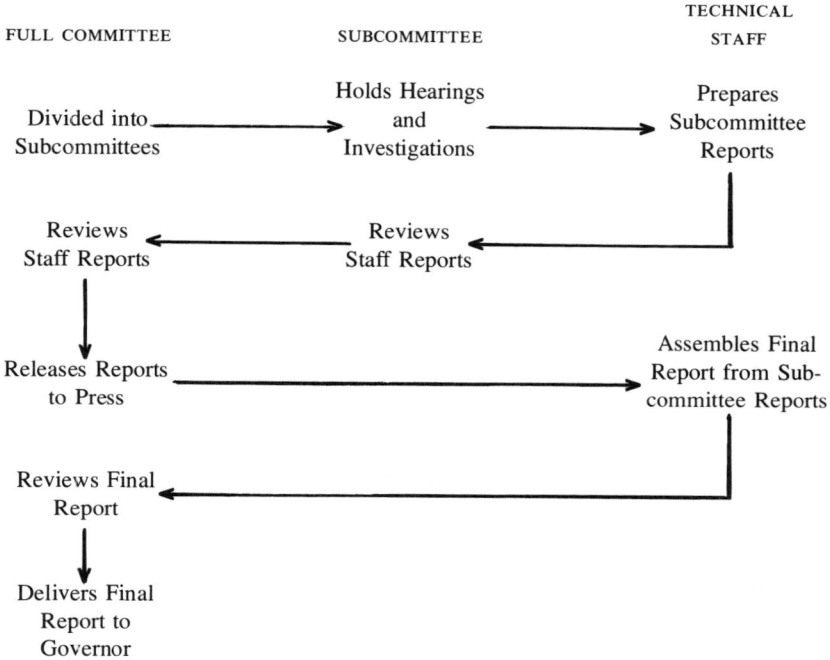

FULL COMMITTEE	SUBCOMMITTEE	TECHNICAL STAFF
Divided into Subcommittees	Holds Hearings and Investigations	Prepares Subcommittee Reports
Reviews Staff Reports	Reviews Staff Reports	
Releases Reports to Press		Assembles Final Report from Sub-committee Reports
Reviews Final Report		
Delivers Final Report to Governor		

SOURCE: Adapted from T. R. Ethridge, "State Administrative Reorganization in Mississippi."

The State Organization in 1950. The Reorganization Committee in 1950 appraised the administrative conditions in Mississippi as "confusion compounded." This did not mean that the confusion had been compounded because of organizational changes since 1930, when the Brookings Report had termed the general administrative situation "chaotic." It meant that the several defects in the government of 1950 compounded the confusion that resulted primarily from the "basic lack of simple and sound organization."[15]

Table 12 shows the nine functional fields into which the Reorganization

[15]Legislative Fact-Finding Committee on Reorganization of State Government, *Mississippi: A Report on State Reorganization* (Jackson, Miss.: Legislative Fact-Finding Committee on Reorganization of State Government, December, 1950), 12.

Table 12

Numbers of Related and Independent Agencies in Each Functional Field of Mississippi Government in 1950

Functional Field	Number of Agencies
General Government	22
Protection of Persons and Property	16
Highways and Transportation	3
Conservation and Recreation	25
Health and Sanitation	8
Hospitals and Institutions	7
Charities and Correction	5
Education	11
Libraries	3
Total	100

SOURCE: Adapted from Legislative Fact-Finding Committee, *Report on State Reorganization,* pp. 2–4. Appendix C lists the 1950 agencies grouped into the functional fields.

Committee grouped the 100 agencies depicted in the organization chart on page 69. That chart illustrates the organization of state administration in 1950 as described by the Reorganization Committee. The basic pattern of the organization is the same as that of 1930, although executive authority and responsibility were more diffused. This diffusion is indicated in Table 13 which shows a 25 percent increase in the number of agencies between 1930 and 1950. The growth in the number of agencies was due almost entirely to statutory action, with only the Board of Trustees of Institutions of Higher Learning becoming a constitutional agency during this period.[16]

While the net increase in total agencies was only 20, the actual increase was much larger because 21 agencies were either abolished or consolidated into new agencies as explained in Table 14.

Between 1930 and 1950, a number of new agencies were created and several others restructured. In the process, as Table 15 shows, the roles of both the governor and the senate in selecting heads of agencies were di-

[16]Mississippi *Constitution,* 1890, Section 213-A. The board was created by statute in 1932 but put into the constitution in 1944.

Chart 1

THE 100 AGENCIES AND OFFICES OF MISSISSIPPI GOVERNMENT STUDIED BY THE LEGISLATIVE REORGANIZATION COMMITTEE IN 1950

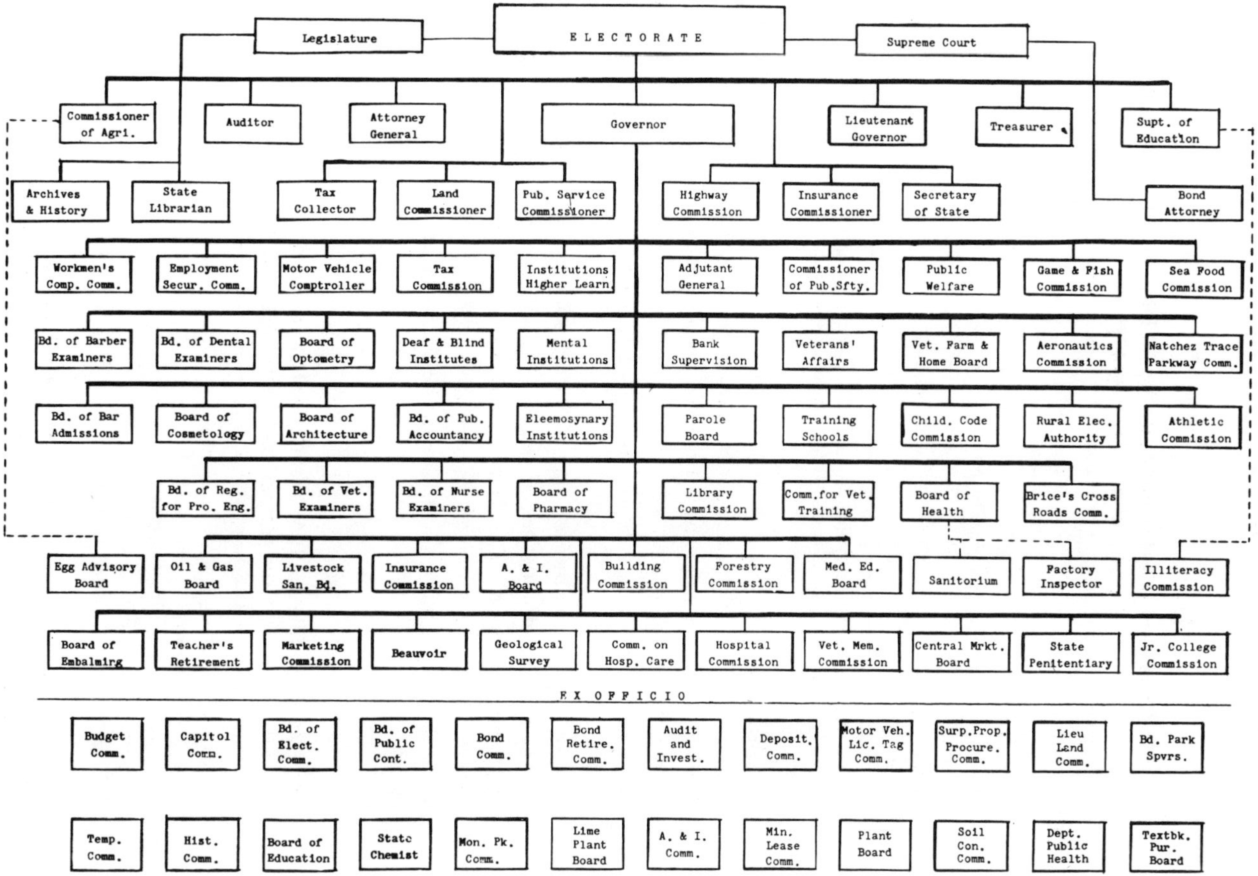

ELECTORATE

Legislature — Supreme Court

Governor — Lieutenant Governor — Treasurer — Supt. of Education

Commissioner of Agri. | Auditor | Attorney General | Land Commissioner | Pub. Service Commissioner | Secretary of State | Bond Attorney

Archives & History | State Librarian | Tax Collector | Tax Commission | Institutions Higher Learn | Insurance Commissioner | Highway Commission

Motor Vehicle Comptroller | Board of Optometry | Deaf & Blind Institutes | Mental Institutions | Commissioner of Pub.Sfty. | Public Welfare | Game & Fish Commission | Sea Food Commission

Employment Secur. Comm. | Bd. of Dental Examiners | Board of Architecture | Bd. of Pub. Accountancy | Eleemosynary Institutions | Adjutant General | Bank Supervision | Veterans' Affairs | Vet. Farm & Home Board | Aeronautics Commission | Natchez Trace Parkway Comm.

Workmen's Comp. Comm. | Bd. of Barber Examiners | Board of Cosmetology | Bd. of Vet. Examiners | Bd. of Nurse Examiners | Board of Pharmacy | Parole Board | Training Schools | Child. Code Commission | Rural Elec. Authority | Athletic Commission

Bd. of Bar Admissions | Bd. of Reg. for Pro. Eng. | Livestock San. Bd. | Insurance Commission | A. & I. Board | Building Commission | Library Commission | Comm. for Vet. Training | Board of Health | Brice's Cross Roads Comm.

Egg Advisory Board | Oil & Gas Board | Marketing Commission | Beauvoir | Geological Survey | Comm. on Hosp. Care | Forestry Commission | Med. Ed. Board | Sanitorium | Factory Inspector | Illiteracy Commission

Board of Embalming | Teacher's Retirement | Bd. of Elect. Comm. | Bd. of Public Cont. | Bond Comm. | Bond Retire. Comm. | Audit and Invest. | Deposit. Comm. | Hospital Commission | Vet. Mem. Commission | Central Mrkt. Board | State Penitentiary | Jr. College Commission

EX OFFICIO

Budget Comm. | Capitol Comm. | Board of Education | State Chemist | Mon. Pk. Comm. | Lime Plant Board | A. & I. Comm. | Min. Lease Comm. | Motor Veh. Lic. Tag Comm. | Surp.Prop. Procure. Comm. | Lieu Land Comm. | Bd. Park Spvrs.

Temp. Comm. | Hist. Comm. | Plant Board | Soil Con. Comm. | Dept. Public Health | Textbk. Pur. Board

Table 13

Growth of Mississippi State Agencies from 1930 to 1950 and Their Legal Bases

Legal Base	Year		Increase	
	1930	1950	Number	Percent
Constitution	10	11	1	10
Statute	70	89	19	27
Total	80	100	20	25

SOURCE: Adapted from the Brookings Report, 443–45; Legislative Fact-Finding Committee, *Report on State Reorganization*, 2–4; Mississippi *Constitution*.

minished. In 1950, the governor's power of appointment extended only to about one-third of the state agencies, whereas in 1930 he had appointed more than half of the agency heads. The selection of agency heads by the *ex officio* method, however, increased considerably between 1930 and 1950, despite the fact that the Brookings Report of 1932 had sharply criticized the *ex officio* method.

It should be emphasized that Table 15 shows "methods" of selecting agency heads and not types of heads, i.e., not whether they were plural or single administrators. The Reorganization Committee found that by far the largest majority of the agencies were headed by plural boards and commissions and that agencies with single heads were primarily those filled by election.

Table 14

The Increase, Elimination, and Consolidation of Agencies of Mississippi Government Between 1930 and 1950

Number of Agencies in 1930	80
Agencies Abolished or Consolidated	−21
Total of 1930 Agencies Minus Consolidations and Abolitions	59
Agencies Created Between 1930 and 1950	+41
Total Agencies Existing in 1950	100

SOURCE: Adapted from the Brookings Report, 456–57; Legislative Fact-Finding Committee, *Report on State Reorganization*, 2–4; Appendix A of Highsaw and Mullican, *The Growth of State Administration in Mississippi*.

Table 15

Primary Methods of Selecting Heads of Mississippi Agencies in 1950 as Compared With 1930

Method of Selection	1950	Percent	1930	Percent
Appointed by the Governor	24	24	23	30
Appointed by the Governor with Approval of the Senate	12	12	18	23
Wholly or Partly *Ex Officio*	40	40	19	25
Elected by the People*	13	13	14	18
All Other Methods	11	11	3	4
Total	100	100	77	100

*Including the governor and lieutenant governor.
SOURCE: Adapted from Highsaw and Mullican, *The Growth of State Administration in Mississippi,* 38. (Although Highsaw and Mullican were consultants to the Reorganization Committee, the committee, in describing the methods of selecting agency heads, used categories and figures different from those presented in Table 15.) Legislative Fact-Finding Committee, *Report on State Reorganization,* 5.

The Defects Noted in the 1950 Organization

In evaluating the state's administrative structure, the Reorganization Committee agreed on a list of nine defects. Three had to do with finances and the lack of statewide personnel or purchasing systems; the other six were more directly related to the structure of the administration. These six defects are listed below:

1. The grouping of nonrelated functions in one agency and the frequent scattering of related functions among several independent agencies.[17]

2. The large number of separate and independent agencies.

3. The extensive use of the long ballot.

4. The administrative weakness inherent in the office of the governor.

5. The extensive use of the *ex officio* device in Mississippi's boards and agencies.

[17]The committee illustrated this point well by referring to the area of conservation where 20 related agencies were independent of each other. The office of secretary of state was cited as an example of the grouping of non-related functions. This point was supported in an interview with the present secretary of state who indicated that his office had responsibilities in a greater variety of areas than any other department or agency of state government. Personal interview, January 12, 1972, Jackson, Miss.

6. The variations in and complexity of internal organization of the administrative agencies.

Generally speaking, the defects found by the joint committee in 1950 were about the same as those found by the Brookings researchers in 1930. For that reason they merit little discussion here. Two of the defects—the weakness in the office of the governor and the use of the long ballot—should be mentioned briefly, however, because the proposals to correct these caused formidable opposition to the reorganization plan. Concerning the long ballot, the committee said, "Popular election of some seventeen administrative officials every four years perhaps has contributed more to the weakness of the present state administrative organization than any other single factor."[18] The committee attempted to discredit the supposed justification for the long ballot, i.e., that popular election of administrative officials makes them responsible to the people. The argument presented was that, even if qualified administrators were offered for election to each post, the most conscientious voter could not be expected to pick them out of a field of thirty or forty candidates. And, the argument continued, since qualified people seldom ran for public office, elective offices were usually filled by second- and third-rate administrators.

In discussing the weakness in the office of the governor, the committee focused on the inherent inability of the governor to supervise administrative operations. It was therefore clear to the committee that "the governor must be vested with broad and significant powers of appointment and removal." The committee noted that while in 1950 the governor was required to make over 250 appointments, he had little effective removal power and could not make appointments to some key administrative positions.

Principles of the Proposed Reorganization

After examining the 1950 organization and [noting] its defects, the committee focused attention on what it called "principles of administration" by which it would be guided in proposing reorganization. The main "principles" were listed as (1) the departmental system, (2) the use of boards and commissions, (3) central service department, and (4) governor.[19]

The Reorganization Committee's discussion of the departmental system and governor was very similar to two principles stated in the Brookings

[18]Legislative Fact-Finding Committee, *Report on State Reorganization,* 7.
[19]*Ibid.,* 15-17. It should be noted that the committee did not necessarily state these items as principles, e.g., "governor."

Report of 1932, namely that (1) related activities should be grouped into a single department, and (2) the governor should be the real as well as the nominal head of the administration.

Use of Boards and Commissions.   On this point the Brookings Report would have eliminated most boards and commissions. However, the 1950 committee felt that the quality of public service would be enhanced if boards and commissions were used to formulate policies but not to do administrative work. The committee emphasized that full authority for administrative management should be vested in a single person and that he should be held accountable for implementing the policies of the board.

Central Service Department.   The committee felt that each major department should be organized so that one section of the department would provide staff services, such as budgeting, accounting, purchasing, and personnel. Such an arrangement was described as an effort to use business methods in the day-to-day operation of the government in order to improve performance and save money.

The Proposals for Reorganization

Using the principles mentioned above, the committee made its proposals for reorganization "in the interest of democratic government in Mississippi and (in) its efficient and economical administration." The organization proposed by the committee is shown in the chart on page 74. Excluding the Executive Office of the Governor, there are 17 departments shown on the chart under the governor. Sixteen of these departments would be headed by policy-making boards. One of the boards would be *ex officio*. The remainder would be appointed by the governor and in some cases subject to the approval of the senate. The governor would appoint the department directors from recommendations made by the boards. All directors would be removable by the governor for cause.[20]

In addition to the 17 departments, the proposed organization chart shows 7 elected officials, an auditor under the legislature, an *ex officio* Board of Election Commissioners, and the Executive Office of the Governor.

The Executive Office of the Governor was to include a bureau of general

[20]*Ibid.*, 16–17. Only the Department of Public Safety would have no board.

Chart 2

ORGANIZATION OF AGENCIES AND OFFICES OF MISSISSIPPI GOVERNMENT AS PROPOSED BY THE LEGISLATIVE REORGANIZATION COMMITTEE IN 1950

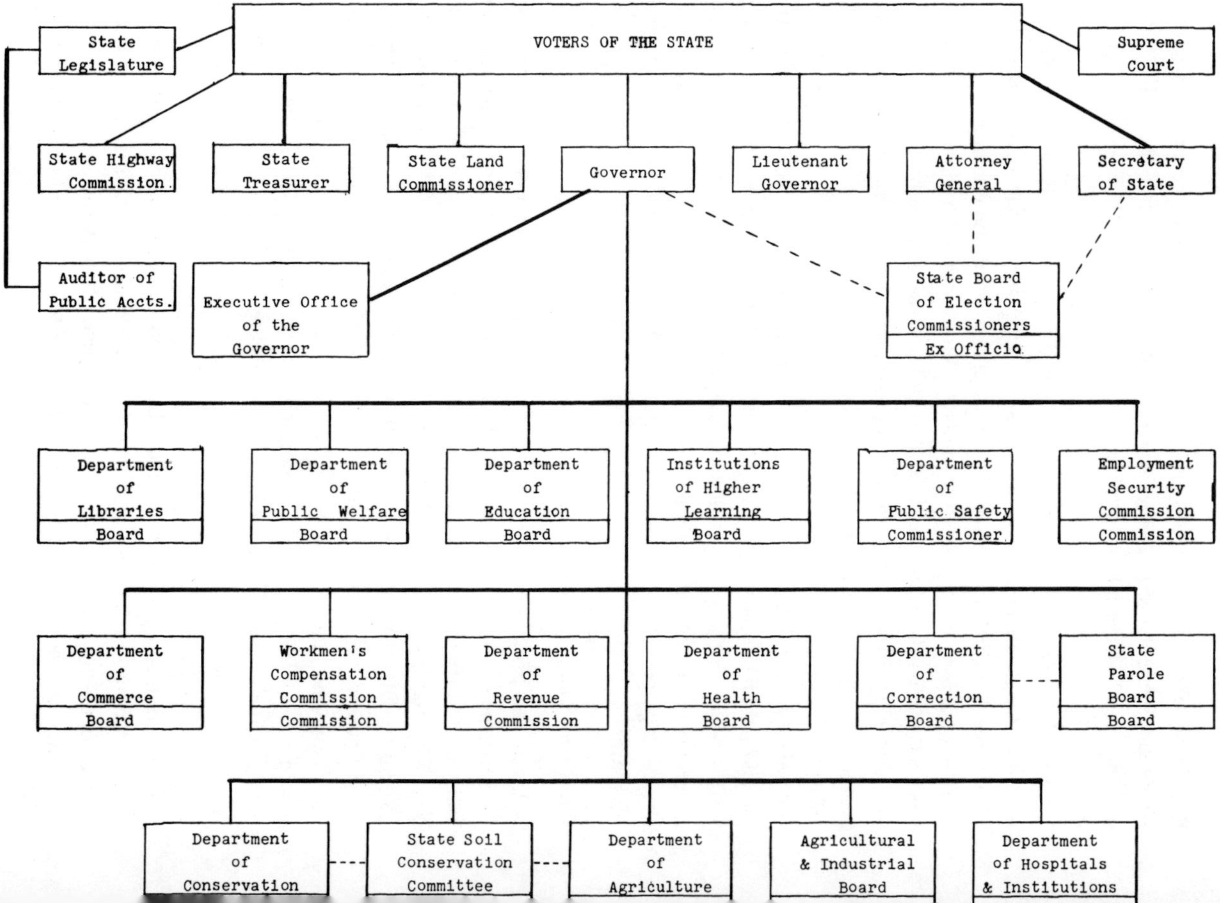

VOTERS OF THE STATE

State Legislature

Supreme Court

State Land Commissioner

State Treasurer

Lieutenant Governor

Governor

Attorney General

Secretary of State

State Highway Commission

Auditor of Public Accts.

Executive Office of the Governor

State Board of Election Commissioners Ex Officio

Department of Libraries — Board

Department of Public Welfare — Board

Department of Education — Board

Institutions of Higher Learning — Board

Department of Public Safety — Commissioner

Employment Security Commission — Commission

Department of Commerce — Board

Workmen's Compensation Commission — Commission

Department of Revenue — Commission

Department of Health — Board

Department of Correction — Board

State Parole Board — Board

Department of Conservation

State Soil Conservation Committee

Department of Agriculture

Agricultural & Industrial Board

Department of Hospitals & Institutions

administration to perform the staff functions of budgeting, accounting, purchasing, and personnel. The centralization of these important functions of state government under the governor would have greatly enhanced his position as chief executive officer of the state. A total of 14 agencies would have been consolidated to form the Executive Office of the Governor.

Altogether, there would be a total of 27 offices and departments in the proposed organization. Several of the proposed departments would have absorbed a half-dozen or more independent agencies, but at least 15 of the 27 existing agencies would have been affected only slightly, if at all, by the reorganization proposals.[21]

Table 16 compares some aspects of the proposed organization with those which existed in 1950 and shows that the total number of agencies was reduced by 73 percent. The number of agencies headed by boards and commissions was reduced more than 78 percent, while the number of boards or commissions with *ex officio* members was reduced by 90 percent.

By reducing the number of agencies and boards, the Reorganization Committee also accomplished its objective of reducing the number of appointed and elected officials. Table 17 indicates that significant reductions were made in all categories. Reducing the number of appointed officials from 279 to 99 reflects the committee's view that the governor was required to make too many appointments and that he could not properly select so many people.

It can be concluded that the reorganization plan of 1950 did not propose as much change in the existing organization as was the case in 1932. For example, the 1950 plan would have eliminated only 8 of 17 elected officials while the 1932 plan would have eliminated 18 of 20. The elimination of elected officials would have required two constitutional changes in 1950 and five in 1932.[22]

With the drastic reduction in the number of elected officials in the 1932 proposals, the governor's power of appointment would have been increased

[21]The fifteen included, in addition to the seven elected offices, the Workmen's Compensation Commission, Soil Conservation Committee, Board of Election Commissioners, Department of Public Safety, Employment Security Commission, Agricultural and Industrial Board, Parole Board, and the College Board. Legislative Fact-Finding Committee, *Report on State Reorganization*, 21–92. Appendix D lists the 27 proposed offices and departments and shows how they were to be set up from the 100 existing agencies.

[22]Table 10 in Chapter II showed that thirteen constitutional changes were required in the 1932 plan. The 1950 study did not indicate what types of changes would be required to implement the plan, but it appears that no more than four or five constitutional changes would have been necessary.

Table 16

Agencies and Boards of Mississippi Government Existing in 1950 Compared With the Number Proposed by the Reorganization Committee in 1950

Factor of Comparison	Number Existing	Number Proposed	Percent of Change
Agencies Headed by Boards	82	18	−78
or Commissions	(40)*	(4)*	(−90)*
Agencies Headed by Single			
Administrators	18	9	−50
Total Agencies	100	27	−73

*Boards or commissions that are wholly or partly *ex officio*.

SOURCE: Adapted from Legislative Fact-Finding Committee, *Report on State Reorganization*, 18–82; Highsaw and Mullican, *Growth of State Administration in Mississippi*, 38.

Table 17

Elected Officials and Governing Authorities Existing in Mississippi Government in 1950 Compared With Those Proposed by the Reorganization Committee of 1950

Variable Factor	Number Existing	Number Proposed	Percent of Change
Number of Elected			
Officials	17	9	−47
Number of *Ex Officio*			
Officials	146	21	−86
Number of Appointive			
Officials	279	99	−68
Total Number of Officials			
in Administrative or			
Governing Positions	442	129	−71

SOURCE: Adapted from the Legislative Fact-Finding Committee, *Report on State Reorganization*, 93. By "Governing Authorities," the committee meant members of boards and other plural bodies.

much more than under the 1950 plan. His appointment power also would have given him more direct control over the administration in 1932, because most of the departments would have had single heads; in the 1950 reorganization plan, nearly all departments would have had plural heads. The governor would make the appointments in both cases but could exercise more control over a single administrator than over a board or commission.

THE FORCES AND FACTORS AFFECTING THE OUTCOME

OF THE 1950 REORGANIZATION EFFORT

The Response to the Subcommittee Reports

As noted, the Reorganization Committee divided its work among nine subcommittees and adopted a policy of releasing the subcommittee reports to the press as they were completed. The release of the subcommittee reports preliminary to the full committee's final report was an effort to keep the public informed on the work of the committee and, hopefully, to prepare them for the changes.[23]

Wilson F. Minor, veteran Mississippi political reporter, termed the committee the best he had ever seen for providing information about its work. As an observer in 1950, Minor said the Reorganization Committee had set such a brisk work pace for four months that it had won the commendations of the state house as one of the hardest working interim bodies ever created. ''But,'' Minor added ''when the Committee . . . announced its plan for making the Highway Commission into an appointive board . . . smiles started changing to frowns.''[24] Actually, the frowns may have begun forming after a news release of September 1, 1950, some two weeks before the announcement of the highway plan. That news report was the only item other than the Korean War that made the headlines of the *Clarion-Ledger* during the months of July, August, and September. The headline indicated that the reorganization plan being prepared would increase the powers of the governor. A committee spokesman, in a rather defensive tone, said the governor might be given more powers but that no dictatorship could develop since the governor could not succeed himself and because he would be checked by the people, the judiciary, and the legislature.

[23]Personal interview with former representative and member of the Reorganization Committee, Ben H. Walley, Jackson, Miss., March 16, 1972.

[24]Personal interview with W. F. Minor, Jackson, Miss., April 13, 1972; *New Orleans Times-Picayune,* September 24, 1950, p. 2.

Two weeks later, the subcommittee on highways issued its report recommending that the three elected highway commissioners be appointed by the governor for overlapping six-year terms. The commission would have only policy-making duties and would appoint a technically qualified director to administer those policies. The Reorganization Committee chairman estimated that the new plan would save the state 30–40 percent of the funds being spent by the Highway Department.[25]

One of the highway commissioners quickly took exception to the report. His letter of reply to the chairman of the Reorganization Committee was reprinted on the front page of the newspaper only two days after the committee report had been released. The commissioner wanted to know how the Reorganization Committee came to be such experts on the Highway Department in such a short time. He promised to take immediate action to make the necessary corrections in the operation of the department if the Reorganization Committee would tell him how they could effect savings of 30–40 percent. Second, he voiced disapproval of the recommendation to make the Highway Commission appointive. The commissioner said the state had good highways because the elected commissioners had to give an accounting to the people every four years. "The people," he said, "are opposed to high-powered bureaus, the centralization of power and political dictatorship by whatever name they are called." With reference to achieving efficiency through centralization, the commissioner commented, "Dictatorships are horribly efficient at times—but isn't that what we are fighting in Korea?"[26]

Another matter of dispute was the proposal to alter the formula for distributing funds to the three highway districts. Each district would get 20 percent of the total, with the remaining 40 percent allocated according to need. The existing allocation was 37.5 percent to the northern and southern districts and 25 percent to the central district.[27]

These events led one writer to report that Mississippi's first effort to reorganize since 1932 appeared to be going up a blind alley. Opposition, he said, "popped up like a jack-in-the-box" when the Reorganization Committee

[25]*Jackson Clarion-Ledger,* September 15, 1950, p. 1.

[26]*Ibid.,* September 17, 1950, pp. 1, 16. Former commissioner S. T. Roebuck said he received no answers to his questions. Personal interview, Newton, Miss., March 13, 1972. In 1932, Roebuck was in the legislature and had been a supporter of Governor Conner up to the effort to pass the so-called "Highway Dictator Bill"; at this point he "broke" with Conner.

[27]*Jackson Clarion-Ledger,* September 15, 1950, p. 1.

announced it would make the three-man Highway Commission appointive by the governor.[28]

Although Governor Wright had given no public statement, his advisors indicated that he disapproved of the changes proposed by the Reorganization Committee involving the replacement of elective officials with gubernatorial appointees. Amid these reports, a committee spokesman admitted that the group should have made an effort earlier in its proceedings to confer with the governor, adding that the committee would soon meet with the governor and try to more fully explain its plan to him.[29]

The Reorganization Committee subsequently met with Governor Wright on September 21, but apparently was unsuccessful in converting him to its way of thinking. No public statement was issued by either party to the conference, but it was ''authoritatively reported'' that Wright had not altered his position of strong opposition to the recommendations that certain elective offices be made appointive by the governor.

Governor Wright was also said to be opposed to the centralization of government. This may have been related to the proposed Executive Office of the Governor which would have combined 14 agencies (including budgeting, personnel, and purchasing) under the governor. This possibility is suggested by the fact that after conferring with Wright, the Reorganization Committee announced a week's delay in the scheduled news release of the report by the Subcommittee on General Government which proposed the Executive Office of the Governor.

One of the members of the Subcommittee on General Government was the editor of the *Kosciusko Star Herald*. An editorial in the *Herald* noted that the Reorganization Committee was sharply divided on the question of increasing the appointive power of the governor. It added that if the governor and the committee could not ''get their heads together and agree on a program, further work of the committee would be a waste of time, money and effort.''[30]

There was little agreement, however, and veteran political observers had begun to compare the 1950 reorganization effort and its underlying issues with the very similar situation of 1932. The committee's recommendations seemed

[28]*New Orleans Times-Picayune,* September 24, 1950, p. 2.

[29]*Jackson Clarion-Ledger,* September 21, 1950, p. 1. The governor met with the committee when it was first organized but placed no limits or restrictions on what they might consider or propose in the way of reorganization. Personal interview with former committee member R. B. Meadows, Jr., Gulfport, Miss., July 14, 1972.

[30]*Kosciusko Star Herald,* September 21, 1950, p. 3.

to follow in many ways those of the Brookings Report, most notably the opinion that the basic needs of the government were for making the governor the real head of the administration. In comparing the 1950 "tug-of-war" over reorganization with that of 1932, it was concluded that the climate had not changed much in eighteen years.[31]

The prospects for reorganization seemed to be dampened considerably by the position of Governor Wright, but the Reorganization Committee continued its work. In a few days, the Subcommittee on Protection to Persons and Property issued its report and recommended that the elective insurance and public service commissioners be made appointive. This suggestion met with a generally unfriendly reaction, as reflected in a newspaper headline which read: "Solons Would Take Four More Offices From The Ballot." This attitude was apparently shared by large segments of the press and public across the state. The editor of one of the leading newspapers said he knew of no state paper that had endorsed the proposed changes. Another leading paper said there were no kind words anywhere for the recommendations involving the Highway Commission and state superintendent of education and stated further that these proposals had aroused a "storm of protest" from the press and public throughout the state.[32]

The general response to the release of the various subcommittee reports can only be described as negative. This attitude was largely determined by the proposals for making elected officials appointive. Before the negative attitude developed, it was generally believed that a special session of the legislature would be called to consider the work of the Reorganization Committee which had been enthusiastically undertaken and encouraged by the governor. Although the optimism once held for reorganization was diminished by the subcommittee reports, there was no statement from Wright concerning the special session, and the suspense as to whether or not there would be one continued.

The Final Report and the Request for a Special Session

Meeting the legislatively imposed deadline, the committee completed its work and delivered the final report to Governor Wright on December 15. In the letter of transmittal attached to the report, Committee Chairman John H.

[31]*New Orleans Times-Picayune,* September 24, 1950, p. 2.
[32]*Jackson Clarion-Ledger,* October 25, 1950, p. 5, September 30, 1950, p. 8, *Jackson Daily News,* October 3, 1950, p. 1.

Culkin asked the governor to call the legislature into special session and give it an opportunity to consider the reorganization report "in whole or in part." Chairman Culkin made it a point to remind Wright that in his biennial address he had promised to call such a session.[33]

It was generally felt, however, that the final report of the Reorganization Committee did not make enough concessions to the governor's view that elective offices should not be made appointive. If the concessions were not enough for the governor, they were also not enough for three of the twelve members of the Reorganization Committee who in separate statements expressed their differences with the full report of the committee as issued in final form. The common theme of the dissenting statements expressed disapproval of the recommendations involving changes in the elective system. It is interesting to note that two of the three dissenters were on the three-member highways subcommittee. The full committee vetoed the first report of that subcommittee, which would have left the Highway Commission on an elective basis. The "revised" subcommittee report on highways, therefore, recommended that the governor appoint the Highway Commission, but this recommendation was greeted with so much opposition that the committee reversed itself and the final report reflected the original position of the two dissenters.[34]

In the letter of transmittal attached to the report, Chairman Culkin attempted to focus the governor's attention on the "most salient elements" of the report by summarizing three aspects of the study. He pointed out, first, the public officials who would continue to be elected (nine) and, secondly, those who would be appointed by the governor (six). The report also emphasized the potential savings of the proposed reorganization which were conservatively estimated at $5,478,571, about 5 percent of total expenditures for 1948–49 ($104,099,267).

Two days after receiving the final report, the governor told newsmen he would spend several weeks studying it, but he gave no indication of his position on the proposed special session. Two weeks later, in a press conference on the eve of a trip to Washington, Governor Wright ended any speculation that he would ask the legislature to consider the reorganization report.

[33]Legislative Fact-Finding Committee, *Report on State Reorganization,* 4.
[34]*Jackson Clarion-Ledger,* December 17, 1950, p. 1; Legislative Fact-Finding Committee, *Report on State Reorganization,* 103–104; T. R. Ethridge, "State Administrative Reorganization in Mississippi," 83.

The governor seemed more interested in reviewing the accomplishments of his administration and stated that "unless international complications and civilian defense force the calling of an extraordinary session of the Mississippi Legislature, I shall consider my legislative program completed." When he returned from Washington two weeks later, Wright said, "I must repeat that I foresee no need for a call of the legislature into extraordinary session this year for any purpose at all."[35]

Governor Wright seemed pleased with the accomplishments of his administration. In proposing the reorganization study, he had spoken of avoiding controversy, and long before the final decision on the special session, it was speculated that the governor wanted to end his administration on a harmonious note and sidestep a legislative struggle over reorganization. He may have been looking to the future, since he was well aware that former governor Mike Conner had led a substantial effort for reorganization and then lost in two subsequent gubernatorial races. Wright himself lost in a 1955 race to regain the governor's office. While Wright's 1950 efforts on behalf of reorganization probably had little impact on the outcome of that race, it is noteworthy that his efforts were not comparable to those of Governor Conner who incurred substantial personal opposition to his stand on reorganization.[36]

The Opposition of the Lieutenant Governor and the Election Year of 1951

Lieutenant Governor Sam Lumpkin, expected to be a candidate for governor in the 1951 election, was, like Governor Wright, concerned with avoiding controversy. He opposed the Reorganization Committee's request for a special session because of the controversial nature of the recommendations for making elective offices appointive. When such recommendations were first made, the lieutenant governor had made a public statement to record his opposition to any effort to increase the appointive powers of the governor. He had added that reorganization was of grave importance but because of the war and the summer elections, reorganization could not, in the proposed special session, receive the careful and unselfish consideration it demanded.[37]

[35]*Jackson Clarion-Ledger,* January 1, 1951, p. 1, January 14, 1951, p. 16.

[36]*Jackson Daily News,* October 3, 1950, p. 1; *Mississippi Official and Statistical Register, 1956–60,* 398.

[37]*Jackson Clarion-Ledger,* September 21, 1950, p. 1, December 15, 1950, p. 20; *New Orleans Times-Picayune,* September 24, 1950, p. 2. It can be noted that Lumpkin voted for the "Highway Dictator Bill" in 1932 as a member of the senate. *Senate Journal,* 1932, p. 1009.

The lieutenant governor's view was given some credence by one political writer who expected the mounting war preparations to temper the campaigning. This apparently meant that, even though reorganization was of "grave importance," to make a big issue of it in the campaign would be to introduce too much controversy. At any rate Lumpkin's strategy fell only 2,000 votes short of getting him into the runoff.[38]

When the reorganization report was submitted to the governor, he was advised to give careful consideration to the time for calling a special session. Presumably one option would have been to call the session after the election. A post-election session would have had disadvantages but would not have forced candidates to face the issue of reorganization. One disadvantage might have been the added factor of a lame duck governor presiding and a governor-elect observing. Returning legislators probably would have been more interested in currying favor with the incoming governor. On the other hand, a lame duck legislature might have been in a favorable position to act on reorganization, since the non-returning legislators would possibly have been subject to less pressure from those opposed to reorganization.

The Reorganization Plan and the Transition to the New Administration

Aside from the desires of candidates or potential candidates that such controversial issues as reorganization not be allowed to complicate their election campaigns, reorganization efforts coming at the end of an administration have other disadvantages. If the reorganization is not completed by the end of the fourth year, it simply gets lost in the transition to the next administration.[39] No matter how dedicated he may have been to reorganization, the governor is replaced at the end of his four years and his replacement may not be at all interested in getting into the fight over reorganization. And without support from the governor, those returning legislators who continue to push reorganization find their jobs more difficult. The ranks of the legislators who supported reorganization may also be thinned from one administration to the next. Such was the case in 1952.

For one reason or another, only half of the twelve members of the 1950 Reorganization Committee returned to the legislature in 1952. Senator Cul-

---

[38]*Memphis Commercial Appeal,* December 31, 1951, Sec. V, p. 8; *Mississippi Official and Statistical Register, 1949–51,* 358.
[39]Personal interview with Representative Edgar Stephens, Jackson, Miss., April 12, 1972.

kin, the committee chairman and possibly the leading advocate of reorganization, was reelected to the 1952 legislature but died before it convened.[40] Culkin almost certainly would have pushed reorganization in the new administration. Other members of the Reorganization Committee who did not return indicated that they too would have supported and pushed reorganization. At least two of them had prepared bills to be introduced in the 1952 session.[41]

As a group, the members of the 1950 Reorganization Committee were rated as average to above average in influence. According to the Bosworth study reported in Chapter I, the relative influence of a reorganization committee is an important factor in the overall reorganization effort. One former legislator who said the relative influence of the 1950 committee was above average discounted the importance of that factor; he felt that reorganization would have to stand on its own merits. Other legislators had a low regard for such interim committees because of the belief that too often the appointment of members to these committees involved political considerations not particularly consistent with the purposes of the committee. Another veteran legislator said interim committees should never be asked to work for lame duck legislatures unless a special session is definitely planned to consider the committee's findings.[42]

Another factor related to the transition that possibly made it difficult for this reorganization effort to succeed was a tactic used by one of the gubernatorial candidates in the campaign of 1951. At his campaign rallies, Paul B. Johnson, Jr., used a large picture of the state office building, turning it upside down and shaking it in a dramatization of his view that some changes in the operations and/or personnel of state government were needed. As a result, state employees became concerned that a renewed economy drive might cost them their jobs. Although Johnson was defeated, his campaign increased the sensitivities of state employees to the reorganization issue. Johnson's personal view was that he was misunderstood in the 1951 campaign. He had not meant to imply that there would be any radical change in state operations nor to create wide-

[40]Chairman Culkin had worked for reorganization in 1932 with Mike Conner and was highly respected. One former colleague described Culkin as outstanding. Personal interviews in Jackson, Miss., with former senator Robert H. Thompson, March 15, 1972, and former senator and present executive secretary to the governor, Herman Glazier, March 14, 1972.

[41]Personal interview with former senator R. B. Meadows, Gulfport, Miss., July 14, 1972.

[42]Personal interviews with former representative William C. Thompson, Forest, Miss., March 13, 1972, former senator Forest D. Copeland, Newton, Miss., March 13, 1972, and Senator Ellis Bodron, Jackson, Miss., March 14, 1972.

spread fear among state employees that their jobs would be in jeopardy if he were elected. Johnson ran for governor again in 1955, and according to one observer, placed less emphasis on the reorganization issue so as not to lose support from state employees.[43]

Opposition of Other Officials and Agencies

Indications are that the most opposition to the reorganization proposals came from the elected officials and from those in sympathy with the long ballot tradition. The agencies and bureaus that might have been changed were also a source of opposition, as Chairman Culkin indicated in the reorganization report. During the course of the study, the various agency heads were interviewed by the committee. Each head was told that the committee sought to reduce the operating costs of state government by eliminating needless bureaus and consolidating where possible without destroying the efficiency or eliminating any functions presently being performed. Asked for their personal reaction to the proposition, they replied "without exception" as follows:

> I think this is one of the very best things that has ever been done in the State of Mississippi and I have long been of the opinion that this work should have been accomplished in the past. However, my department is of a type, character and kind that cannot be consolidated with any other agency, as its duties and functions are unique, and a reduction in the personnel or a transfer of any of the duties of this department would work a hardship and prevent certain citizens from receiving benefits to which they are entitled.[44]

Senator Culkin was undoubtedly considering this type of agency response when he said in a public appearance that everyone was in favor of economy except those affected by the changes.[45]

Over three weeks before Culkin expressed his views, one newspaper confidently predicted that if the reorganization plan ever went to the legislature, it would meet with strong resistance from the agencies affected.[46] Many agencies, however, opposed the reorganization proposals even before they were presented in final form, and several were able to get the Reorganization Committee to alter its proposals more to their liking.

[43]Personal interviews with former governor Paul B. Johnson, Hattiesburg, Miss., August 28, 1972, and Wilson F. Minor, capital correspondent for the New Orleans Times-Picayune, Jackson, Miss. April 13, 1972.

[44]Legislative Fact-Finding Committee, Report on State Reorganization, 2–3.

[45]Jackson Daily News, October 26, 1950, p. 9.

[46]Ibid., October 3, 1950, p. 1.

As discussed earlier, the opposition of the Highway Commission caused the committee to reverse its position concerning the appointment of the highway commissioners. The Reorganization Committee also reversed itself on its initial proposal concerning the Health Department. That proposal would have allowed the governor to appoint laymen to the State Health Board and also appoint its chief administrative officer, who would not be a member of the board. "Strong insistence" by the medical profession, however, led the committee to reverse itself, and the final committee report recommended no changes in the makeup of the board, nor in the methods of selecting board members or the chief administrative officer.[47]

Opposition came from other officers and agencies as well. The secretary of state opposed changes proposed for his office and strong protest also arose from the Department of Agriculture and Commerce. One former committee member said opposition was encountered from every state agency.[48] Another committee member recalled that at times the most minor changes were opposed. Such experiences led him to conclude that the opposition to reorganization resulted primarily from jealousy.[49]

After the Reorganization Committee made its report, the governor became the focal point for the agency opposition. Governor Wright, of course, had promised to call a special session of the legislature to consider the report but did not do so. He explained to the committee that he had changed his mind about calling the special session for reorganization. He did not say he was influenced by agency opposition, but some members of the Reorganization Committee reportedly formed the opinion that this was the reason he changed his mind.[50]

To repeat an earlier point, Governor Wright seemed to be philosophically and staunchly opposed to the committee's proposals to shorten the ballot and

[47]*Jackson Clarion-Ledger*, October 14, 1950, p. 1; T. R. Ethridge, "State Administrative Reorganization in Mississippi," 87; Legislative Fact-Finding Committee, *Report on State Reorganization*, 58–60. The committee did make recommendations in the final report affecting the internal organization of the Health Department.

[48]Personal interviews with Sam Allred, Jackson, Miss., April 14, 1972, and Wilson F. Minor, Jackson, Miss., April 13, 1972, Letter from W. Dave Womack of Tequesta, Florida, dated July 10, 1972.

[49]Personal interview with R.B. Meadows, Jr., Gulfport, Miss., July 10, 1972. Regarding Meadow's observation, it is interesting to recall David Easton's statement that politics is the constant reallocation of the available values, and then to consider Webster's definitions of jealousy, i.e., being resentfully suspicious of a rival or a rival's influence and being watchful in guarding or keeping.

[50]Telephone interview with Thomas R. Ethridge of Oxford, Miss., July 18, 1972.

increase the appointive power of the governor. As the chairman of the Highways and Highway Financing Committee in 1932, Fielding Wright had opposed the Highway Director Bill as a move to make the governor the "Czar of
the Highways." The effect of the agency opposition, therefore, may have
been secondary to Governor Wright's personal views.

Agency opposition certainly had an impact on the work of the Reorganization Committee, however, and would undoubtedly have had an effect on any
legislative action. The relevant question seems to be that, while agency opposition to reorganization may be inevitable, is it necessarily sufficient in and of
itself to thwart reorganization? As the next chapter will indicate, many con-
temporary leaders of state government in Mississippi believe that reorganization involving the consolidation of agencies with no particular changes in the
elective system is possible and can be achieved.

Does this mean that reorganization not involving changes in the elective
system could have been achieved in 1950? Possibly so, but under the circumstances, with the furor over shortening the ballot, it would have been difficult.
The Reorganization Committee hoped that at least part of the plan, if not all,
might be adopted. However, the committee was unwilling to retreat from its
position that several elected officials should be made appointive.

The Practicalities of the Reorganization Plan

The unwillingness of the committee to retreat from its position that several
elected officials should be made appointive was a serious liability to the 1950
effort. As earlier analyses of state reorganization efforts have shown, a common factor in the unsuccessful attempts has been that the tendencies to propose the most desirable organization from a theoretical standpoint are not
balanced with proper consideration for the political practicalities. Although
the proposals regarding the appointment of elected officials were not nearly as
drastic in the 1950 plan as they were in that of 1932, the 1950 plan still failed
to strike an acceptable balance between desirable theoretical features and
politically practical and achievable features. The Reorganization Committee,
at its first meeting, decided to propose what it felt would be the best theoretical organization rather than what might be feasible politically. The decision to
propose the "ideal" was not unanimous, however, and it is doubtful that the
ideal always took precedence over the practical or that the practical was
always ignored. In this regard, it is interesting to note that, on the one hand,
the commissioners of insurance and agriculture were made appointive (in the

proposed plan) while, on the other hand, the land commissioner and treasurer were left in the elective category.[51]

When the 1950 study was in progress, one observer said the question was whether the final report would be practical enough to warrant the calling of a special session. According to the report, it was well known that the governor was "loath to call a special session that may ultimately prove impractical."[52]

The Importance of Public Support

Senator Culkin, chairman of the Reorganization Committee, emphasized the importance of public support for reorganization when he said, "Only through a campaign of instruction and on the demand of the public will the existing conditions be changed."[53] Obviously the public demand was not sufficient in 1950. With the exception of a few legislators, there was not much "follow-up" interest in reorganization after the plan was submitted. The enthusiasm that had led to the study was largely absent after its completion. The initial momentum for reorganization was lost when the special session was not called to consider the 1950 report. Interested legislators attempted some piecemeal changes in the regular sessions of 1952 and 1954, but the momentum had been lost and there was not much support for reorganization.

Even the Mississippi Chamber of Commerce, which later supported the 1970 report, took a "hands-off" policy on the 1950 study. The chamber prepared a pamphlet summarizing the 1950 study and distributed it widely "to insure that a maximum number of civic-minded citizens knows its substance." However, the chamber advised that it was taking *no* position on the report and that the response to the pamphlet could determine whether or not a position should be considered. A search through the chamber minutes of the period yielded no evidence that the matter was ever considered further.[54]

The reorganization plan of 1950 not only lacked support but, aside from the policy of the Reorganization Committee to publicize the subcommittee reports, there was no discernible effort to create any support for the plan.

[51]Personal interviews with Ben H. Walley, Jackson, Miss., March 16, 1972, and Sam Allred, Jackson, Miss., March 15, 1972; Legislative Fact-Finding Committee, *Report on State Reorganization,* Letter of Transmittal, 4.

[52]*Jackson Clarion-Ledger,* October 3, 1950, p. 6.

[53]*Jackson Daily News,* October 26, 1950, p. 9.

[54]Letter of Transmittal from Chamber President A. F. Chisholm in *What the Reorganization Committee Found and Recommended by the Mississippi Economic Council,* Jackson, Miss., April, 1951; letter from Bob W. Pittman, manager, Mississippi Economic Council, July 14, 1972.

Further, the credibility and appeal of the main argument for the 1950 effort, i.e., economy, was diminished considerably by the surplus that existed at the time in the state treasury.[55]

The discussion on support for reorganization can be concluded with a brief reference to the views of a former legislator and gubernatorial candidate, who believes that if the governor favors reorganization, he can and he should exercise the leadership to build the support necessary for the passage of reorganization. This former legislator, now a state-level elected official, believes that the governor can gain legislative approval of almost anything he is willing to fight for and compromise on with the legislature. This view was also expressed by former governor Paul B. Johnson, Jr.

The 1950 Reorganization Study and the Hugh White Administration

When Hugh White became governor in 1952, the reorganization study was about thirteen months old and had never been considered by the legislature. Governor White told the legislature in his inaugural message that the Joint Legislative Reorganization Committee had issued its report. He urged the legislature to consider carefully its many excellent recommendations. "We should," he said, "eliminate duplication of effort and overlapping of state commissions and departments" and save every possible dollar of state expense. The governor announced his endorsement of many of the suggestions made by the Reorganization Committee and said he would await with interest the legislative action on these recommendations.[56] Governor White's speech, which filled about nine pages in the *Journal of the House,* included only nine lines on reorganization. Comparatively, this was not a very strong plea for reorganization and, accordingly, the legislative response was not very enthusiastic.

Practically the only people interested in the reorganization report during the first legislative session of the Hugh White administration were the veterans who had served on the Reorganization Committee; and only six of them returned to the legislature in 1952. Altogether, seven reorganization bills were introduced in 1952 by four of the six returning legislators. These bills proposed the creation of the Executive Office of the Governor, Department of

---

[55]Chapter I indicated that the recent trend in state reorganization studies, including the 1970 Mississippi study, is to emphasize the objective of improving the service of government and not that of making the government more economical.

[56]*House Journal,* 1952, p. 104.

Revenue, Department of Public Safety, and the consolidation of archives and library services.[57] Another bill went beyond the recommendations of the reorganization report and proposed the appointment of the highway commissioners.[58]

None of these bills was ever reported out of committee. The only successful maneuver on behalf of reorganization in the 1952 legislature was the adoption of House Concurrent Resolution 28 to purchase 500 additional copies of the reorganization report. The resolution was authored by the three house members who had served on the Reorganization Committee—Representatives Womack, Howell, and Holmes.

The second legislative session of the Hugh White administration, held in 1954, saw these same legislators advance other reorganization bills. This time they picked up more support in the House of Representatives and also from the governor who came out much stronger for reorganization in his biennial address than he had in his inaugural address. Governor White said that, because of the increasing costs of government and the increasing demands made of government, it was "of urgent importance" that the lawmakers give continuing and serious study to the reduction of government expenditures: "Therefore, I express the hope and strongly urge that the legislature at this session give careful and serious study to a program for effecting economies in the operation of state government."[59]

The governor offered three alternative approaches to economizing in state government: first, the consolidation of boards and agencies; second, the strengthening of budget laws to provide for stricter supervision in budgetary matters; and third, the establishment of a central purchasing agency. Governor White said the legislature might find other acceptable ways to economize but he indicated his preference for the central purchasing agency.

While only four reorganization bills were introduced in that session, they embraced all three approaches offered by White for economizing in state government. A senate bill proposing the consolidation of boards of eleemosynary institutions received a favorable committee report but was not called up for floor action. A similar house bill was never reported from its committee.[60]

---

[57]See House Bills 457, 771, 772, *House Journal,* 1952 and Senate Bills 409, 410 and 611, *Senate Journal,* 1952. See also House Concurrent Resolutions 51, 52, 53, 54.

[58]Senate Bill 612, *Senate Journal,* 1952, p. 436.

[59]*House Journal,* 1954, pp. 13-14.

[60]*Senate Journal,* 1954, p. 468, Senate Bill 1616; *House Journal,* 1954, p. 220, House Bill 534.

Twenty-three other house members joined Representatives Womack, Holmes, and Howell in introducing two other bills that were more successful. House Bill 245 creating a division of contracts and purchases under the supervision of the governor passed the house by vote of 94 to 20 but was never reported out of committee in the senate. House Bill 244 creating the Executive Office of the Governor and consolidating certain state bureaus passed by vote of 123 to 2. It went to the senate and was referred to two committees, Judiciary and Finance. No reason for this double referral is known. It is apparent, however, that such a move would make it more difficult for the bill to get to the floor of the senate since it would have to be approved by two committees instead of one.[61] The Judiciary Committee did not report the bill out but the Finance Committee reported it "Do Not Pass" on April 29, 1954, five legislative days before the end of the session.

Senator T. R. Ethridge, a member of the Finance Committee, felt that the committee had so much other work in the form of revenue and appropriations bills that there was no time to consider anything else in the regular session. In 1954, the Finance Committee handled both appropriations and revenues and Senator Ethridge, who was secretary for the committee, said, "It was frantic up there all the time."[62]

The committee was obviously very busy in the closing days of the session, for in the last three committee reports—those of April 27, 29, and 30—it reported out 78 bills. Only the Judiciary Committee reported more than 78 bills during the entire session. Altogether, the Finance Committee considered approximately 220 bills.[63]

Thus, with the failure of the house-passed executive office bill, the Hugh White administration ended with little or nothing accomplished in the way of reorganization. The next administration was that of Governor J. P. Coleman. Coleman said in his inaugural address of January, 1956, that he advocated strict economy in government, but he offered no specific proposals and made no direct references to reorganization. Although very little of the 1950 study had been implemented, a senate bill in 1956 proposed that a new reorganiza-

[61]There is no written senate rule covering double referrals. The secretary of the Mississippi Senate says the rules governing double referrals are informal ones based on precedence. Telephone conversation, February 11, 1972.

[62]Telephone interview, July 18, 1972. The senate in 1964 created a separate committee to handle appropriations. Ethridge had served on the Reorganization Committee and had introduced several reorganization bills in the senate.

[63]*Senate Journal,* 1954, pp. 894–913.

tion study be made. One of the main reasons given for the proposed study was the tremendous increase in the number of governmental departments, bureaus, commissions, and agencies. This was similar to the rationale offered for the 1950 study. The 1956 proposal paralleled the one setting up the 1950 study except that the recess committee would have had the additional responsibility for studying the existing inequities in the state's tax structure. The bill won speedy approval in committee, which was chaired by the bill's author, but died on the senate calendar.[64]

The Expected Results of the 1950 Study

The Reorganization Committee listed ten "consequences" that could have been expected to result from the adoption of the proposals of the 1950 study. These consequences are presented in the following paragraphs, along with a brief statement of whether or not the proposals were adopted.

1. Grouping of related functions. Related functions were not grouped.

2. Reduction in the number of agencies. The number of agencies was not reduced.

3. Short ballot. Except for the abolition of the office of tax collector in 1964, the ballot was not shortened.

4. Central supervision and direction in the governor's office. This objective has not been achieved.

5. Personnel and purchasing systems. In 1962, a supervisor of state purchasing was established in the office of the Budget Commission. The purchasing supervisor is "to adopt purchasing regulations governing the purchase by any agency of any commodity or commodities and establish standards and specifications for a commodity or commodities and the maximum fair prices of all commodity or commodities." This arrangement does not comply with the Reorganization Committee recommendation that a division of purchasing be a part of the executive office with responsibility for purchasing all goods and materials.[65]

Twenty years after the 1950 study, the Mississippi Classification Law of 1970 was enacted. The provisions of that law were similar to the recommendations of the 1950 study regarding the testing of applicants and the

---

[64]*Ibid.*, 1956, p. 55, 556–647; of *Original Senate Bills,* 1901–1989, Regular Session of 1956, Senate Bill 1980.

[65]Legislative Fact-Finding Committee, *Report on State Reorganization,* 85–101; Mississippi *Code,* 31-7-9.

compensation of employees. The 1970 law, however, is more directly a product of the Joint Committee on Salaries and Expenses, 1964–65. The 1970 law did not provide for employee security nor did either of the committees make such a recommendation.[66]

One objective of the Reorganization Committee was to make the state service more attractive. A significant step in that direction was taken in 1952 when the state's retirement system was set up. It is interesting that the retirement system was the first part of the reorganization report to receive favorable legislative action, yet the retirement proposal was mentioned in the reorganization report only in two sentences which were in the letter of transmittal attached to the report.

6. Sound fiscal management. Some improvements have been made but no changes in budgeting and pre-audit controls have given the governor full responsibility and control in these areas as was recommended.

7. Limited special fund financing. The committee recommended that the independence of agencies be reduced by making them more dependent on general fund financing rather than on their own special funds. The legislature addressed itself to this problem in 1962 by passing a law requiring all special fund agencies to submit estimates of their expenses to the Commission of Budget and Accounting. The commission would then review the estimates and make recommendations to the legislature regarding the agencies' proposed expenditures.

8. Elimination of *ex officio* agencies. This objective has not been achieved.

9. Sound internal organization. The Reorganization Committee proposed for each agency a standardized internal structure following a hierarchical pattern of departments, bureaus, divisions, and sections. This standardization has not been achieved.

10. Estimated expenditure reductions. The committee summarized the expenditures of 57 of the state's agencies and estimated savings in two areas: (1) general administrative costs and (2) purchasing expenditures. (The estimated savings are shown in Table 18.)

The foregoing comparison of the consequences expected to result from the adoption of the proposals of the 1950 study with actual results has shown that,

[66]*Report of the Joint Committee on Salaries and Expenses* (Jackson, Miss., 1964–65), 4–11; personal interview with James D. Cox, executive director of the State Classification Commission, Jackson, Miss., August 3, 1972.

Table 18

The Reorganization Committee's Estimated Savings from Purchasing and General Administration in 57 State Agencies Based on Expenditures for 1948–49

Item	1948–49 Expenditures*	Estimated Reductions
General Administration	$10,556,900	$ 844,551
Purchasing	$31,087,351	$4,634,020
Total	$41,644,251	$5,478,571

*Expenses for all items in 1948–49 were $104,099,267.
SOURCE: Adapted from Legislative Fact-Finding Committee, *Report on State Reorganzation,* 99–101.

in terms of producing the proposed organizational change, the reorganization effort of 1950 was a failure.

It is safe to say therefore that the estimated savings expected to accrue from the area of general administration (See Table 18) have not been realized. These savings were forecast to result from the integration of related functions, but the related functions were not integrated.

The record is not quite as clear on the matter of purchasing, but it appears the 1950 effort also failed to produce the proposed improvements in purchasing. It is interesting to note from Table 18 that the majority (85 percent) of the savings projected from the 1950 proposals would have come from the centralized state purchasing system. It is unlikely, however, that savings from changes in purchasing procedures have reached the expected level. A supervisor of purchasing was established in 1962 under the Commission of Budgeting and Accounting, but he does not function as an agent for the central purchasing of all goods and materials for state agencies as proposed in the 1950 study. A preliminary review of the 1970 reorganization report indicates that much remains to be done in the area of purchasing if it is to reach the proficiency advocated and predicted in the 1950 study.

As noted, 85 percent of the dollar savings from the proposed reorganization would have come from the central purchasing system. One should not conclude because of this, however, that the best solution to the problem of reorganization would be to push for central purchasing and ignore the structural changes which normally cause the defeat of reorganization. While it is true that structural changes or the integration of functions would have produced only 15 percent of the projected savings, saving money was not the total objective of the reorganization effort. Another important point is that, without making basic organizational changes and integrating the various functions of government, it would be very difficult to implement and operate centralized purchasing in a generally disorganized system. The analysis of the 1970 reorganization proposals will show that although many of the defects cited in the existing system were not structural defects, most of the solutions proposed to correct the deficiencies were structural changes.

The reorganization proposals of 1970 were a product of the third major effort to improve the administrative structure of Mississippi government. That effort, initiated under the leadership of Governor John Bell Williams, is the subject of the next chapter.

4 / The Third Major Effort to Reorganize Mississippi Administration

Before getting into the third major reorganization effort, a study of a joint legislative committee of 1964–65 will be reviewed briefly. Although that work is sometimes referred to as a reorganization study, its scope was more limited than the reorganization studies of 1932, 1950, and 1970.

REPORT OF THE JOINT COMMITTEE ON SALARIES AND EXPENSES, 1964–65

In 1964, a joint legislative committee was established and charged with making a detailed investigation of (1) the salaries and duties of state officers and employees, (2) the possibility of waste and overstaffing in all agencies and departments, (3) the possible need for reorganization in order to cut out duplication of effort and expenditures, and (4) travel expenses, convention costs, and related matters. That committee is popularly referred to as the Hooker Committee, after its chairman, Representative Wilburn Hooker.

As originally set up, the committee was supposed to complete its study during the regular legislative session of 1964. The committee began its work but soon discovered that it faced a "monumental task . . . and that it was an utter impossibility for the committee to even begin its operations satisfactorily during the stress and strain of the legislative session." The legislature apparently agreed with this, for it extended the life of the committee until the next regular session and appropriated $25,000 for its expenses.[1]

The Hooker Report is sometimes called a reorganization study, but the depth of its research did not approach that of either of the other three studies considered in this book. The depth of the Hooker study was limited by the comparatively smaller appropriation it received and by the broader range of

[1] Mississippi Legislature, *Report of the Committee on Salaries and Expenses in State Government* (Jackson, Miss., 1964–65), 2, hereafter called the Hooker Report, *Laws of Mississippi,* 1964, C-592, C-660.

duties with which it was charged. The 1950 reorganization study had $40,000 to work with and the estimated cost of the 1970 study exceeded $250,000.[2]

The Hooker study gave more consideration than the other studies to the internal operations of agencies and also prepared legislation for some of its recommendations—such as the committee's investigation of the salaries and duties of state employees. In contrast with the 1950 study, which provided no details with its recommendation for the adoption of a personnel classification system, the Hooker Committee made specific recommendations for the classification of state jobs and also provided a compensation plan. These recommendations resulted in the creation of the Mississippi Classification Commission in 1970.[3]

Although the Hooker Committee held hearings and looked into the operations of every state agency, its report did not discuss or make specific recommendations for many of the agencies. Altogether, 21 topics were discussed in the report but less than half of these dealt with specific agencies. Many of the topics covered such general operational or administrative matters as "Communications," "Office Space," "Storage or Destruction of Records," and "Public Printing." Two other topics—"Consolidation" and "*Ex Officio* Boards"—more nearly dealt with overall organization. In the six and one-half pages devoted to consolidation, the committee mentioned six bills that it drafted in "attempting to coordinate various functions of state government." Each bill proposed the consolidation of the functions of two agencies. One bill would have abolished the elected state land commissioner and transferred his duties to the secretary of state. Consolidations recommended in two of the six bills were later accomplished. In one case the Boards of Trustees of the Deaf and Blind Schools were combined and in another case the functions of the State Medical Education Board were transferred to the Board of Trustees of Institutions of Higher Learning.[4]

On the matter of *ex officio* boards, the committee stated that several officials were on so many boards that they could neither meet with all of them nor make any contribution to their operations. The committee therefore recommended that the practice of putting officials on *ex officio* boards which were

[2]*House Jouranl*, 1971, p. 70. The 1970 study was done by a group of private businessmen at no cost to the state.
[3]Joint Legislative Fact-Finding Committee, *Report on State Reorganization*, 95, Hooker Report, 4–11; personal interview with James D. Cox, director, Jackson, Miss., August 3, 1972; *Laws of Mississippi*, 1970, C-394.
[4]Hooker Report, 18–24; *Laws of Mississippi* 1966, C-423; *Laws of Mississippi*, 1968, C-415.

unrelated to their official duties should be discontinued. Specific recommendations removing two officials from the Forestry Commission and two officials from the Board of Public Contracts were offered. Both of these changes were subsequently made, the latter by abolishing the board.[5]

Although the work of the Hooker Committee may not be considered part of any large-scale reorganization attempt, relatively speaking, it may have accomplished more than the so-called "major" reorganization efforts.

THE FORCES LEADING TO THE THIRD MAJOR REORGANIZATION EFFORT

The third major reorganization effort was formally initiated by Governor John Bell Williams in December of 1969, when he issued an executive order setting up the Mississippi Commission on Efficiency and Economy in State Government. Apparently there was no public demand nor interest group pressure involved in the governor's decision. Herman Glazier, Williams' executive assistant, reported that the governor's experiences in performing his executive duties during the first year or so of his administration had prompted him to begin the reorganization effort.[6] Aside from Governor Williams' own interest in administrative reorganization, the only influence on his decision to inaugurate the third reorganization effort seems to have come from the legislature. A special legislative committee set up in 1968 had employed the Eagleton Institute of Politics to study the organization of the Mississippi legislature.[7]

The preface to the Eagleton study, issued in December of 1969, contained a pertinent observation on the executive branch. It stated that, compared with many other states, the Mississippi legislature was strong but its strength was "attributable less to its own ability and competence than to the notable weakness of executive institutions in the state." Although the executive branch was beyond the scope of the study, the consultants said they "could not fail to take note of the institutional incapacity of the Office of the Governor in Mississippi, especially its lack of managerial control and fiscal authority."

[5]Hooker Report, 24–25; *Laws of Mississippi* 1964, C-241; *Laws of Mississippi* 1968, C-506.
[6]Mississippi Executive Department, *Executive Order No. 52* (Jackson, Miss.: December 1, 1969); personal interview with Herman Glazier, executive assistant to Governor Cliff Finch, Jackson, Miss., March 14, 1972. Glazier, also a colleague of the late governor Fielding Wright, reports that Governor Wright was similarly influenced when the reorganization effort of 1950 was launched.
[7]David B. Ogle, *Strengthening the Mississippi Legislature* (New Brunswick, New Jersey: Eagleton Institute of Politics, Rutgers University, 1969), iv, hereafter called the Eagleton Report.

The Eagleton study reported that "strong majorities" of legislators considered an examination of the executive branch necessary. Some members of the Mississippi House of Representatives who were particularly interested in the prospects for legislative reorganization later met informally with Governor Williams to express their view that administrative reorganization might also be undertaken. The legislators mentioned three possible ways to study the problem: (1) with a study group made up of lay and business leaders, (2) with a study group made up of legislators, or (3) with some combination of the two.[8]

After deciding that something had to be done, the governor began considering the alternative approaches for a study of the executive branch. He considered the reorganization study of 1950 and that of the Hooker Committee, both of which were made by joint legislative (recess) committees. Williams also looked at other states to see how they were handling the problems of executive reorganization. His research into the matter was facilitated by his personal contacts with other governors. He found that other states had recently used study groups of lay leaders and obtained excellent results. Partly as a result of the success other states were having with lay groups and partly as a result of the legislature's past reluctance to follow up on legislative studies, Governor Williams decided that the best approach would be to have a group of business and lay leaders make a study of the state's administrative system.

On December 1, 1969, Governor Williams called together the chief executive officers (or designated representatives) of 93 corporations and asked them to form a team called "The Mississippi Task Force on Government Efficiency and Economy." His purpose in asking for the study of the organization and operation of the state departments and agencies was to get suggestions for improving and promoting the manageability of the executive branch. For example, Williams said it was impossible for the governor to analyze reports from all the agencies, noting that there was overlapping in the jurisdictions of some groups and that the governor did not have the time or staff to mediate and coordinate the activities of so many agencies. It was also noted that lines of authority from the agencies to the governor were not clearly defined and that many agencies were under the control of the legislature.[9]

The business leaders responded favorably to the governor's request. They

[8]*Ibid.*, 3; personal interview with Representative Kenneth Williams, Jackson, Miss., April 12, 1972.

[9]Personal interview with former governor John Bell Williams, Jackson, Miss., August 3, 1972.

agreed to form the task force on efficiency and economy and pledged to use their funds, personnel, and expertise to make a study. The business executives subsequently held an organizational meeting and chose a five-member committee which was charged with the overall responsibility and guidance for the study. The workers were then divided by the executive committee into two major research groups—(1) on business systems and (2) on organization. As the study turned out, by far the largest part of the report consisted of the findings and recommendations of the "organization" group.[10]

THE PROPOSALS FOR REORGANIZATION

Before examining the 1970 reorganization proposals, analyses will be made here of (1) the 1970 organization outlined by the Commission on Efficiency and Economy, (2) the defects in the organization the commission identified, and (3) the principles upon which the commission based its proposals for reorganization.

The State's Organization in 1970

The chart on page 101 pictures the organization of the state administration outlined by the commission in 1970. This discussion of the commission's findings is primarily a comparison of those findings with the findings of the Reorganization Committee of 1950. Since the reorganization effort of 1950 produced little or no structural changes, the organizational pattern in 1970 is the traditional one of diffused executive authority and responsibility. Table 19 shows how the number of independent agencies in the nine functional fields of government used in the 1950 study had increased by 1970.

The increase in the number of independent agencies in two of the nine functional fields was rather marked—"Conservation and Recreation" went from 25 to 32 and "Health and Sanitation" rose from 8 to 14. Two other fields experienced more moderate net increases and three fields had no net increase. Two fields—"Education" and "Charities and Correction"—had net decreases in the number of agencies.

As indicated in both Tables 19 and 20, 11 agencies were abolished between 1950 and 1970. During the same period 26 new agencies were created, leav-

---

[10]*House Journal,* 1971, p. 70; The Mississippi Commission on Efficiency and Economy in State Government, *Report to the Governor* (reproduced by Mississippi State University, Starkville, Miss., 1970).

THE 112 AGENCIES AND OFFICES OF MISSISSIPPI GOVERNMENT STUDIED BY THE COMMISSION ON EFFICIENCY AND ECONOMY IN STATE GOVERNMENT IN 1970

ELECTORATE

LEGISLATURE

GOVERNOR

SUPERINTENDENT OF EDUCATION

TREASURER

LIEUTENANT GOVERNOR

INSURANCE DEPARTMENT COMMISSION

PUBLIC SERVICE COMMISSION

ATTORNEY GENERAL

LAND COMMISSIONER

STATE AUDITOR

SECRETARY OF STATE

COMMISSIONER OF AGRICULTURE

PLANT BOARD

STATE FAIR COMMISSION

ARCHIVES & HISTORY

LIME PLANT BOARD

STATE LIBRARIAN

INTERAGENCY COMM. ON MENTAL ILLNESS & RETARDATION

DEAF & BLIND INSTITUTIONS

MENTAL INSTITUTIONS

ELEMENTARY INSTITUTIONS

FEDERAL PROGRAMS

HOSPITAL REIMBURSEMENT COMMISSION

BOARD OF REG. FOR SANITARIANS

FORESTRY COMMISSION

HOSPITAL COMMISSION

BOARD FOR SANITARIANS

A & I BOARD

COMMISSION ON HOSPITAL CARE

BOARD OF AGRICULTURAL AVIATION

HIGHWAY COMMISSION

BOARD OF ANIMAL HEALTH

AIR & WATER POLLUTION

RURAL ELECTRIC AUTHORITY

BOARD OF PUBLIC HEALTH

AUTHORITY FOR EDUCATIONAL TELEVISION

CENTRAL DATA PROCESSING AUTHORITY

BUREAU OF MEDICAID

BUDGET COMMISSION

PERSONNEL CLASSIFICATION

BOARD OF TRUSTEES HOSPITAL FOR CEREBRAL PALSY

AERONAUTICS COMMISSION

REAL ESTATE COMMISSION

MARINE CONSERVATION COMMISSIONERS

VETERAN'S MEMORIAL COMMISSION

BOARD OF WATER COMMISSIONERS

VETERAN'S AFFAIRS

GAME & FISH COMMISSION

VETERANS FARM & HOME BOARD

JUNIOR COLLEGE COMMISSION

TEXTBOOK PURCHASING BOARD

EDUCATIONAL FINANCE COMMISSION

A & I BOARD

STATE SOVEREIGNTY COMMISSION

LIBRARY COMMISSION

DEPT. OF CIVIL DEFENSE

BUILDING COMMISSION

INSTITUTIONS OF HIGHER LEARNING

COUNCIL ON AGING

PUBLIC WELFARE

PUBLIC RETIREMENT

ADJUTANT GENERAL

BOARD OF WATER SAFETY COMMISSIONERS

CENTRAL MARKETING BOARD

MARKETING COUNCIL

TAX COMMISSION

EMPLOYMENT SECURITY COMMISSION

GEOLOGICAL SURVEY

WORKMEN'S COMPENSATION COMMISSION

MOTOR VEHICLE LICENSE TAG COMMISSION

ATHLETIC COMMISSION

COMMISSIONER OF PUBLIC SAFETY

TRAINING SCHOOLS

MOTOR VEHICLE COMPTROLLER

BOARD OF REGISTRATION FOR PRO. ENG.

BOARD OF PUBLIC ACCOUNTANCY

BOARD OF NURSES EXAMINERS

BOARD OF VETERINARIAN EXAMINERS

BOARD OF OPTOMETRY

BOARD OF DENTAL EXAMINERS

BOARD OF BARBER EXAMINERS

BOARD OF BAR ADMISSIONS

BOARD OF ARCHITECTURE

BOARD OF COSMETOLOGY

BOARD OF PSYCHOLOGICAL EXAM.

BOARD OF PHYSICAL THERAPY

POLYGRAPHIC EXAM. BOARD

BOARD OF EMBALMING

BOARD OF PHARMACY

MEMORIAL STUDIUM COMMISSION

MONUMENT PARK COMMISSION

NATCHEZ TRACE PARKWAY-RIGHT OF WAY COMM.

STONEWALL JACKSON MEMORIAL BOARD

GRAND GULF MILITARY MONUMENTS

OIL & GAS BOARD

NATCHEZ TRACE PARKWAY COMMISSION

COAST COLISEUM COMMISSION

PARK SYSTEM

PAROLE BOARD

STATE PENITENTIARY BOARD

BRUCE'S CROSSROADS COMMISSION

BOARD OF ELECTION COMMISSIONERS

SOIL CONSERVATION COMMISSION

MINERAL LEASE COMMISSION

SURPLUS PROPERTY PROCUREMENT COMMISSION

BOND RETIREMENT COMMISSION

BOND COMMISSION

BOND ATTORNEY

DEPT. OF PUBLIC HEALTH

LIFE LAND COMMISSION

STATE CHEMIST

DEPOSIT COMMISSION

CAPITOL COMMISSION

BOARD OF SAVINGS & LOAN

EX-OFFICIO

101

Table 19

Changes From 1950 to 1970 in the Numbers of Agencies in Nine Functional Fields of Mississippi State Administration

Functional Field	Total 1950	Abolished 1950–70	Created 1950–70	Total 1970
General Government	22	2	4	24
Protection to Persons & Property	16	1	4	19
Highways & Transportation	3	—	—	3
Conservation & Recreation	25	1	8	32
Health & Sanitation	8	—	6	14
Hospitals & Institutions	7	2	2	7
Charities & Correction	5	1	—	4
Education	11	4	2	9
Libraries	3	—	—	3
Totals	100	11	26	115*

*This number (115) exceeds the 112 agencies studied in the 1970 reorganization effort because some agencies were not included in both studies. See Table 20.
SOURCE: Adapted from Legislative Fact-Finding Committee, *Report on State Reorganization*, 2–4; Commission on Efficiency and Economy, *Report to the Governor*, 9, 53–61.

Table 20

Agencies Studied in 1950 and in 1970 and Those Abolished and Created in the Interim

Agencies Studied in 1950	100
Agencies Abolished Between 1950 and 1970	− 11
Subtotal	89
Agencies Created Between 1950 and 1970	+ 26
Subtotal	115*
Agencies Studied in 1950 but not in 1970	− 5
Subtotal	110
Agencies Studied in 1970 but not in 1950	+ 2
Total Agencies Studied in 1970	112

*Net increase in the number of agencies from 1950 to 1970 is fifteen.
SOURCE: Adapted from Legislative Fact-Finding Committee, *Report on State Reorganization*, 2–4; Commission on Efficiency and Economy, *Report to the Governor*, 9.

ing a net increase of 15 agencies between 1950 and 1970. The difference between the number of agencies studied in 1950 (100) and the number studied in 1970 (112) is only 12, however. This number (12) is not equal to the net increase (15) in the number of agencies between 1950 and 1970 because the 1970 study did not consider a few of the agencies studied in 1950. This is explained in Table 20.

Of the eleven agencies that were abolished, as noted in Tables 19 and 20, the functions and duties of five were discontinued. The functions and duties of the six other abolished agencies were transferred to existing agencies.

The 112 agencies studied in 1970 are shown in the organization chart on page 101. It should be noted that two entries on the chart—the "Natchez Trace Parkway Commission" and the "Natchez Trace Parkway Right-of-Way Commission"—seem to represent a single agency. Another entry on the chart, the "Insurance Department Commission," represents two distinct agencies—the Insurance Commission (dealing with fire and casualty insurance rates) and the Insurance Department, headed by the commissioner of insurance.[11]

In comparing the organization chart of 1970 (page 101) with that of 1950 (page 69), it is interesting to note that in 1950 only two agencies—Archives and History and the Office of State Librarian—are shown under the legislature, while on the 1970 chart, eight agencies are shown under the legislature. Most of the six additional agencies shown under the legislature are agencies created since 1950. The one exception is the Budget Commission which was set up in 1932. Under that law, however, the state operated with an "executive budget" until 1955 when the law was changed to have the governor act only as *ex officio* chairman of a new commission made up of four legislators. When the Central Data Processing Authority was first set up in 1968, it was composed of six members, mostly *ex officio* administrative officials. The legislature felt this arrangement was unsatisfactory and rewrote the law in 1970 so that all six members of the Data Processing Authority would be legislators.[12]

In another case, the governor gave the legislature the controlling membership on an agency's board. The (personnel) Classification Commission shown

[11]Mississippi *Code,* Sections 55-13-1, 83-1-1, 83-3-1.
[12]*Laws of Mississippi* of 1932, C-320; *Laws of Mississippi* of 1955, C-24; *Laws of Mississippi* of 1968, C-499; *Laws of Mississippi* of 1970, C-466. In 1968, six more legislators were added to the membership of the Commission, *Laws of Mississippi* of 1968, C-513.

in Chart 3 on page 101 was set up in 1970 with the provision that the lieutenant governor and speaker of the house appoint four legislators to the eight-member board. The other four members were to be appointed by the governor from the "citizens of the state." Membership on the very first commission was evenly divided—four legislators and four non-legislators. The succeeding governor, however, used his appointments to name three more legislators to go with the four legislators appointed by the lieutenant governor and speaker. The Classification Commission, therefore—like the Budget Commission, Central Data Processing, and the Medicaid Commission—is dominated by legislators. The Medicaid Commission was created in 1969 with the stipulation that four of its seven members be legislators.

A review of state statues raises the question as to why the Interagency Commission on Mental Illness and Mental Retardation, Archives and History, and the Authority for Educational Television are shown in Chart 3 under the legislature.[13] It is obvious, however, from comparing Charts 1 and 3 that since 1950 the legislature has gained prominent, if not controlling, positions on several important state agencies whose functions are normally thought of as administrative or executive.

The Defects Found in the 1970 Organization

Basing their deliberations primarily on data from interviews with officials responsible for the day-to-day administration of the state's business, the Commission on Efficiency and Economy in State Government identified several problems that it said must be overcome. The commission did not elaborate on the problems, however, stating that it was not the purpose of the report to be critical of the state's operations. The problems listed were:

1. The lack of a systematic approach in overall program planning and budgeting.

2. The absence of effective information processing and administrative procedures for effective management control.

3. The lack of uniform policies and procedures in personnel, finance, and purchasing.

[13]*Laws of Mississippi* of 1970, C-394; *Laws of Mississippi* of 1968, C-31, C-37. Although there is some question about the agencies shown under the legislature in the chart prepared by the 1970 reorganization study (chart 3), Appendix E lists 10 agencies that in 1976 were controlled by the legislature.

4. The variations in departmental practices and procedures and the absence of standardization in management control methods.

5. The large number of independent operating units, many of which could perform more efficiently if consolidated with related functions.[14]

There is some notable difference between these problems and those cited in the 1950 study. Overall program planning and information processing (Items 1 and 2 above) were not mentioned in the 1950 study. Conditions, of course, had changed considerably by 1970, and it is understandable why there was a concern for overall program planning in 1970 when expenditures of the state had increased from $134,463,878 in 1950 to $924,178,184 in 1970. Some problems noted in 1950 but not in 1970 were the long ballot, the extensive use of the *ex officio* device, and the inherent administrative weakness in the office of the governor. The preceding analysis of the 1970 organization shows that these conditions, noted as problems in the 1950 study, still exist.

The Principles for the Proposed Reorganization

As with the defects, the principles for the reorganization noted by the commission were listed with no elaboration except to say that "certain guiding management principles have shaped the formation of conclusions within this report." The principles outlined by the Commission on Efficiency and Economy included:

1. Existing functions cannot be arbitrarily eliminated. Their purpose and effectiveness should be evaluated in the light of current and potential needs.

2. Unnecessary duplication of effort must be avoided, and lines of authority must be clear and nonconflicting.

3. The number and variety of activities which can be effectively controlled by an individual administrator are limited.

4. Combination of related functions and activities for management purposes is desirable whenever practical.

5. Information systems serve as a management tool for recording data essential to decision-making in program planning and management.

6. An organization, whether government or business, cannot realistically establish a permanent, unchanging administrative structure. It must be capable of responding to changing problems and needs.

Three additional "considerations" were noted:

[14]Commission on Efficiency and Economy, *Report to the Governor*, 3–4.

1. The growing demands on state government resources make it essential to coordinate program planning of related functions.

2. It is necessary to provide the governor, legislature, and Budget Commission with reliable, documented budget proposals supported by well-defined statements of program objectives.

3. The increasing complexity of the governor's office makes it necessary that he have immediate access to specialized staff assistants.

Of the five problems identified by the commission, only one of them (the fifth) was a problem of structure or organization. Conversely, five of the six management principles listed above that were to guide in the formation of the report's conclusions seem to be principles or guides for organizational or structural change. The important point here is that structural changes are offered as solutions to problems that are not necessarily structural in nature.

The Proposals for Reorganization

Based on the analysis of the problems and using the management principles noted above, the commission attempted to outline some specific courses of action. The following recommendations were made:

1. Restructuring of organizational relationships.

2. Establishment of a systematic approach to long-range planning.

3. Modification of the state's management information system.

4. Modification of policies and practices in the field of financial management.

5. Restructuring the state's purchasing practices.

6. Development of a personnel management system to provide career opportunities for state government personnel.[15]

These recommendations were outlined in more detail in the remaining 58 pages of the report. Forty-three of those pages were devoted to proposals for restructuring the organizational relationships within the government (No. 1 above). Items 2 through 6 were outlined in the last 15 pages of the report. The commission's view was that organizational structure determines in large part the effectiveness of any government or business activity. The commission felt the activities of government or business would be easier to control, more efficient, and less costly with related functions grouped, non-essential units eliminated, and the lines of authority and the reporting relationships clearly

[15]*Ibid.*, 4–5.

defined. The commission recommended that the 112 agencies studied be restructured into 32 departments and that the legislature charge the governor with the continuing responsibility for the economy and effectiveness of the state's organization. It was not the purpose of the commission, however, to outline the legislature's role and/or its relationship to the recommended structure. The proposed organization is shown in Chart 4 on page 108.

The recommended changes proposed by the 1970 study were similar to those proposed in 1950 (shown in Chart 2 on page 74).

The major feature of both reports was the consolidation of 100 or more agencies into some smaller number. The objectives in each case were to make the lines of authority clearer and to give the governor a more manageable span of control. The proposed organizations in each case showed 17 agencies directly under the governor. Altogether, excluding the governor and the lieutenant governor, the 1950 report proposed 24 agencies and offices for the executive branch. In 1970, again excluding the governor, 32 agencies were proposed for the executive branch. Five of the 32 agencies were newly established since the 1950 report,[16] and 3 others in the 1970 chart were not proposed as separate agencies in 1950. Except for these 8 agencies, there would be only 24 agencies and offices in the 1970 proposed organization, the same as in the 1950 proposal.

The most notable difference in the two reports was in the number of elected officials to be eliminated. The 1950 report proposed the elimination of 8 of the 17 elective officials (47 percent), while the 1970 report proposed to eliminate only 2 of 16 elective officials (12 percent). Mainly because of the proposals to eliminate more elective officials in 1950, the structural changes proposed in the 1970 study were not as far-reaching as those in 1950.

FORCES AND FACTORS INVOLVED IN THE EFFORTS
TO EFFECT THE REORGANIZATION

Presentation of the Reorganization Report

The Commission on Efficiency and Economy in State Government worked for about a year on its report and delivered it to the governor for the beginning of the 1971 legislative session. Governor Williams did not mention the report

[16]The five new agencies include the Stadium Commission, Department of Federal Programs, Educational Television Authority, Employee Retirement, and the Department of Alcohol Beverage Control.

Chart 4

ORGANIZATION OF AGENCIES AND OFFICES OF MISSISSIPPI GOVERNMENT AS PROPOSED BY THE
COMMISSION ON EFFICIENCY AND ECONOMY IN STATE GOVERNMENT IN 1970

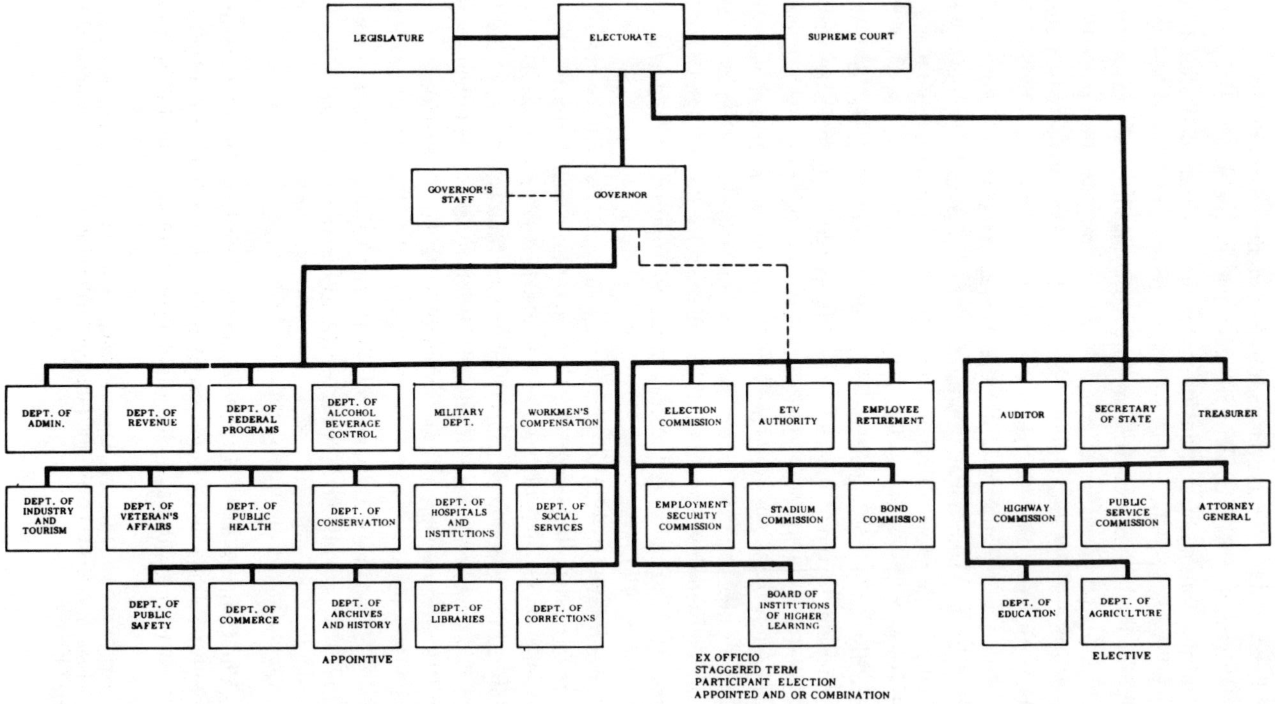

directly in his annual message to the legislature (January 7) but chose to present it in a special message on January 13, 1971. The purpose of the message was to ''earnestly'' solicit the cooperation and support of the legislature on the matter of reorganization. In his message, the governor made several comments on the need for reorganization, although it was his belief that the need for better management of state government had been adequately demonstrated before the study by the ''Blue Ribbon Commission.'' Williams spoke of the ''hodge-podge'' of state agencies which followed no planned pattern and which sprang up without regard for the overall structure. A major difficulty with the resulting structure, he said, was the absence of a clear line of executive authority. The executive was forced to share administrative functions with the legislature. To Governor Williams, the problem was ''in the structure and the solution must be in the improvement of that structure.''[17]

In presenting the report to the legislature, Governor Williams made no specific recommendations and asked the legislators for no commitment at that time other than their interest. Williams stated, ''Under our Constitution, the executive proposes and the legislature disposes.'' He noted that the task was huge and complicated and that he did not expect all the improvements to be made by the present or even the next legislature. The governor's reference to the complexity and difficulty of the task, however, was not offered as an excuse for inaction on the matter.

Governor Williams also used the occasion to emphasize some key points in the new report. He wanted it clearly understood by the legislature, by state employees, and the public at large that reorganization would in no way be a drive to cut the number of state employees. Further, the governor said it was a narrow view to see the reorganization solely as an economy move. The important point was, he stressed, to give the state a more manageable and responsive government. The strategy, said Williams, would be to use the ''umbrella'' approach which would consolidate related agencies into an umbrella type department where the various agencies would be incorporated intact, retaining all their powers.[18]

To the casual observer, reorganization by the ''umbrella'' approach may not appear to be much of an improvement. The editor of the 1970 reorganization report said the grouping of agencies under umbrella departments would

---

[17]*House Journal,* 1971, pp. 41–50, 69–72.
[18]*Ibid.* Chapter I discussed the interest in the umbrella approach to state reorganization found in recent literature.

give the agencies a greater feeling of rapport. Improved administration would result indirectly and gradually after the initial change in the formal organization. Phase II of the reorganization and the continuing organizational and administrative improvement under the "umbrella" approach would depend on the development of informal relationships. The department head would pursue the development of these informal relationships because of his interest in securing better administrative control over the loosely knit department. Initially he would have little or no formal authority over his department, but as he strengthened his position through informal means, he would expect this to be reflected ultimately in changes in the formal organization.[19]

It is apparent that the umbrella approach to reorganization would initially minimize the structural changes of the reorganization process, and that the 1970 reorganization plan did not propose nearly as much change as had the other reorganization studies. This point was not readily apparent, however, in the newspaper account of the 1970 plan which was said to have "recommended massive consolidation of state commissions to thirty-three departments." The headline that "John Bell Williams Reveals Proposal to Shake Up Agencies" was hardly the point Governor Williams made when he said "the strategy would be one of incorporating intact the existing agencies with all their powers into 'umbrella' type departments."[20]

Two days after the governor presented the report, the *Clarion-Ledger* asked its readers the following question in its "Your Opinion Counts" weekly survey: "Do you favor the immediate implementation of the business and professional plan to reorganize state government?" Sixty-five percent of those responding said "yes."[21]

A week later, the first reorganization bills were introduced in the legislature. Commenting on these in a press conference, the governor said he did not know if the legislature would have time to consider his proposals in the 90-day session but said, "there has to be a beginning before there can be any conclusions."[22]

Some explanation of the "90-day session" is in order. A constitutional amendment was adopted in 1968 requiring the legislature to meet annually in sessions of limited duration. The first session of a new administration could be

---

[19]Personal interview with Charles Sewell, Jackson, Miss., August 30, 1972; Council of State Governments, *Reorganization in the States*, 15.

[20]*Jackson Clarion-Ledger*, January 14, 1971, p. 1; *House Journal*, 1971, p. 71.

[21]*Jackson Clarion-Ledger*, January 15, 1971, p. 1, January 22, 1971, p. 1.

[22]*House Journal*, 1971, p. 202; *Jackson Clarion-Ledger*, January 29, 1971, pp. 1, 16.

125 days in length, while the three other sessions of the administration were limited to 90 days. The 1971 session was the first "annual" session of the legislature held after the adoption of this amendment, and because it was the fourth year of the administration, the session was limited to 90 days. Governor Williams later suggested that the reorganization legislation introduced in 1971 received less attention than it would have had the legislature not been concerned with adjusting its procedures to the new limited session. This point is reinforced by the fact that, largely as a result of the "annual session" amendment of 1968, the Eagleton Institute of Politics was employed to make a study of the legislature and recommend changes.[23] Such a study was thought necessary because the "annual session" amendment was viewed as a challenge to the customary habits and procedures of the legislature.

As a result of the annual session amendment, the legislature in 1971 was meeting for the first time in regular session in an election year. Newspaper analyst Charles M. Hills concluded that the solons "were heading into an election year and decided to leave the matter (of reorganization) alone."[24] As was shown in Chapter III, too much enthusiasm for and involvement in reorganization could be costly in an election campaign.

The legislative reluctance to take up reorganization in an election year was probably intensified by the amount of reorganization that was proposed. The legislature was being asked via the bills that were introduced to do more reorganizing than it had ever before been asked to accomplish. Most of the reorganization was proposed in House Bill 1121 which would have created 9 departments.[25] These departments would have been under the governor and would have been more than half the departments proposed for the appointive category by the reorganization report of 1970. Further analysis shows that the 9 departments proposed in House Bill 1121 would have provided for nearly half the changes necessary to produce the organization pictured in Chart 4 (see page 108). Thirteen of the 32 offices or departments shown in the chart were existing departments for which little or no change was recommended in the reorganization report.[26]

[23]Personal interview, Jackson, Miss., August 3, 1972; Eagleton Report, iv.

[24]*Jackson Clarion-Ledger,* January 16, 1972, Sec. F, p. 1.

[25]The companion bill in the senate was Senate Bill 2172, *Senate Journal,* 1971, p. 169.

[26]Commission on Efficiency and Economy, *Report to the Governor,* 8. The thirteen departments with little or no change were the Public Service Commission, Highway Commission, Treasurer, Secretary of State, Auditor, Bond Commission, Stadium Commission, Employment Security Commission, Employee Retirement, Educational Television Authority, Election Commission, Workmen's Compensation, and Military.

That legislators were reluctant to attempt such large-scale reorganization in the face of upcoming elections is supported by the research into the 1950 reorganization effort, which was also affected by an election. It will be recalled that the governor was considering a special session for reorganization in the election year of 1951. The lieutenant governor, Sam Lumpkin, aspiring to the gubernatorial office, spoke out on several occasions against the reorganization effort. Former governor Paul B. Johnson, Jr., who opposed Lumpkin in the gubernatorial race of 1951, said Lumpkin sought to disassociate himself from the reorganization effort and the 1950 report because it would have been impossible for him to have explained his support of reorganization in the election campaign.[27]

As implied in Johnson's assessment, reorganization is a complicated matter. The general idea of governmental reorganization for economy and efficiency may be widely supported, but when proposals for specific changes are mentioned reorganization becomes a controversial issue with opposition arising over every proposed change. Because Lumpkin was a part of the administration which produced the detailed reorganization proposal in 1950, he could not come out for reorganization in the 1951 campaign without being burdened with the opposition generated by the specific changes proposed in the 1950 report. The practical politics of situations such as that Lumpkin faced generally leads many political candidates to predictable conclusions. They avoid the controversy and hopefully the opposition and thereby offer unending illustrations of the axiom that it is much more difficult to be for something than to be against something.

A Special Session of the Legislature

Although the 1971 legislature did not act on the reorganization proposals, Governor Williams did not give up. On August 14, 1971, he announced that he was considering calling the legislature into special session to take up the reorganization question. The governor referred to the election campaign then in progress in which he said there was much talk of "trimming the fat" from government operations. A special session, he said, could provide the opportunity for doing that, but he hastened to add that the most important variable in the final decision on the special session call would be the attitude of the legislators. The news report of the possible special session pointed out that the focus of the reorganization effort would be the consolidation of agencies and

[27]Personal interview, Hattiesburg, Miss., August 28, 1972.

suggested that moves to strengthen the governor's power of appointment would be objectionable. Williams felt it would be more feasible to attempt reorganization in a special session where it would be the only matter before the legislature. He was considering the special session for November, after the general election, at which time a number of legislators would be participating as "lame ducks." Governor Williams indicated that such a situation might be more conducive to dealing with reorganization since political pressures would be less on a man going out of office.[28]

However, in the middle of November and after the general election, the governor announced that he would not call the special session for reorganization. Newspaper accounts of the announcement said that Williams had decided not to call the session because there would not be enough time to complete the job of reorganization before the new administration took office in January. The reports said the decision came after numerous conferences with Lieutenant Governor Charles Sullivan, House Speaker John Junkin, and other legislators. One newspaper stated plainly that Sullivan and Junkin were opposed to the special session and another intimated the same. The *Clarion-Ledger* said an adverse reaction from legislators and the knowledge that the governor-elect was interested in working for reorganization contributed to Williams' decision not to call the special session.[29]

It is highly probable that there was another reason why the special session plans were cancelled. In the gubernatorial election the well-known lieutenant governor lost to William Waller, a candidate who had never held state office and who was not particularly well known. Because the legislators did not know the views of the governor-elect, they were hesitant to take up executive reorganization in a special session prior to the beginning of the new administration.

In his retiring message on January 12, 1972, Governor Williams referred to his previous messages on reorganization and renewed "the suggestion that consideration and study be given to a needed reorganization." Although Williams made only a brief reference to reorganization, the topic was one of five items in his speech that drew applause from his audience.[30]

---

[28]*Jackson Clarion-Ledger,* August 14, 1971, pp. 1,7.

[29]*Jackson Daily News,* November 17, 1971, p. 1; *Hattiesburg American,* November 17, 1971, p. 1; *Jackson Clarion-Ledger,* November 17, 1971, p. 1; *Memphis Commercial Appeal,* November 17, 1971.

[30]*Message of Governor John Bell Williams to the Joint Assembly of the Mississippi State Legislature,* January 12, 1972 (Jackson, Miss.), 29–30; *Hattiesburg American,* January 13, 1972.

The First Year of William Waller's Administration

William Waller was inaugurated as governor one week after Williams' retiring message. Governor Waller expressed the view in his inaugural address that he had received a "mandate for progress from the people." According to Waller, one area of challenge would be the efficient operation of state government. He proposed that "we attack the problem now and initiate modern management practices in state government." The problem was, he said, too complex to handle in one limited annual session, but the new governor was optimistic that a large part of the laws could be passed.[31]

The following week, Waller addressed a joint assembly of the legislature to outline his "thoughts regarding a legislative program for the year." Again he stated his view that the program was in response to a public mandate. State government reorganization was one of nine topics in the governor's proposed legislative program. Governor Waller said that sweeping reorganization was too complex to consider in that session of the legislature but named three specific areas that he felt could and should be considered—(1) a new Department of Administration, (2) an expanded Department of Revenue, and (3) expansion of the functions of the Department of Public Safety.[32]

These departments which Waller proposed to create or change were 3 of the 24 agencies shown under the governor in the organization chart on page 108. Such changes, if accomplished, would have provided only a small part of the proposed organization, but as Governor Williams had said, there had to be a beginning. Of the several bills introduced to make the suggested changes, only one became law. The successful bill transferred the Bureau of Narcotics from the Health Department to the Bureau of Public Safety. Passage of this bill came at a time when widespread public feelings forced all sorts of action in the area of drug abuse. Such actions ranged from investigations by local grand juries to national commissions studying marijuana. Mississippians, therefore, faced the drug situation firsthand, but also were frequently reminded of the scope and seriousness of the problem by the national news media. Passage of the narcotics bill indicates that the public concern over the drug problem did not go unnoticed by political figures and also suggests that the remainder of the reorganization bills, all of which failed, could have benefited from more public interest in their passage.

[31]*House Journal,* 1972, pp. 82–84.
[32]*Ibid.,* pp. 101–94.

Unlike the narcotics bill, three other bills establishing various bureaus in the Department of Public Safety died in house committees after passing the senate.[33] Two of the bills went to the Ways and Means Committee and one went to the Judiciary "A" Committee. The bills were not reported from committee and the common view of the committee members was that the bills were given little or no consideration. Some said there was not enough time to study the bills because they were received during the last month of the session, when the committees had other important and unfinished business. Other committee members felt that Governor Waller's rapport with the house was poor at the time and they were not inclined to consider "his" reorganization bills. Still others were not particularly receptive to the idea of reorganization. In this regard, it should be mentioned that several legislators and other observers did not believe the objectives of and the need for reorganization had been clearly established or explained. The generalities of reorganization for economy and efficiency may be appealing, but they provide no answer for those who want to know more specifically what savings or other benefits can be expected.

Another of the three changes suggested by Waller in his legislative program was the establishment of a Department of Revenue. The senate's Finance Committee gave a favorable report to a bill designed to reorganize the revenue collection functions of state government, but the bill died on the senate calendar. A similar bill in the house was never reported from the Ways and Means Committee. Some house members felt the bill received scant consideration because it was 2¼ inches thick, contained 443 pages, and weighed 5½ pounds. According to Roman Kelly, then clerk of the House, it was the longest bill ever introduced in the Mississippi House of Representatives.[34] The sheer size and length of the bill undoubtedly reduced its chances for success, but it may not have been as complicated as suggested by its physical appearance. The thickness of the bill, which would have amended approximately 150 sections of the Mississippi *Code of 1942*, was due to the constitutional prohibition on amending existing laws by referring only to their titles. In other words, when a bill proposes to amend a law, the entire section of the law has to be inserted in the proposed bill even if only two or three words in

---

[33]Senate Bills: 1606, Create Bureau of Vehicles; 1607, Create Bureau of Law Enforcement; 1610, Create Bureau of Administrative Services. *Senate Journal,* 1972, pp. 1486–87; *House Journal,* 1972, pp. 749, 782, 1528, 1555.

[34]*Senate Journal,* 1972, pp. 244, 949; *House Journal,* 1972, p. 318; personal interview, Jackson, Miss., August, 1972.

the law are to be changed. In the Department of Revenue bill, approximately 150 sections of the *Code* were being amended, so all 150 sections were reproduced in the proposed bill, thus accounting for its thickness.

A third change Waller felt could be made involved the establishment of a Department of Administration in the executive branch. Bills to accomplish this were introduced in the house and senate. The overall purpose of the senate bill was to "coordinate the activities of the executive branch, plan the reduction of costs, and increase efficiency."[35] The Department of Administration would undertake long-range planning and make studies for the consolidation and reorganization of the executive branch of the government.

Proponents of the senate bill said it would provide the vehicle for streamlining the executive branch. Opponents said the bill would create a super-agency and give the governor dictatorial powers. One senator remarked that he too wanted to save money but that he also wanted to "save the state from a dictatorship."[36]

Nevertheless, the bill passed and went to the house where it was referred to the Appropriations Committee. Governor Waller and Earl Evans, a special assistant who had drafted the bill and helped it gain passage in the senate, met with members of the Appropriations Committee to answer questions about the measure. The committee, however, did not report the bill out for floor action. Evans felt the committee objected to the bill because it was perceived as an effort to increase the power of the governor.[37] One of the bill's authors said important leaders in the house opposed the legislation because the first version of the bill proposed that the Department of Administration would perform staff functions for state agencies. Some of these functions, e.g., purchasing, would have been taken away from existing agencies dominated by the legislature.[38]

In a discussion on reorganization, Representative Edgar Stephens, then chairman of the House Appropriations Committee, stated that any proposals to give the governor more power would be seriously questioned by the legisla-

---

[35]House Bills 336, 725, 818, *House Journal,* 1972, p. 1557. None of these house bills was ever reported from committee. Senate bill 1860, *Senate Journal,* 1972, p. 1503.

[36]*Jackson Clarion-Ledger,* March 22, 1972, p. 1, April 2, 1972, p. 1.

[37]*House Journal,* 1972, p. 749; personal interview, Jackson, Miss., April 16, 1972. Earl Evans served in the senate as chairman of the Appropriations Committee and was later director of the Commission of Budgeting and Accounting.

[38]Personal interview with Senator George Yarbrough, co-author of the bill, Jackson, Miss., March 27, 1972. As suggested by the governor in his legislative program, the Department of Administration would have been set up to perform the staff functions of purchasing, personnel, budgeting, and accounting. *House Journal,* 1972, p. 103.

ture because it felt it had a continuing responsibility (as opposed to the single four-year term of the governor) for the proper administration of state programs. Concerning the Department of Administration bill, Stephens indicated that a possible point of concern among committee members was the feature allowing and requiring the director of the proposed department to investigate state administrative operations and recommend changes.[39] With the authority "to request employees of the . . . agencies of state government to assist him in the performance of his duties," the director of the proposed department would have had rather broad powers. In effect, the department would have served as a sort of continuing reorganization study committee.

Some members of the Appropriations Committee felt it was not necessary to create a new department for the purpose of studying reorganization. They felt that the legislature could study and plan reorganization. To this end, the vice-chairman and four other members of the committee introduced a resolution proposing the creation of a reorganization study committee, to be made up of 14 legislators and a member of the governor's staff. The governor would have been an *ex officio* member of the committee.[40]

The house resolution represented a preference for the legislative approach to studying and planning reorganization as opposed to one more directly involving the governor through the proposed Department of Administration. Unable to get the administration bill out of committee and having been unsuccessful with the other reorganization proposals in his legislative program, Governor Waller apparently decided the legislative approach to studying reorganization was the most he could hope for. Though the governor made a personal appeal to the House Rules Committee for approval of the resolution setting up the legislative reorganization study committee, his decision was probably too late, for the legislature adjourned only a few hours afterwards.[41]

One other bill of the 1972 session should be mentioned—House Bill 430, referred to as the legislative post audit bill. The lawmakers felt that a post audit committee should be established to audit state agencies, and thereby keep them informed as to whether the agencies were administering their programs in accordance with the intent of the legislature. The state auditor strongly opposed the house bill but generally favored a senate substitute which

---

[39]Personal interview, Jackson, Miss., April 12, 1972.

[40]House Concurrent Resolution 110, Mississippi Legislature, Regular Session, 1972; personal interviews, Jackson, Miss., April, 1972.

[41]Interview with Representative Betty Long, April 7, 1973.

he said could improve the "communications between the executive branch and the legislative branch so far as legislative intent is concerned."[42]

One highly respected veteran of state government, with service in both legislative and executive branches, felt very strongly that the post audit was one key to the eventual passage of a reorganization program.[43] Many legislative leaders were also of the opinion that with an effective post audit the legislature would be more receptive to reorganization efforts designed to give the governor more control over the administrative processes of state government. The post audit bill passed in the senate by a vote of 49 to 2 and in the house by 102 to 12.[44]

Governor Waller, however, vetoed the bill, stating three reasons why he believed it to be unconstitutional:

1. The bill removed authority from a constitutional officer elected by the people.

2. The bill on its face was vague.

3. The transfer of power from the constitutional office of state auditor to a legislative committee clearly required that the legislature take over certain functions of the executive branch.

Waller said he did not oppose the principle of the bill, however.

> [M]ost all political leaders recognize the urgent need for additional controls over the performance and efficiency of state agencies so as to require more businesslike management of tax dollars. I will seek passage of new laws modernizing and reorganizing the functions of state government at the very beginning of the next session of the legislature. I hope the legislature will allow passage of these bills.[45]

At the time of the veto, the legislature had adjourned and could not review the governor's action but, at Waller's request, nearly a third of them returned to Jackson to give him their views on the post audit. Of the 59 legislators present, only 3 took the governor's side and opposed the bill. Waller knew he was risking alienating members of the legislature but felt they would "cool off" before the next session and would not be negative toward his programs.[46]

A couple of months later, state legislator Robert Arrington predicted that

---

[42]*Jackson Clarion-Ledger,* March 24, 1972; *Hattiesburg American,* April 6, 1972.

[43]Personal interview with Earl Evans, Jackson, Miss., March 16, 1972. The other key was establishment of a merit system for state employees to offer them job security in any consolidation or reorganization of agencies.

[44]*Senate Journal,* 1972, p. 701; *House Journal,* 1972, p. 385.

[45]*House Journal,* 1972, pp. 1394-96.

[46]*Jackson Clarion-Ledger,* May 28, 1972, p. 1.

the first thing the Mississippi lawmakers would do in the 1973 session would be to repass the post audit bill over the governor's veto. Arrington's prediction was based on his poll of 72 colleagues—69 of them wanted to repass the post audit bill. His conclusions were that the legislature would not be very cooperative concerning Waller's reorganization proposals in 1973.[47] The legislature certainly had not been cooperative in the governor's initial efforts on reorganization, which were totally unsuccessful.

In December, 1972, at the end of his first year in office, however, Governor Waller issued a 66-page "Summary of Accomplishments" in which he reiterated his belief that reorganization was one of "the two top needs of Mississippi." The legislature had already put into motion a program to meet the other of the two top needs, i.e., highways.[48] With the highway problem provided for, it was reported that reorganization would not only be the number one issue for the remaining three years of the Waller administration but was in fact considered of even greater import than the need for highways.[49]

Not everyone, of course, agreed with the view from the governor's office on the priority of issues facing the state and the legislature. As the beginning of the 1973 legislative session approached, a powerful senate committee chairman said the priority problem for 1973 was the "sensible expenditure of the funds available for the next fiscal year, as well as a determination of whether modest tax relief might be afforded to the tax-payers."[50] Other issues which seemed to concern legislators more than reorganization included the state penitentiary, the equal rights amendment, no-fault insurance, public kindergartens, and salaries for teachers.

Another example of the differing opinions on the priority of issues came from the chairman of one of the most important house committees. He listed the reenactment of the post audit bill as the top item for legislative consideration. Second on his list of priorities was simply the enactment of appropriation bills, followed by early adjournment. The governor's main concern was low

[47]Personal interview with Robert Arrington, Hattiesburg, Miss., July 20, 1972.
[48]William L. Waller, "Summary of Accomplishments During 1972," A Report of Governor Bill Waller's First Year in Office (Jackson, Miss., 1973), 23–24; *Jackson Daily News,* December 28, 1972, p. 2. Some of the groups that lobbied for the highway bill were: HOPE (Highways, Our Pressing Emergency), Delta Council, East Mississippi Council, Northeast Mississippi Council, Mississippi Association of Supervisors, Mississippi Farm Bureau, Mississippi Petroleum Industry Council, and the Mississippi Automobile Dealers Association.
[49]Personal interview with David Fleming, executive assistant to Governor Waller, Jackson, Miss., August 4, 1972.
[50]*Tupelo Daily Journal,* December 27, 1972.

on this lawmaker's list because he said "the reorganization of state government or consolidation of various agencies, will not increase the per capita
income of Mississippians or save taxpayers money."[51]

The sentiments of legislators on the matter and their perceptions of the
relative priority of current issues offered little encouragement for reorganization on the eve of the 1973 session. On the first day of the session the
Mississippi House of Representatives expressed its feelings on the priority of
the post-audit bill. No more than fifteen minutes after convening, the house
passed by vote of 91 to 21 a revised version of the post audit bill vetoed by
Waller in 1972.[52]

Later the same afternoon, Governor Waller was given only a lukewarm
reception when introduced to the legislature to deliver his State of the State
report. He received a nice round of applause, however, when he asked if he
correctly detected "a slight reduction in enthusiasm over last year." Waller
said in his formal remarks that "purveyors of doom" cherished a division
between the governor and the legislature, but he expected the session to be
positive. He referred to a "continuing obligation to eliminate the waste of tax
money."[53]

As one illustration of the "vast need" to consolidate and reorganize, the
governor said the number of health care agencies had increased from 52 in
1970 to 65 in 1973, with an accompanying increase in appropriations of
nearly 100 percent ($69 million). Waller said he had "long championed the
modernization of state government to save tax dollars" and that new methods
and procedures were needed in the operation of state government in 1973.

The governor was apparently not too confident of his ability to win passage
of proposals relating to his number one issue, however, for there was decidedly less push for reorganization in 1973 than there had been the year
before. It was almost as if the legislature's response to the matter in 1972 and
its current attitude were too intimidating.

Waller's approach to reorganization (based on widely accepted principles
of organization) was in fact challenged by a series of bills introduced in the
senate. Referred to as the "cut the governor" bills, the three proposals would
have (1) given a legislative committee control over federal-state programs,
(2) affected the governor's control of the Building Commission, and

[51]*Memphis Commercial Appeal,* October 17, 1972.
[52]*New Orleans Times Picayune,* January 3, 1973; *Jackson Daily News,* January 3, 1973.
[53]*New Orleans Times Picayune,* January 3, 1973; *House Journal,* 1973, pp. 31–32.

(3) amended the Classification Commission Act to provide for a legislatively dominated commission.[54]

It became obvious early in the 1973 legislative session, therefore, that governmental reorganization would not get very far. The governor's "legislative priorities" speech of January 31 indicated that he realized the difficulties facing the issue, because it was the ninth of ten topics covered in the speech. The only specific reorganization recommendation included was for the creation of joint committees to study health care delivery services and government administration.[55]

Aside from the facts that the governor had been soundly defeated in his efforts in 1972 and that his honeymoon period was largely over, the chances for reorganization were diminished in 1973 by the substantial cash balance in the state treasury. Governor Waller drew attention to this situation when he declared in his State of the State speech that the projected cash balance for June 30, 1973 was an "historically high" $83 million. Under such circumstances it was difficult to explain the need for any change, especially since several legislators were naturally suspect of claims that the proposed reforms would produce economy in government.

Although a new Department of Mental Health was created in 1974 to consolidate the duties of the Board of Trustees of Mental Institutions, the Interagency Commission on Mental Illness, and the mental health work of the State Board of Health, the Waller administration accomplished very little of the reorganization proposed by the 1970 blue ribbon study or by the governor himself.

In 1975, the fourth year of his term of office, the thrust of Governor Waller's reorganization efforts was to address various problem areas through constitutional amendments. Of several amendments offered, those most directly relating to reorganization were ones to create a lay board of education, allow the governor and state treasurer to succeed themselves in office, and to limit the number of state agencies to 50. Waller made little headway in convincing the legislature that it should approve the amendments and then let the people decide whether the proposed changes should be made. In support of the measures Waller said he would "get out and stump" for the amendments. The legislature, however, did not give the people the opportunity to vote on the issues. Perhaps the question of gubernatorial succession gained the

---

[54]*Jackson Daily News,* January 28, 1973.
[55]*House Journal,* 1973, p. 237.

most attention in the news, as Waller's unsuccessful attempts to get the proposal out of committee were given considerable publicity. The feeling of many observers was that if the amendment had been advanced so that it would not have enabled Governor Waller to immediately succeed himself it could have received a more sympathetic hearing.[56]

Although Waller was unable to effect much change, he did make a noteworthy contribution to the reorganization effort. His consistent support of reorganization during his entire term of office helped keep the issue alive. Some measure of the popular interest generated from the attention Waller has given to reorganization is evidenced from a sampling of newspaper editorials throughout the state supporting the effort.[57] In addition, the Mississippi Economic Council (MEC) devoted considerable time to the issue. The council presented a half-hour television program on the issue and sponsored a leadership development seminar which focused on the need for reorganization. The chairman of the MEC Governmental Affairs Committee said in June of 1975 that state government reorganization was one of the most pressing needs facing the state.[58]

Although state government reorganization as revived in the third major reorganization effort persisted as a political issue for more than five years, that effort has been no more successful than the first in 1932 or the second in 1950.

In comparing the three efforts for similarities, other than the fact that each was unsuccessful, it is interesting to note that in 1932 in Mississippi's first reorganization effort the governor encouraged the legislature to act on the matter because the state of Georgia, he said, had just undergone a reorganiation with resulting savings of $1 million. Another governor, more than 40 years later, trying to make Mississippi's third reorganization effort its first successful one, also referred to reorganization in the state of Georgia which he said had saved $60 million in its first year.[59]

The latter Georgia reorganization (1972) was accomplished under the leadership of Jimmy Carter. Subsequently, Carter made a convincing demonstra-

[56]*Jackson Clarion-Ledger,* January 16, 31, 1975.
[57]*Greenwood* (Miss.) *Commonwealth,* January 10, March 27, July 10, 1975; *Hattiesburg American,* February 3, 1975; *Pascagoula Mississippi Press,* November 14, 1974, December 21, 1975; *Biloxi Daily Herald,* July 1, 1975; *Tupelo Daily Journal,* April 22, 1976; *Biloxi South Mississippi Sun,* April 14, 1976; *Simpson County News,* February 12, 1976; *Laurel Leader Call,* October 12, 1976.
[58]*Jackson Clarion-Ledger,* June 15, 1975; *Jackson Daily News,* June 15, 1975.
[59]Senate Journal, 1932, p. 75; *Jackson Daily News,* June 16, 1973.

tion that government reorganization is a potent political issue. When Carter announced his candidacy for president of the United States, a newspaper in the Georgia capitol asked with bold headlines "Carter for what?" It was inconceivable to most observers how a former governor of a southern state, a man almost totally unknown on the national level, could entertain the thought of running for president. Carter, however, unlike his detractors, realized that the public was sensitive to the need for government reform. Reorganization of government, is a very complicated and difficult task, and this factor, taken with Carter's reorganization of state government in Georgia, helped establish his credibility as a candidate for national office. As a candidate, he was very bold in pointing out that he had reorganized state government in Georgia and that he could do the same thing to the national government in Washington. It is the considered opinion of this writer that Jimmy Carter's campaign for president would never have gotten off the ground—in fact he probably would not even have entered the race—if he had not been in the position to use the reorganization issue as he did.

5 / The Third Reorganization Effort Continues

It has been suggested that the third major effort to reorganize state government in Mississippi began with the study commissioned by former governor John Bell Williams in December of 1969. That study got underway in 1970 and has been the point of reference out of which the third reorganization effort has emerged. The study was completed in the latter part of 1970, and either the study or more often its general subject matter has been an issue of some importance in Mississippi politics since then. The issue was presented to the legislature in 1971, the last session of the legislature in the Williams administration. 1971 was an election year and the legislature did not spend much time with reorganization nor was it a particularly big issue in the gubernatorial campaign or in legislative races. William Waller, however, made reorganization one of his major concerns during his term of office. His efforts were unsuccessful in terms of accomplishing the goals of the reorganization plan, but his efforts probably were responsible for the heightened public awareness of the issue. The candidates running for election in 1975 were certainly sensitive to the interest the reorganization issue had created among the electorate. One legislator observed that everybody from governor to constable was running on reorganization in 1975.

REORGANIZATION AS A CAMPAIGN ISSUE

As Governor Bill Waller was making his final reorganization appeal to the last session of the legislature during his administration, leading candidates to succeed him in office introduced state government reorganization as a major issue in the gubernatorial campaign of 1975. In March, fully four months before the August primary elections, candidate Maurice Dantin indicated that curbing the growth of state government might be the theme of his campaign. Dantin referred to previous reorganization studies which, he said, indicated that state government could function effectively with 50 percent fewer agencies. His view was that it was essential to consolidate state agencies in order to stop their "helter-skelter" growth.[1]

Dantin continued to debate the issue, and said in April that he favored the amendment process rather than the constitutional convention as an approach to the reorganization of state government. Like Dantin, the Republican candidate for governor, Gil Carmichael, came out strongly in favor of government reform. Dantin's position on the amendment process was in contrast with Carmichael's view that a constitutional convention was necessary in order to achieve the needed reform in state government. Dantin's position, whether calculated or not, was potentially less controversial than advocating a constitutional convention. In proposing the consolidation of agencies, however, he found it desirable to emphasize that he was "not talking about wholesale firing of people from state payrolls".[2]

To some extent the issue of state government reorganization was refined to mean the consolidation of state agencies. In May of 1975, the *Greenwood Commonwealth* reported that such a consolidation was a clear issue in the gubernatorial campaign. Reviewing the positions of some candidates, the *Commonwealth* said candidate Cliff Finch promised to reduce the number of departments and agencies through consolidation of state agencies and that candidate William Winter promised to "cut the frills and fats out of state government."[3]

At least four of the leading candidates for governor in the 1975 election—Dantin, Winter, Finch, and Carmichael—in varying degrees advocated state government reorganization. Of these, Carmichael's candidacy was distinctive because of his advocacy for constitutional revision. Dantin made reorganization a major part of his campaign; Winter is remembered for the premium his campaign placed on experience, and Finch was more clearly identified as the "working man's candidate" than for his positions on state government reorganization. Although Finch's election was a surprise to many observers, his defeat of the candidates who were more vocal on the issue of reorganization was not an indication that the issue was not of concern to the voters or to Finch.

[1]*Columbus Commercial Dispatch,* March 26, 1975.
[2]*Biloxi South Mississippi Sun,* April 9, 1975.
[3]*Greenwood Commonwealth,* May 20, 1975.

Governor Finch expressed his interest in the efficient operation of state government by making the issue one of the first topics covered in his State of the State address. "Now, more than ever, we (state government) must show innovation, ingenuity, determination, and resourcefulness in the way we use our money," he affirmed. The new governor also said he hoped that more than $60 million a year could be saved through greater efficiencies in the operation of state government. The plan to achieve the savings was to first "make a full, hard determination of what the people really need from state government. Where we find the state is not meeting these needs, we should do something about it,—but at the lowest possible cost that will get the job done. Where we find fat, or waste, it must be cut out and the cost savings used to meet new needs or to improve present programs. It is my hope that such an examination would result in increasing efficiency that would save at least 10%."

The governor underscored the seriousness of his concern as he continued, "Let me make clear that what I propose is not just another study. This is a deep, sweeping, fact-finding examination of where all our money is being spent and how much it buys. I propose to start this evaluation with the governor's office and the programs for which the governor is directly responsible." Finch said the evaluation would then move to other departments and agencies under such authority as his office possessed for such work. He also urged committees of the legislature to conduct studies so that nothing would be left undone.[4]

Governor Finch actually began his examination before assuming office by engaging the Research and Development Center to begin providing him with information about state agencies and programs. Likewise the legislature, through the legislative audit committee (Performance Evaluation and Expenditure Review Committee—PEER), had begun to consider reorganization prior to Finch's initial message to the legislature. The PEER group revealed a plan in October of 1975 for consolidating state agencies. According to the committee spokesman, the legislature could accomplish reorganization by "simply authorizing the transfer of one agency to the control of another existing agency

[4]*Jackson Clarion-Ledger*, January 22, 1976.

or to a new coordinating agency.'' Additionally, a concurrent resolution had been introduced in the state senate about a week before Finch spoke. The resolution called for the creation of a joint study committee to examine the organization of the executive branch of state government. One of the coauthors of the measure noted that there was ''a lot of duplication and overlapping of agencies.'' He acknowledged that studies had been done in the past but said since the legislature must pass judgment on any consolidation, there needed to be a legislative study of the issue.[5]

Other senators apparently shared the view that a legislative study was needed, for a second resolution was introduced a month later calling for the creation of a committee to study reorganization of the executive branch of state government. The stated purpose of this resolution was the same as the first. Notable differences were apparent, however, in the proposed member-ships for the study committees. The first resolution had proposed a committee made up of 10 members, all legislators, while the second proposed a commit-tee made up of the governor, lieutenant governor, attorney general, and sec-retary of state plus ten legislators. Of more interest, perhaps, was that the second resolution was authored by 27 of the 52 members of the senate. Although a majority of the senate authored the proposal, that was not enough to insure its passage. The resolution died in the senate's Appropriations Committee, which was made up of 21 members, 10 of whom were authors of the resolution.[6]

LEGISLATIVE EFFORTS AT REORGANIZATION

Although the resolutions proposing studies of the executive branch of gov-ernment were unsuccessful, several efforts were made to reorganize this or that department or to consolidate various functions and agencies. Proposals were offered to consolidate conservation agencies in order to develop the expertise said to be needed to control strip mining operations; others sought to reduce the number of commissioners on the Game and Fish Commission from 11 to 5 and to allow the commission to appoint a director of conservation. Some legislators attempted to abolish the Park Commission and other agen-

[5]*Ibid.,* October 22, 1975, January 13, 1976; Mississippi Legislature, Senate Concurrent Resolution No. 515, Regular Session 1976.
[6]Mississippi Legislature, Senate Concurrent Resolution No. 551, Regular Session, 1976.

cies as part of a proposal to create a new Recreation and Tourism Commission
and to abolish the Motor Vehicle Comptroller's office.[7]

A more sweeping proposal for agency consolidation was introduced and
ultimately passed in the senate. This proposal, similar to ones introduced in
the Waller administration, would, by constitutional amendment, place a
maximum limit on the number of state agencies. Such a plan would not only
halt what some advocates of reorganization referred to as the uncontrolled
growth of state agencies, but it would also require that the existing agencies be
combined or abolished so there would be no more than 40 agencies.[8] This
amendment, which required a two-thirds approval of the senate, passed without a dissenting vote.

The measure died, however, in the house Constitution Committee, despite
advice from its author that the people would vote overwhelmingly for the
amendment if the legislature would but give them the opportunity.[9] The
senator believed the constitutional amendment approach was the only way to
achieve a consolidation of agencies, and told the house committee that if
approving the amendment "is all we do in this administration, this administration will go down as a successful one." He made no claims that any such
consolidation would save money although he suspected it would. Improved
efficiency and better service to the public would more certainly result, he
said.[10]

Other advocates of reorganization, on the other hand, have pointed out that
reorganization of state government could save money. The reorganization
proposal by the PEER Committee in October of 1975 suggested that as much as
$20 million a year could be saved. In December, a house member advocating
reorganization said it would save at least $30 million "and probably more."
With teacher pay raises a major topic of debate in 1975, one newspaper
editorial said reorganization could probably save enough money to give
teachers the salary increases they were demanding. Also in 1975, one of the
gubernatorial candidates reportedly said that "over a period of several years

[7]*Jackson Clarion-Ledger,* January 28, 1976, February 25, 1976, March 11, 1976, April 10,
1976.
[8]Mississippi Legislature, Senate Concurrent Resolution No. 524, 1976.
[9]Amendments to the state constitution require two-thirds approval of both houses of the
legislature followed by voter ratification in a statewide election.
[10]*Jackson Clarion-Ledger,* March 30, 1976; *Jackson Daily News,* March 30, 1976.

some 50 percent of the state payroll could be reduced."[11] A savings of this magnitude could amount to over $100 million because, typically, personnel costs are in excess of half of an agency's total expenses. For example, if all agencies spend $600 million, and if only half of that amount is required for the "payroll," that would be $300 million. Reducing the payroll by 50 percent would, in this case, reduce expenditures by $150 million.

It is possible that the above claim was a misquoted, or misunderstood "campaign statement." Claims of possible savings from reorganization continued to be made, however. In a "first of its kind" appearance by a Mississippi governor on educational television in November of 1976, Governor Finch mentioned reorganization proposals he planned to submit to the 1977 legislature which, he said, would save taxpayers $70 million. Other impressive opinions regarding the importance of reorganization were not stated in terms of savings. For example, Lieutenant Governor Evelyn Gandy, in assessing the outcome of the 1975 legislative session, said perhaps her "top disappointment" was the inability of the legislature to do anything about governmental reorganization. She expressed optimism, however, that something could be done next time. She felt it was necessary to study the issue in more depth during the recess months to become better prepared to answer questions raised about reorganization. A member of the house also voiced concern that the legislature was unprepared on the issue. He said he was "sure there's overlap and double expenditures," but pointed out the need for expert advice if reorganization was to be undertaken by the legislature.[12]

The reorganization issue, as in 1932, still continues to have its detractors though, as evidenced by the defeat of innumerable proposals. During the course of the several reorganization efforts, it is occasionally observed by advocates with various degrees of commitment to the issue that reorganization cannot be accomplished all at once. This statement is seldom construed as the viewpoint of obstructionists. On the other hand, advocates of reorganization have accomplished so very little that they sometimes wonder if anything at all will ever be done. Indications of such an attitude were evident in the senate

[11]*Jackson Clarion-Ledger*, October 22, 1975; *Pascagoula Mississippi Press Register*, December 21, 1975; *Greenwood Commonwealth*, January 10, 1975; *New Orleans Times Picayune*, May 6, 1975.
[12]*Jackson Clarion-Ledger*, November 24, 1976, May 12, 1976; *Bolivar Commercial*, February 6, 1976.

debate over the proposal to abolish the Motor Vehicle Comptroller's (MVC) office. One senator who argued for the measure said if that bill to abolish only one out of all the state agencies failed, "then there just isn't going to be any reorganization in Mississippi and we might as well admit it." The same sentiment was expressed by another senator as the debate on the MVC bill continued one week later: "If we can't reorganize the Motor Vehicle Comptroller's office, then we might as well admit we're not going to have any reorganization of state government in Mississippi."[13]

JOB SECURITY AND AGENCY CONSOLIDATION

One feature of the MVC bill was that it prohibited the termination or demotion of any of the current employees of the three agencies involved. The job protection this feature provided seemed to be evidence that the proponents of change were concerned that agency workers, fearing for their jobs, would make it difficult for reform legislation to pass. Such an attitude was also recognized in senate debate when the sponsor of the MVC bill told his colleagues, "The problem with reorganization—and we all know it—is that we all have friends working for state agencies. These friends say let's start by reorganizing some other department."[14]

As in the MVC measure, assurances that existing employees would not lose their jobs as a result of reorganization also appeared in other reorganization bills introduced in 1976. For instance, Senate Bill No. 2294, proposing the grouping of about two dozen agencies into a Department of Natural Resources, stated that it was the "sense and intent" of the legislature that, "when reorganization abolishes positions, the individuals affected, when otherwise qualified, should be given priority consideration for any new positions created by reorganization or for vacant positions in state government." In discussing the philosophy of this provision, a coauthor of the measure said "there would be tremendous resistance by these agencies because of people losing their jobs." The sponsor explained that while the bill proposed the *merging* of a number of agencies no agencies would be *abolished* because of a "moral consideration."[15]

---

[13]*Jackson Clarion-Ledger,* April 2, 9, 1976. The MVC bill passed in the senate but died in the house. A similar bill was also passed by the senate in 1972.
[14]*Jackson Clarion-Ledger,* April 9, 1976; *Jackson Daily News,* March 19, 1976.
[15]*Biloxi Daily Herald,* January 28, 1976.

The "sense and intent" clause in Senate Bill 2294, however, includes enough room for interpretation that it may not have provided much protection to employees in case of reorganization. Legally, as in practical application, there is considerable difference in the words shall and should. Had the clause read "affected employees *shall* be given priority," it would have given the affected workers more assurance that they would have a job in case of agency reorganization.

Though not necessarily in reaction to reorganization, state employees' concern for their future is clearly evident in the announcement by the State Employees Association of Mississippi (SEAM) that it would ask the 1977 legislature to pass laws to provide better job security for state workers. SEAM cited firings and demotions in the Mississippi Highway Patrol which had resulted from the organizational changes in that agency when appointments were made by the new (1976) administration. The association president was quoted as saying dismissals were happening statewide, and people were "very, very concerned about their jobs and the security of them."[16]

Those lawmakers and other advocates of reorganization who are concerned with the question of job security for existing employees believe that through the normal process of attrition, the number of employees in state government can be reduced. The idea is that by reorganizing along functional lines, activities will become more efficient and can be carried out with fewer people. With this approach, however, the extra employees would not be fired but the overall work force would be reduced as vacancies were created by deaths, retirements, etc.

The attrition principle has also been introduced as a method for reducing the size of state government separate and apart from any reorganization effort involving organizational changes in specified agencies. In March of 1976, it was reported that the senate Appropriations Committee would place an amendment in each appropriations bill to set a ceiling on the number of employees for each agency of state government. Such an approach, it was estimated by the committee chairman, would allow the legislature to reduce the "padding" in agency salary budgets and produce savings in the range of $7 million. A typical agency appropriation bill for the 1977 fiscal year included a section similar to the following example from the State Highway Department appropriation.

---

[16]*Jackson Clarion-Ledger,* November 5, 1976.

It is the intention of the Legislature to provide in this appropriation for a maximum of 3,318 full-time and 400 part-time seasonal employee positioins in said agency for the fiscal year 1977. In the event any employee position within said agency shall become vacant during the fiscal year as the result of the death, resignation, retirement or discharge of an existing employee, no funds appropriated or authorized to be expended hereby shall be expended for the payment of the salary of a new or replacement employee until the same shall have been certified to be necessary and essential to the efficient operation of such agency by the agency head or governing board thereof and submitted to and approved by the chairman and director of the Commission of Budget and Accounting. If the action of the said chairman and director, in the judgment of the executive head of such agency, jeopardizes the effectiveness and efficient operation of said agency, appeal may be made by the agency to the full commission at its next regular or special meeting. Even if such vacancy shall be filled, the funds authorized hereby and not expended for payment of the salary of the employee position during the period of the vacancy shall not be spent for increased salaries due to reclassification of employees.

One criticism of the use of the amendment was that it would discriminate against agencies which had a high rate of employee turnover. The idea here was that agencies with high turnover would have to seek more frequently the approval of the chairman and director of the Commission of Budget and Accounting. It is noteworthy that this approval power is essentially shared by legislative forces in control of the commission and by the governor's office. (The governor is chairman of the commission.) Another criticism of the amendment was that agency heads would be more reluctant to fire inefficient employees because of a concern with the possible difficulties in getting approval to fill the resulting vacancies.[17]

There are others, probably just as interested in state government reorganization, who do not believe reorganization could be effective by relying on the attrition theory. One member of the house Constitution Subcommittee which considered the constitutional amendment proposed by the senate to limit the number of state agencies felt such a move would simply cause existing agencies to be grouped under new superagencies. In her view this would not accomplish very much and, if it did not save money, the shifting of agencies would be an exercise in futility. She said "we are going to have to bite the bullet and cut employees."[18]

In a more earthy tone another lawmaker said he hoped the legislature would

[17]*Jackson Daily News,* March 10, 1976; *Laws of Mississippi,* 1976 C-222, p-330.
[18]*Jackson Daily News,* March 30, 1976.

"have the guts" to avoid taking the painless way out—simply combining agencies and letting attrition get rid of unnecessary employees. When agencies were combined, he said, the people who were no longer needed would simply have to be "let go." To let attrition do the dirty work would in his view make reorganization prohibitively costly in the beginning.[19]

TRADITIONAL CONCEPTS OF REORGANIZATION AND ALTERNATE PROPOSALS

Since the Brookings Report on the organization of Mississippi government was issued in 1932, reorganization to most people has meant the consolidation of state agencies. In earlier periods consolidation was taken to mean that a number of agencies would be combined to form a single agency—for example, 15 agencies would be combined to form a single agency. More recently, the grouping of independent agencies under a single "umbrella" department—such as Natural Resources—has gained increasing acceptance by the advocates of reorganization. Using the umbrella approach, agencies may for all intents and purposes maintain their separate identities but, by counting only the "umbrellas," proponents claim a net reduction in numbers of agencies. This approach represents a considerable compromise from earlier approaches which were more rigid in their standards as to what constituted reorganization and consolidation.

While many people have historically viewed reorganization as the consolidation of agencies, most of the professional studies have emphasized the need for administrative improvements along with the structural changes. Popular interest and efforts to implement the studies have tended to focus on the dramatic aspect of the issue, reducing the 100 plus agencies, boards, and commissions to a more fathomable 25 or so. As suggested by the lieutenant governor, however, the problem is more complicated and proposals to reorganize cannot be defended simply on the basis that they will reduce the number of agencies.

In light of some of the difficulties experienced in the traditional approaches to reorganization, other suggestions have been offered in recent years as alternate methods. In 1976, the Mississippi Economic Council (MEC) noted the emergence of proposals for zero-based budgeting, "sunset laws," and

[19]*Jackson Clarion-Ledger,* January 18, 1976; *Jackson Daily News,* January 18, 1976.

reduction of agencies by constitutional amendment and urged the legislature to appoint a special committee to examine the potential paths to reorganization.[20]

The PEER Committee in December, 1976, recommended that the legislature adopt a sunset law and proposed that the state adopt a program approach to budgeting in place of the existing object of expenditure or line item method of budgeting. The sunset law would provide that state agencies (with some exceptions) be abolished after a period of four years unless recreated by law. Each agency could be recreated by appearing every fourth year before legislative committees and demonstrating the need for its continued existence. It was expected that a sunset law would curtail the growth of the state bureaucracy, allow greater legislative oversight, abolish useless agencies, and streamline state government. The main threat of the law, according to the report of the proposal, would be to small, useless agencies, but it would also increase efficiency and accountability of larger agencies and make all agencies more responsive to the needs of the people.[21]

Formalizing the sunset concept may be a good idea and will, if publicized, probably gain considerable public support. Public support is important to effect reform in government, and a concern over this approach might be that the sunset legislation would be regarded as a panacea or be viewed as the culmination of forty-four years of effort to bring about state government reorganization. Public concern over the effectiveness of state government must not diminish with passage of sunset legislation, at least not if the findings and recommendations of previous studies can be accepted.

There is a possibility that passage of a sunset law could be looked upon as an admission by the legislature that it has not, up to this point, exercised its power to abolish state agencies no longer serving useful purposes. One response by a legislator to the PEER proposal was that duplication in state agencies certainly ought to be eliminated but that there already was a method for doing that. "All it takes now," he said, "[is] for legislation to be introduced to abolish an agency and have it passed by the legislature." This lawmaker also expressed reservations about giving so much power over the continued existence of state agencies to legislative committees.[22]

Another point to note is that responsibility for implementing the program

---

[20]Mississippi Economic Council, "News Release" (Jackson, Miss., November 4, 1976).
[21]*Jackson Daily News*, December 6, 1976.
[22]*Hattiesburg American*, December 7, 1976.

budgeting concept would rest with the Commission of Budget and Accounting, which is made up largely of legislators. In the last few years, considerable attention, including at least two court cases, has been focused on the question of legislators serving on boards and commissions of state government. The Budget Commission and a few other boards and commissions are dominated by legislators. Many other agencies of state government are governed by boards and commissions on which members of the legislature serve. In such cases it is possible conflicts would arise over the prospect that the legislature, operating with the sunset concept, could take the expected critical view of state agencies on which members of the legislature serve.

SEPARATE MAGISTRIES—LEGISLATIVE AND EXECUTIVE

Senator Theodore Smith filed suit in Hinds County Chancery Court to challenge the practice of legislators serving on boards, commissions, and agencies which are instruments of the executive branch of the government.[23] It was Smith's contention that legislators have unconstitutionally crossed the line dividing the legislative and executive branches of state government.

The legal basis for Smith's suit is Article 1 of the Mississippi Constitution (1890) which outlines the "Distribution of Powers" in the following two sections.

> Section 1. The powers of the government of the state of Mississippi shall be divided into three distinct departments, and each of them confided to a separate magistracy, to-wit: those which are legislative to one, those which are judicial to another, and those which are executive to another.
> Section 2. No person or collection of persons, being one or belonging to one of these departments, shall exercise any power properly belonging to either of the others. The acceptance of an office in either of said departments shall, of itself, and at once, vacate any and all offices held by the person so accepting in either of the other departments.

In Smith's view, the constitution was clear on the matter and to allow legislators to serve on boards and commissions did not "bend" the constitution, "it tears it to shreds."[24]

Smith filed his suit in October, 1974, and it is probably not an unfair assessment to say the case was not given a speedy hearing. One of the legislators serv-

---

[23]*Jackson Daily News,* October 1, 1974.
[24]*Columbus Commercial Dispatch,* October 7, 1976.

ing on state boards and commissions and against whom the Smith suit was filed, requested that the case be shifted to his home county for disposition. The original petition and accompanying paperwork were transferred to chancery court in Lowndes County in October of 1976.

After the change of venue in the case and some related publicity it was suggested by one newspaper, outside of both Hinds and Lowndes counties, that there was growing concern over the "overlapping interests" of some state legislators. Primary focus of the article was to comment and elaborate on the 30-minute documentary produced by a Jackson television station a few days before. The subject of the television program was power politics, and it explored the possibilities of conflicts of interest arising when the private interest of legislators overlaps or gives the appearance of overlapping with legislative activity or public interest.[25] Such conflicts of interest were not addressed by the Smith suit and are not necessarily related to the question of reorganization.

There is a distinction between conflicts of interests pertaining to one's personal interests and those pertaining to the separation of legislative and executive powers. There is a good possibility, however, that adverse publicity about one type of conflict tends to have an additive effect in the face of adverse publicity of the other.

Nevertheless, there is a growing concern about the conflict of interest question. For example, about one month after the Smith suit was transferred to Lowndes County, a second petition was filed there seeking the removal of a senator from either the legislature or from the Medicaid Commission and Budget Commission. The petition questioned the constitutionality of legislators serving simultaneously in both the legislative and executive branches of government. As in the Smith case, the second case charged that such simultaneous service violated Sections 1 and 2 of the state consitution.[26]

The petition was filed in behalf of James V. LeLaurin of Lauderdale County, reportedly the head of a citizens' organization to support the effort. LeLaurin's group, the Mississippi Constitutional Defense Fund (MCDF), was formed in an effort to establish a broad base citizen group to raise funds to finance legal challenges to the constitutionality of legislators sitting on execu-

[25]*Meridian Star*, October 24, 1976.
[26]*Columbus Commercial Dispatch*, November 5, 1976.

tive boards. The philosophy offered by LeLaurin was that the long-standing principle of separation of executive and legislative powers must be reaffirmed. This would, in his view, restore the balance among the three branches of government in Mississippi. The imbalance or concentration of power in the legislative branch, according to LeLaurin, has frustrated progress in Mississippi and is responsible for the state's low economic standing.[27]

Since formation of the MCDF it has been estimated that as many as 50 legislators could be forced out of their seats. If one assumes the courts will uphold Smith's point of view in his case, the basis for the belief that legislators would lose their posts is that part of Section 2 of the state constitution which stipulates, "The acceptance of an office in either of said departments shall, of itself, and at once, vacate any and all offices held by the person so accepting in either of the other departments." Smith predicted the final decision on the issue will come from the state supreme court. Such a decision upholding the position taken by the MCDF would, according to Smith, be the most far-reaching decision ever made by the Mississippi Supreme Court. His confidence in the ultimate outcome has been bolstered by the formation of a constitutional defense group in which reportedly about 50 Mississippians are actively involved. The group has helped raise about half of the $80,000 Smith said would be necessary to take the issue to the supreme court. Smith also made the observation that most of the legislators now on boards and commissions remain unaware that a court decision favorable to him would cause them to be ousted from the legislature. As he put it, "These legislators don't seem to know it, but they will no longer be senators or representatives after we win this suit."[28]

Smith himself served on the Medicaid Commission as a legislator. His membership on the commission was set out in the law establishing the Medicaid Commission. Three of the seven members of the commission are appointed by the governor with the advice and consent of the senate. The other four members are selected because of their positions on legislative committees—chairman of the Senate Appropriations Committee, chairman of the Senate Public Health and Welfare Committee, chairman of the House Pensions, Social Welfare, and Public Health Committee, and chairman of the

[27]*Jackson Daily News,* November 11, 1976; *Jackson Reporter,* November 11, 1976.
[28]*Greenville Delta Democrat Times,* December 12, 1976.

House Appropriations Committee. An additional provision of the law is that no legislative member of the commission may be a provider or representative of a provider of services considered by the commission.[29]

Senator Smith, as chairman of the Senate Public Health and Welfare Committee, after serving for a time on the commission as specified by the law, disqualified himself from the commission by purchasing a token interest in a drug store. Another senator has been appointed from the Senate Public Health and Welfare Committee to serve on the Medicaid Commission in place of Smith.

The Medicaid Commission was set up to administer a statewide system of medical assistance for indigents, including health care and remedial and institutional services, as specified under Titles XVIII and XIX of the Social Security Act. As a result of the commission's policies in administering the program, many poor people receiving drugs from the Medicaid program became very upset with the commission in 1976. Their concern was over decisions by the commission to require a 50 cent charge on all drugs previously paid for under Medicaid and to remove some anti-arthritic medications from the list of drugs paid for by Medicaid. These decisions, made effective July 1, 1976, proved so unpopular that by the end of the year a class action suit challenging them was to be filed in federal court. Not only did the suit question the legality of the 50 cent payment and the removal of drugs from the program, but it also challenged the constitutionality of four state legislators serving as members of the Medicaid Commission. As in the Smith case and the action filed by the Mississippi Constitutional Defense Fund, the suit against the Medicaid Commission said it was a violation of the constitution for legislators to serve in the dual roles.

The traditional theory of the doctrine of separation of powers was based on the belief that the formation of policy could and should be the responsibility of a legislative body and that the implementation of that policy should be the responsibility of the executive or administrative branch of government. Sections 1 and 2 of the state constitution, the basis for the Smith and MCDF suits, were written to incorporate the separation of powers principle in the fabric of state government in Mississippi.[30] It is expected that the courts will help

[29]*Mississippi Code,* Section 43-13-107.
[30]It can be noted that some political scientists in recent times have observed the difficulties involved in always making a clear distinction between policy and administration. While the two are sometimes indistinguishable, the separation of powers as a principle of government remains a valid

resolve questions arising in this case which are more involved than at first they appear. The Medicaid program received approximately 75 percent of its $153 million 1977 budget from the federal government, which has specific guidelines the program must adhere to. State law, however, established the Medicaid Commission and assigned it the duty of administering a statewide system of medical assistance. In this respect the commission takes on the trappings of an element of the executive branch of government. Members of the legislative branch, however, are in a majority on the commission. Some of the public comments resulting from the controversy about the commission's recent actions also point out a close connection between the commission and the legislature. One of the legislative members of the commission said he could not, when the commission considered repealing the controversial decisions, vote for repeal because of a previous commitment he made with the legislature in an earlier session. He indicated that he would, however, as a legislator, introduce a measure in the 1977 session of the legislature to restore the anti-arthritic drugs to the Medicaid list and to repeal the 50 cent charge for other drugs.[31]

In a related separation of powers question also bearing on the organization of state government, a Hinds County circuit court judge was asked to resign from the Game and Fish Commission. In making the request of the judge, Senator Smith referred to a 1971 opinion by the state attorney general which said Mississippi law prohibited persons from holding offices in two branches of state government. The opinion was reportedly rendered in response to an inquiry by a chancery judge who wanted to know if it was legal for him to also serve as a member of the board of trustees of a junior college. The attorney general arrived at his decision by determining it was "beyond question" that the office of chancery judge was in the judicial department and "almost as indisputable" that the board of trustees for a junior college is in the executive branch of government. Therefore, one person holding office in both branches was in conflict with the state constitution.[32]

The Hinds judge may not have responded immediately to the request that he resign but, less than six months later when he voluntarily left his post, approximately one and one-half years remained in his term of office. A news account

---

concept. In addition, the cases under discussion are not questioning the theory or philosophy of the matter, only the application of Sections 1 and 2 of the Mississippi Constitution.

[31]*Jackson Clarion-Ledger,* December 15, 1976; *Jackson Daily News,* December 10, 1976.

[32]*Jackson Clarion-Ledger,* February 20, 1976.

of the move indicated the judge resigned because the governor had not responded to an earlier request by the judge that the governor make appointments to the vacant positions on the commission.[33]

Another recent case involving the question of the propriety or desirability of legislators serving in the executive branch of state government surfaced in 1973. One state senator reportedly was on the payroll of the Highway Department as an administrative assistant in a district office earning $1,000 per month. The senator denied any conflict of interest between his legislative and administrative positions. When the conflict of interest question arose, the senator explained that he was "completely resigned from and never connected with" the Highway Department when the legislature was in session and that his pay from the administrative post was stopped while he was in session with the legislature. The department reportedly received the approval of the attorney general's office before employing the senator.[34]

It seems "indisputable" that the person involved in this case was connected with the legislative and executive branches, as distinguished in Section 1 of the state constitution. Some of the public debate surrounding this case indicates that the flexibility in interpreting and applying Section 2 of the constitution is in whether an office holder in one branch is also an office holder in the second branch or merely an employee of the second branch. Upon a second reading of Sections 1 and 2 it becomes obvious why various parties have seen the need to seek opinions and even court decisions on the matter. For convenience the two sections are repeated here:

> Section 1. The powers of the government of the state of Mississippi shall be divided into three distinct departments, and each of them confided to a separate magistracy, to-wit: those which are legislative to one, those which are judicial to another, and those which are executive to another.
> Section 2. No person or collection of persons, being one or belonging to one of these departments, shall exercise any power properly belonging to either of the others. The acceptance of an office in either of said departments shall, of itself, and at once, vacate any and all offices held by the person so accepting in either of the other departments.

The lawmakers themselves from time to time have indicated their awareness of and concern for the provisions of Sections 1 and 2. In a law passed in

---

[33]*Jackson Daily News,* September 13, 1976.
[34]*Biloxi South Mississippi Sun,* November 1, 2, and 14, 1973; *Jackson Daily News,* November 6, 1973.

1968 dealing with the membership on the War Veterans Memorial Commission, the legislature specified that "No member of either branch of the legislature nor any state officer or employee shall serve on the commission."[35] By this action the legislature made it clear that the question of legislators serving on executive branch commissions could not be raised. It also provided that no other state officer or employee could be eligible for appointment to the commission.

A 1970 law providing for four legislative members to serve on the Marine Resources Council seemed to be anticipating a separation of powers type of challenge. The law stated, "It is specifically provided that the legislative appointees shall serve by virtue of their office and shall not be deemed public officers in the executive branch of state government."[36] The 1968 law precluded the possibility of a constitutional challenge by restricting membership on the War Veterans Memorial Commission to non-legislators. By contrast, the 1970 law apparently attempts to reduce the possibility of a successful constitutional challenge by suggesting that the Marine Resources Council not be considered a part of the executive branch of government. Another possible interpretation could be that, since the legislative members of the council were not to be considered *public officers* in the executive branch (note use of the term "office" in Section 2), they were to be considered *employees* of the executive branch.

This latter interpretation is of interest when considered in light of a 1957 Mississippi Supreme Court case which in effect said that if the legislature did not designate as an "office" an administrative position authorized by legislative action, the person employed in that position did not hold an office within the meaning of Section 45 of the constitution.[37]

Since chapter 365, Laws of 1956, creating the State Sovereignty Commission, rests authority in the Commission to employ necessary personnel, but is silent as to the creation of any office or that of Executive Director, one occupying the position of Executive Director is a mere employee working at the pleasure and under the direction of the Commission, and does not hold "office" within the meaning of Mississippi Constitution # 45 providing that no member of the legislature, during the term in which he was elected, shall be eligible to any office of profit which shall have been created during the time the member was in office, except to such offices

[35]*Mississippi Code*, Section 35-3-23.
[36]*Ibid.*, Section 57-15-11.
[37]*Ibid.*, Section 3-1-27.

as may be filled by an election of the people. Golding v Armstrong, 231 M 889, 97 So 2d 379.

This case was unrelated to the meaning of the term "office" in Section 2 of the constitution, except that it is an indication of a court decision that takes a narrow or restrictive view of the meaning of "office."

It will be remembered from Chapter 2 that the question of legislators holding jobs in other departments of government was of major concern in the reorganization efforts of the 1930s. The issue gained prominence in 1934, when Governor Mike Conner faced strong opposition from the Highway Department on his reorganization plan. The charge was made that many legislators were employed by the Highway Department and that they worked from their positions in the legislature to kill the reorganization plan for fear the Highway Department would be adversely affected. No less a figure than the distinguished former speaker of the state house of representatives, Walter Sillers, reportedly worked on a resolution asking the Highway Department to furnish the legislature a list showing the number of legislators and their relatives appearing on the department's payroll. Another resolution, introduced in the house, would have declared it "the sense of the Mississippi legislature that no member of the legislature during his tenure should accept employment by, with, or in, any other department of state government."[38]

One expression of the sentiment of the resolution proposed in 1934 was evident in a section of a 1938 law stating that "No member of the legislature shall be eligible to serve as an officer or employee or in any other capacity under the provisions of the Highway Safety Patrol and Driver's License Law of 1938.[39]

As in 1934, when Governor Conner had experienced frustration over the practice of legislators serving in other departments, Governor Waller also was concerned about similar practices during his administration. He made clear his support for Senator Smith's position. Waller appeared to be inconsistent in taking such a stance, however, because he appointed legislators to executive boards and commissions. The appointments were necessary, said Waller, because he "feared severe recrimination" if he had done otherwise. The governor pointed out that he had a forty-year tradition to deal with in naming

[38]*House Journal,* 1934, p. 175.
[39]*Mississippi Code,* 45-1-7.

legislators to the state Building Commission, and said he knew of no other state where legislators "hold the executive persuasion."[40]

Governor Waller undoubtedly was among those who feel the executive branch is too much under the control of the legislature. Governmental control or power is of course the root issue in the reorganization effort. The central purpose of reorganization has been to enable the chief executive officer of the state to be a more effective administrator of the executive branch as it attempts to discharge its constitutional responsibilities, i.e., to implement the policies decided upon by the legislative branch. To make the chief executive a more effective administrator means that the Mississippi legislature will have to yield to the governor more power than he now has. The crux of the problem is that the additional power given the governor would reduce the relative power of the legislature. In strengthening the governor, the legislature would lose power both directly and indirectly.

The area of personnel management offers an example of power shifting both directly and indirectly. Legislators presently control the state (personnel) Classification Commission, but Senator Smith's suit could result in legislators being removed from the commission. Presumably the vacuum left by the removal of the legislators would be filled by the executive branch and the governor would have more authority over the management of personnel in the executive branch. In this instance the governor's authority would increase at the direct expense of the legislature.

An example of the governor's increased control causing only an indirect power loss in the legislature is taken from a recent study of personnel practices of state agencies. The study commissioned by Governor Waller found that 86 different agencies of state government, all located in Jackson, operated independently of each other in staffing their agencies. Waller said it was a ridiculous situation when a person interested in working in state government faced the prospect of applying at 86 different personnel offices in order to exhaust the possibilities of locating a state job.[41] Remedying this situation would of course strengthen the ability of the governor in state personnel administration while affecting the prerogatives of the legislature in a more indirect manner than in the case of the (personnel) Classification Commission.

[40]*New Orleans Times Picayune,* October 3, 1974.
[41]*Ibid.,* August 9, 1973.

The legislative preference for the fragmentation represented by the 86 personnel offices undoubtedly contributes to the belief of some that state government is in a precarious position. One state senator appearing on the platform with Governor Waller in one of his "move the capitol" programs said the state's 160 agencies and 36,000 employees leave state government "almost out of control."[42]

Whether or not state government is almost out of control is a matter of opinion. It is more nearly a fact, however, that, since the beginning of the 1932 reorganization effort, the size of state government in terms of agencies has more than doubled, and the state budget is more than 100 times what it was in 1932.

As noted earlier in this chapter, a private citizen filing suit to force a change in the balance of political power in state government between the legislative and executive branches charged that the organization of state government was holding back the economic development of the state. Governor Finch, in his State of the State address on January 5, 1977, did not make such a direct charge. His comments and recommendations for reorganization, however, were preceded by this statement: "The hard, cold truth is we are behind and getting further behind other states in income, health care, housing, education, and other areas vital to the good life for our people."[43] The governor's comments seemed to imply that Mississippi is behind other states because of the nature of the organization and operation of its state government.

[42]*Jackson Daily News,* November 13, 1974. Although there is not universal agreement as to the "number" of state agencies, the number 160 has been frequently cited in recent discussions. See Chapter VI for additional comments regarding numbers of agencies. A list of agencies is given in Appendix E.

[43]*Jackson Clarion-Ledger,* January 6, 1977.

6 / Summary and Conclusions

The state government reorganization movement has persisted as a phenomenon of American state government since the first successful state reorganization in 1917. In recent times, the guiding principles of the reorganization movement's earlier years have been showing signs of change. The politics of reorganization now receive more and more consideration in the development of reorganization plans. As a result, relatively less time is spent considering the most desirable organization from a theoretical standpoint. The plans no longer as a matter of course propose the shortest possible ballot or the wholesale elimination of boards and commissions. Reorganizers are more willing to compromise and are turning more and more to the piecemeal approach.

From the review and analysis of reorganization efforts in the states, it is concluded that successful reorganization efforts generally have several elements in common. For example, it is almost always necessary for a state's governor to take a leading role in the reorganization effort, particularly providing strong follow-up after the reorganization proposals are released by the study group. It is also important that the reorganization effort have popular support. The issue must often be strong enough to survive one or more setbacks and persist, sometimes for several years. The reorganization plan must not ignore the traditions in the state and make proposals that require overly drastic changes. Proponents of reorganization must be willing to compromise both in developing the proposals and in getting them approved by the legislature. Chances for success are increased when the reorganization plan is not prepared by out-of-state consultants and when it contains drafts of the legislation that will be necessary for implementation.

In large measure, reorganization has failed in Mississippi because these elements of successful reorganization have largely been absent from state efforts. Although the governor provided strong leadership for the 1930 effort, the changes proposed by out-of-state consultants were so drastic that they stimulated widespread and insurmountable opposition. Popular support for reorganization was, therefore, negligible. In the absence of popular support and support from Governor Conner's successor, reorganization was unable to survive its setbacks and persist as an issue. While there was no compromise between the ideal and the practical in the preparation of the reorganization report, the governor repeatedly stated that he was not advocating the blanket adoption of that report. Legislation was not presented with the report, but the extreme nature of the report would have made that useless anyway.

Other factors having a significant effect on the outcome of the 1930 reorganization effort were (1) the simultaneous proposals for rather drastic reorganization of state and county government which substantially broadened the opposition to state reorganization; (2) the urgency of the financial problem facing the state and the associated struggle to pass the sales tax; (3) the substantial opposition to the efforts stirred up by the lieutenant governor with his charges of dictatorship; and (4) the very bold and forceful opposition of the Highway Department.

A second major reorganization effort was begun in 1950, but it too lacked most of the elements found in the successful reorganizations discussed above and in Chapter I. The opposition in 1950, as in 1930, focused on the proposed changes in the elective system despite the fact that the changes proposed in 1950 were modest in comparison with those proposed in 1930. For example, in 1950 only 8 of 17 elected positions would have been eliminated, but in 1930 18 of 20 such posts would have been abolished.

The proposed changes in the elective system and related increases in the power of the chief executive caused the governor to withdraw his support from the 1950 reorganization effort. This was a significant factor in its failure. Another factor was the opposition of state agencies, notably a few agencies headed by elected officials. There was no citizen or interest group campaign associated with the 1950 reorganization effort either to urge adoption of the proposals that were presented or to maintain interest in the reorganization issue after the idea was abandoned by Governor Wright in 1951. With a new term of office beginning in 1952, the legislature lost several of its reorganization advocates and the new governor showed relatively little enthusiasm for the matter. As a major issue, therefore, reorganization had faded away by 1955, but it reappeared some fifteen years later.

The third major reorganization effort has been distinguished by the reorganization study and report of 1970. Since the main objections to the earlier reports were their proposals to eliminate 90 percent of the elected officials in 1930 and 47 percent in 1950, it is important to note that the 1970 report proposed the elimination of only 12 percent of the elected officials (2 offices).

Though the 1970 report minimized the more objectionable aspects of the earlier reports, it was not well received by the legislature. The feeling was that the report would have been much more acceptable if it had been prepared with legislative participation.

Table 21 presents a summary of the factors determined to have been significant elements of successful reorganizations in other states and shows whether each factor had a positive or negative effect in each of the major reorganization efforts in Mississippi.

With the one exception noted in Table 21, i.e., executive leadership, the factors or variables significantly related to the outcome of reorganization had negative impacts on the reorganization effort of 1930. The only variable of the ten with a positive impact on the reorganization effort of 1930 was the leadership provided by the governor.

In the 1950 effort, seven of the ten variables, including executive leadership, had negative impacts on the outcome of the reorganization. The prepara-

Table 21

Positive and Negative Effects of Ten Variables on Mississippi Reorganization Efforts

Variable	Year of Reorganization Effort		
	1930	1950	1970
Popular Interest and/or Support	−	−	+
Persistence of the Issue	−	−	+
Avoidance of Proposals Requiring Drastic Change	−	−	+
Willingness to Compromise*	−	−+	+
Preparation of Legislation for the Plan	−	−	−
Executive Leadership	+	−	−+
Use of In-state Consultants	−	+	+
Legislative Involvement	−	+	−
Role of the Media	−	−	−+
Strategy and Timing	−	−	−+

*When a variable is marked − + it means that the variable has not had a preponderantly negative (−) or a preponderantly positive (+) effect.

tion of the 1950 reorganization report by in-state consultants and the involvement of the legislature in the preparation of the report were two positive aspects of the 1950 reorganization effort. A negative-positive rating is ascribed the compromise factor because compromises were made in the report even though they were not entirely acceptable to the governor.

As assessed in Table 21, only two of the ten variables have been negative factors in the 1970 effort—the lack of involvement of the legislature in the preparation of the reorganization report and the failure to prepare legislation to be submitted with the reorganization report. On the other hand, five factors rate positive in the 1970 effort. First, popular interest has been shown in reorganization, and second, the issue seems to have developed an element of persistence. Third, preparation of the report was by in-state consultants. Fourth, compromise was evident in the efforts to avoid the most objectionable features of the previous reports. Fifth, the recommendations of the report have not been too drastic. The recommendations have met with objections, but the report does not ignore traditions of the state to the point that the report is an albatross to the reorganization effort as was the case with the Brookings Report in the 1930s.

The other three variables of Table 21 (i.e., executive leadership, the role of the media, and strategy) have not had preponderantly positive or negative effects on the 1970 reorganization effort.

As the reorganization effort of 1970 continues, its fate will probably be determined by whether in the near future these three factors become negative or positive. It should be emphasized that the role of the media does not necessarily refer to editorial positions, but to the overall tone and attitude toward an issue that the media can establish in its reporting. For example, Governor John Bell Williams presented the 1970 reorganization report to the legislature and made every effort to explain that the proposals for reorganization were designed (using the umbrella theory)[1] to minimize the disruptive effect of the reorganization on the system. However, the *Clarion-Ledger* (Jan. 14, 1971) said Governor Williams revealed a plan for the "massive consolidation of state agencies." Reports of this kind are conducive to the creation of negative attitudes toward change and to the reinforcement of natural reluctance toward change.

No attempt will be made here to predict the positive or negative effects of these variables in a future reorganization effort, but predictions can be offered

---

[1]For an explanation and discussion of the umbrella theory, see Chapters I and II.

as to the probable outcome of reorganization efforts wherein the effects of these factors are assumed.

Any reorganization effort in which every variable of Table 21 could be rated positive in its effect on the effort has a very high probability for success. This, of course, is not to say that reorganization could not occur without a positive rating on every variable. It is concluded, however, that no effective reorganization can occur without a positive rating for leadership. In fact, the most important single conclusion of this study is that gubernatorial leadership is the most critical of all factors involved in a reorganization effort.

The importance of leadership is magnified because of the influence the governor can have on the other variables listed in Table 21. For example, it has been shown that some of the difficulty experienced in implementing the last reorganization study occurred because of the lack of legislative participation in the preparation of the report. It has been proposed several times since 1970 that a new study be made by a group composed in part of legislators. This writer is not suggesting that a new study is needed, but if a new study is made the governor should be a party to that decision and should use his influence to insure the necessary participation by the legislature. In any reorganization effort, the governor should also exercise strong leadership to control four other factors that would be related to the study or effort—the willingness to compromise, the preparation of legislation, the use of in-state consultants, and the avoidance of proposals requiring drastic changes. (Note that three of these factors were rated positive in the 1970 effort.)

Clearly, a decision for a new study would be an aspect of the timing and strategy element, another important factor the governor can influence. The governor, however, must develop his strategy under some limitations. His term is limited to four years, the most productive part of which is the first year or two. It would not be easy for a governor, upon assuming office in January of his first year, to present a reorganization plan that had been prepared with proper consideration for the factors discussed above. This suggests, of course, the importance of continuity of effort between the outgoing and the incoming governor. It also suggests that if a governor gets himself elected on a strong platform of reorganization, he will be better prepared to take advantage of his "honeymoon" period with the legislature, which would be the best time to push his program.

It is obvious that an important element in the development of a strategy for reorganization is planning. Unfortunately, evidences of proper planning in previous efforts are obscure. The rhetoric of modernizing government and eliminating waste and duplication can be appealing, but when the skeptics ask for specifics a definite, workable, and defendable plan must be produced.

Strategy must also be calculated to minimize opposition and maximize support for the effort. A study of the reorganization process indicates that it is counterproductive to push reorganization with announcements that there are too many employees in state government and that the number should be reduced by so many thousand workers. The number of employees who fear that their job will be one of those eliminated will be substantial. This approach creates instant and eventually intense opposition to the plan from those apprehensive about losing their jobs. Such an approach could conceivably stimulate public opinion in support of the effort to streamline state government by eliminating unnecessary jobs, but in order to offset the instant resistance of state employees, other strong complimentary reasons should be available for use in a concerted public opinion campaign. Short of this, it is not good strategy to announce that reorganization is needed because there are too many state employees.

Although there are restraints on the governor's ability to develop reorganization strategy, these may be somewhat minimized by the overall positive influences that the factors of popular interest and persistence could have on the reorganization effort. The two factors are interrelated and in large measure are products of the governor's leadership. If the governor's leadership is positive, persistence will probably be a positive factor also, since persistence was shown (by definition) in Chapter I to be dependent upon the role of the governor. To date, Governors Williams and Waller have combined to reintroduce, for the third time in this century, governmental reorganization as a major political issue. Governor Finch, successor to Waller, has also become a vocal advocate of reorganization thereby creating an unprecedented situation wherein three successive governors have pushed for reorganization. As a result, the prospects are brighter than they have ever been that the administrative branch of Mississippi government will undergo substantial improvement.

The recent downturn in the economy causing the state to operate with a much tighter budget could also draw attention to the question of reorganization. There are those who believe the pressures on the state budget are mounting and that these pressures will be felt more and more in the future, even with a healthy economy. The reasoning is that changes are occurring in Mississippi politics as a result of the "one-man one-vote" court decisions and of the voting rights laws. In part because of these changes, the old guard which has admirably held the rein on the state budget since 1932 will inevitably be replaced with a "new guard."

It is feared that this new guard will not be able to withstand the increasing pressures to expand the budget and raise taxes. Therefore, the thinking is that this seems an opportune time for strengthening the office of governor in Mississippi—from the standpoint that the increasing pressure on the budget makes people more interested in economy and efficiency (reorganization) and from the standpoint that a strengthened executive office could help carry on the fiscal philosophy of the "old guard."

The prospects for reorganization within the next few years are very good—provided the reorganization effort has leadership comparable to that exhibited by Governor Conner from 1932 to 1936. This assessment may appear inconsistent with the data in Table 21 which shows that Conner's leadership was the only positive aspect of the unsuccessful effort of the 1930s. It will be remembered, however, that Governor Conner's efforts were stymied by an inherited reorganization plan that heavily influenced the negative ratings on all other factors. Such a major tactical mistake or misfortune can and should be avoided in the present effort. Based on the experiences of previous efforts both in Mississippi and elsewhere, the key seems to be leadership.

Aside from the significance of leadership as suggested from the history of reorganization efforts, several examples of the importance of leadership can be noted from the recent public discussions of the matter. In the last session of the legislature under the Waller administration, then lieutenant governor William Winter, commenting on reorganization, said it would take some "really tough leadership."[2] Winter's remark was reported in the context of debate at the start of the 1975 legislative session when the teachers were expecting a large pay increase. The teachers' insistence on pay raises was often countered with the question of where the money for the raises would come from. Sometimes it was suggested that if state government could be reorganized, the money would be available for teacher pay raises.

The teacher salary increase was granted, but the money did not come from savings from reorganization. And one year later when the legislature met again, the difference between the demands on the state budget and the available resources had not lessened. The so-called "tight money" situation again

[2]*Jackson Clarion Ledger,* January 13, 1975.

added to the debate about reorganization. The chairman of the Senate Finance Committee said he thought the legislature would be "forced to look at some form of reorganization." With this element of urgency attached to the issue, Winter's successor as lieutenant governor echoed his view of the importance, if not indispensibility, of the role of leadership. Lieutenant Governor Gandy said reorganization would be accomplished only if the state's legislative and executive leaders "push it."[3]

A review of the major reorganization efforts in Mississippi indicates that many proposals have been made but that very few have been "pushed" through. One isolated example is the recurring recommendation that the state land commissioner's office be abolished. Under such plans, the duties of the office would be transferred to another state office and the election of a state land commissioner would no longer be necessary. Previous reorganization studies, Governor Waller, the PEER Committee, and others have made such recommendations.[4] While such proposals have met only limited opposition, there is little evidence they have been pushed very hard.

Ironically, one holder of the office many have advocated abolishing has given some indication of what is involved in providing leadership and in "pushing" for a proposed change. According to reports, John Ed Ainsworth entered the 1975 campaign for land commissioner almost as a joke and campaigned for a time on the promise that, if elected, he would help have the position abolished. Soon after the election, his attitude, as expressed in response to legislative initiative to have the office abolished, was that the office should be upgraded. He asked for an opportunity to make a complete study to see how the office could be upgraded. It was his belief that with proper direction the office could provide more revenue for government operations.[5]

The new land commissioner began his work in earnest and proved he was quite serious about providing direction for the office. In the process, Ainsworth met with such opposition as that from some members of the Commission of Budget and Accounting who balked at approving the use of $7,000 in state funds for the land commissioner to complete and publish a report of sixteenth-section school lands. One member of the commission said publishing the report would be to waste the appropriation. This commission member described the matter as a hot political issue and the report as unnecessary.

[3]*The Clarion Ledger Jackson Daily News,* January 18, 1976.
[4]*Jackson Clarion Ledger,* May 5, 1975.
[5]*Greenwood Commonwealth,* January 29, 1976, August 1, 1976; *Natchez Democrat,* December 3, 1976; *Brookhaven Daily Leader,* July 14, 1976.

Despite this setback, Ainsworth said he would publish the information "one way or another." He emphasized his determination by stating that he was "not going to roll over and play dead. We are going to get the information out." Other members of the commission voiced support for the report and said any information Commissioner Ainsworth could provide the legislature on sixteenth-section lands would be helpful. Sixteenth-section lands were described as a "constant problem" that needed to be resolved. Meeting a month later, the Budget Commission, with only one dissenting vote, decided to approve expenditure of the $7,000 for the report.[6]

The additional support on the Budget Commission for Ainsworth and his report may well have been a reflection of the popular support apparently generated by his staunch stand and refusal to "play dead." After Ainsworth's first attempt to get approval for the report, one newspaper ended a rather complimentary article about the land commissioner by proclaiming "Ainsworth for Governor." The opening statement of the article announced that the commissioner "was in the process of becoming our favorite state official, simply because he—finally, at last, after decades of public neglect and indifference—is trying to do something about the scandal of the mishandling of sixteenth-section school lands."[7]

A Brookhaven paper said Ainsworth was developing as the "political sleeper" of the current state administration. Seemingly impressed by the commissioner's actions, the paper felt he was on a collision course with virtually the entire political establishment. A third newspaper described John Ed as a "find out of a grab-bag" who was making a nothing job in state government take on some meaning. That paper concluded that "people generally are hungry for courage in political office" and that John Ed "captured public opinion as being a rare stand up guy looking out for taxpayers' interests."[8]

The discussions stimulated by Ainsworth included some very critical comments about past practices in the management of sixteenth-section lands. The *Natchez Democrat* ran a series of articles on the land question in November and December of 1976. That paper's managing editor said John Ed had stirred up widespread support in his efforts to clean up the longest, dirtiest scandal in the history of Mississippi—"the giving away, the stealing of sixteenth section lands." An article in this series traced the problem back to 1840. It

[6]*Jackson Clarion Ledger,* July 4, 1976; *Memphis Commercial Appeal,* August 12, 1976.
[7]*Greenwood Commonwealth,* August 1, 1976.
[8]*Brookhaven Daily Leader,* July 14, 1976; *Jackson Reporter,* August 12, 1976.

noted that in 1890 the question had surfaced briefly when the state superintendent of education reported that "the leasing of sixteenth section properties
was a lamentable squandering of our children's heritage . . . a lasting shame to
our state."[9]

The problem is an old one and the complexities of it are sometimes lost in
the emotionalism that often arises when it is discussed. Ainsworth is apparently aware of the complexities, such as those arising over rights of
sixteenth-section homesteaders. He recognizes that there are legitimate griev-
ances involved in certain instances and has advised homesteaders to "stand by
your guns."[10]

John Ed's philosophy seems to be that just because the problem is difficult
that is no reason to neglect it. His actions in his first year in office indicate his
willingness to face the issue squarely and to pursue his objective in spite of
adversity and opposition.

Leadership has been demonstrated to be the most critical factor in a state
government reorganization effort. The leadership displayed by Commissioner
Ainsworth has certainly involved courage and determination. A not-to-be-
overlooked factor, however, is the emphasis placed on doing a "complete
study" so that the information necessary for decision-making could be made
available. As this is written, however, it seems that much information pertinent to the issue of reorganization in Mississippi has not found its way into the
debate. For example, some people have said, in pointing out the need for
reorganization, that no one knows how many state agencies there are and that
in itself substantiates the need for reorganization. It is not difficult to find
others who authoritatively announce the number of state agencies; there is
great variability, however, in the numbers, which have ranged from 110 to
271.

The Question of Counting and Reducing the Number of Agencies

The secretary of state's *Directory of Mississippi Commissions and Boards,
1972–1976,* contains 138 entries.[11] That document includes a number of
agencies which have only local or regional jurisdiction, for example, the
Harrison County Parkway Commission and the Tombigbee Valley Authority.

[9]*Natchez Democrat,* November 29, 1976, December 3, 1976.
[10]*Ibid.,* December 1, 1976.
[11]Heber Ladner (comp.), *Directory of Mississippi Commissions and Boards, 1972–1976*
(Jackson, Miss.: Secretary of State).

Although bodies of this type were generally excluded from the 1970 reorganization study, there are two reasons why they sometimes are counted as state agencies. One is that legislation creating an agency with less than statewide jurisdiction often stipulates that it "shall be an agency of the state." A second reason is that the governor frequently appoints one or more members to its governing board. At present, there are more than two dozen such agencies to which the governor appoints members.

Another consideration in "counting" state agencies is whether to include entities created by executive order. A few of these, such as the Health Planning Advisory Council, are included in lists of state agencies such as that prepared by the secretary of state; but most of the executive order agencies usually are not listed.

A third group of agencies, those created to participate in interstate compacts to which Mississippi is a party, also raises questions when efforts are made to identify and count all state agencies. At least two such agencies—The Gulf States Marine Fisheries Commission and the Tennessee-Tombigbee Waterway Development Authority—are included in the *Directory of Mississippi Commissions and Boards, 1972–1976;* but several other agencies of this type are excluded, even though the governor is either a member or appoints representatives.

In addition to the types of agencies discussed above, Table 22 categorizes numbers of agencies headed by elected officials, agencies controlled by the legislature, ex-officio agencies, and other agencies that belong in none of these groups. (See Appendix E for an itemized list of agencies in each category.)

While Table 22 accounts for more than 200 agencies, an analysis of the state budget indicates that appropriations were recommended only for approximately 120 of the agencies categorized.[12] Another approach to counting state agencies, therefore, might be to consider only those with separate allocations of funds in the state budget.

In terms of the manageability of Mississippi government, however, it makes little difference whether the number of agencies is 120 or 210. On the other hand, citing large numbers of agencies tends to draw attention to the problem of state government organization. This can be good, since considera-

---

[12]The 120 agencies counts the Governor's Office of Federal-State Programs but not any of the activities that are considered divisions of the office.

Table 22

Number of State Agencies, by Type, Mississippi, January 1, 1976

Type	Number
Agency headed by elected official	12[a]
Agency controlled by legislature	10
State agency with one or more members appointed by governor	95
Agency with local or regional jurisdictions to which the governor appoints one or more members	26[b]
Interstate-compact agency on which governor serves or to which he appoints a representative	12
Executive-order agency	19[c]
Ex officio agency	26
Other agencies	10
Total	210

[a]Includes the lieutenant governor.
[b]Does not include 11 local port commissions.
[c]An approximate number which does not include about 8 agencies that may be considered as divisions of the Governor's Office of Federal-State Programs.

ble public interest seems to be necessary in order to stimulate action on the matter. But, unfortunately, while attention focuses on numbers, other important aspects of the problem can go unnoticed. As a result, some advocates of reorganization are not fully prepared to explain the need, or to defend their proposals, for reorganization. There is also the danger that reducing the number of agencies is mistakenly assumed to be the objective of reorganization. The real objective is to produce a more effective and responsive government, and there is much more involved in accomplishing this goal than reducing the number of agencies.

For example, until just recently, the debates, discussions, plans, and reorganization studies gave very little attention to the comparative budgets of the various state agencies.[13] It appears to this writer that budgetary information of this nature is essential in order to develop a clear perspective of the

---

[13]See Thomas E. Kynerd, "Budgetary Analysis and the Problem of State Government Reorganization in Mississippi," *Public Administration Survey* 24, (November, 1976). Much of the material presented here, beginning with the section on counting and reducing agencies and continuing through the discussion of the relative budgets of state agencies is taken from the *Public Administration Survey* article.

problem of state government organization. As pointed out earlier, a common objective of past reorganization efforts has been the reduction in the number of agencies. Developing information relating to the relative budgets of each state agency, however, might suggest to decision-makers that any reform efforts should look closely at those few agencies that use the bulk of the state's financial resources. The results in this area could be more beneficial than trying to significantly reduce the overall number of agencies by dealing with scores of agencies that use only a small percent of total resources.

An examination of the fiscal year 1977 budget as recommended by the Commission of Budget and Accounting helps illustrate the possibilities.[14] For example, the budget recommended only $1,500 for the Mineral Lease Commission but $452 million for the State Department of Education (including the minimum education program and junior college funding). One perspective on the relative size of these two budgets is that one is over 300,000 times larger than the other. This comparison immediately suggests that the largest part of the state budget is allocated to a relatively small number of agencies and functions.

That this is true is confirmed from Table 23, which indicates the number of agencies through which various percentages of the state budget are allocated. It is obvious that a few agencies have large expenditures, since a single agency accounts for 27 percent of total expenditures, 2 agencies account for 48 percent, and 12 agencies are responsible for 90 percent of the total $1.654 billion budget. It is also apparent from Table 23 that most of the agencies have comparatively small if not insignificant expenditures since 98 percent of all monies is allocated to only 35 agencies. As a result, the remaining 175 agencies account for no more than 2 percent of the budget.

One question raised by Table 23 is whether the usual approaches to reorganization which emphasize a reduction in the large number of agencies focus too much attention on the 175 agencies with 2 percent of the budget and allow many of the 35 agencies which together account for 98 percent of the budget to escape serious review. The effect of a situation where the large agencies would escape serious review is further illustrated by drawing additional conclu-

---

[14]This discussion considers the total of all money available to administrative-type agencies, whether the source is the general fund (mainly taxes), special funds (mainly fees generated by the agencies), or federal funds. The total budget for all expenditures is $1.711 billion. This discussion deducts from that figure $57 million for the legislative and judicial branches, local assistance, tax refunds, and debt service and uses the figure of $1.654 billion as the total budget.

Table 23

Budget Allocations to State Agencies, Fiscal Year 1977

Cumulative No. of Agencies	Cumulative % of Budget Allocated	Cumulative Amount in Millions of $ Allocated
1	27%	$ 452
2	48	791
3	59	983
4	69	1,136
5	73	1,211
6	78	1,279
7	81	1,340
8	84	1,391
9	86	1,429
10	88	1,462
11	89	1,480
12[a]	90	1,492
35	98	1,623
210[b]	100	1,654[c]

[a]The 12 agencies are: State Department of Education, Highway Commission, Board of Trustees of Institutions of Higher Learning, Medicaid Commission, Office of Federal-State Programs, Welfare Board, Employment Security Commission, State Aid Engineer, Department of Mental Health, Board of Health, Public Safety Commission, and Penitentiary Board.

[b]The 210 agencies classified in Table 22 and Listed in Appendix E.

[c]This figure includes general, special, and federal funds for all administrative type agencies. It excludes expenditure for the legislature and the judiciary along with money for local assistance, tax refunds, and other miscellaneous items which make up the overall state budget ($1.711 billion).

sions from Table 23. For example, of the 12 agencies accounting for 90 percent of the budget, the average allocation per agency is $124 million, as compared to an average of $177 thousand per agency for the 175 agencies with two percent of the budget. Thus, the average agency budget in the 90 percent group is 700 times larger than the average agency budget in the two-percent group. Actually, the Department of Education's budget alone is nearly 15 times larger than the combined budgets of all 175 agencies in the two-percent group. Put another way, if the budget for the Department of Education receives an annual increase of 7 percent, that would be equivalent to the combined budgets of all 175 agencies in the two percent group in Table 23.

It is entirely possible, therefore, that a significant reduction could be made in the large number of agencies so as to quiet the clamor for state government reorganization without making state government significantly more productive or effective. This would be a serious setback for those interested in modernizing state government; for the primary objective of state government reorganization is not to reduce the number of state agencies, but rather to make state government more effective, responsive, and efficient.

The large number of agencies was only one of several problems of state government organization identified in the reorganization studies of 1932, 1950, and 1970. Problems noted in the areas of planning, budgeting, personnel administration, purchasing, and other administrative procedures are also important, and while structural changes often must precede administrative type changes, structural change without a plan or a mechanism to effect needed administrative changes is insufficient.

Another serious problem noted in the reorganization studies relates to the make up of the governing bodies of many state agencies. For example, as shown in Table 22, of the 210 state agencies, 26 are headed by governing boards that are made up predominantly of *ex officio* members. Some of the 26 are made up entirely of *ex officio* members. An *ex officio* board member is a person, who, because of the position he holds as a full time state official, is required by law to serve on the governing board of one or more other agencies.

Two examples of *ex officio* boards that should be familiar to most interested citizens are the Savings and Loan Associations Board and the State Board of Education. The former is a 5-member board made up of the Attorney General, Secretary of State, State Auditor, State Treasurer and the Commissioner of Insurance. Two of these officials, the Attorney General and the Secretary of State, along with the State Superintendent of Education make up the Board of Education. The Attorney General serves as an *ex officio* member on approximately 14 statutory boards while the Secretary of State and the State Superintendent of Education serve as *ex officio* members on approximately 7 to 10 statutory boards.

It will be remembered from earlier chapters in this study that the *ex officio* device as a governing board of a state agency has been sharply criticised. The 1950 reorganization report was very critical, saying in part that:

"At its best, the use of an *ex officio* board or commission is a haphazard means of administering state affairs; at its worst, it results in flagrant interference with proper administration of the given function, for never can there be assurance that an administrative officer, competent in one activity, will have the capacity or the interest required for the discharge of his *ex officio* duties. It is not the usual practice for a full-time administrative officer to devote full efforts to the requirements of his primary office and yet contribute effectively to the performance of another agency. He must neglect one or the other, or more frequently, both. Thus, use of the *ex officio* device not occasionally has resulted in high administrative costs because of the lack of effective supervision which it involves.''

Some would say now that ''high administrative costs'' are not the only results of the use of the *ex officio* device. In the aftermath of the closing of the Bankers Trust Savings and Loan Association it has been charged that the use of the *ex officio* device in the form of the State Savings and Loan Associations Board has resulted in personal financial difficulties for many thousands of citizens. The *ex officio* savings and loan board apparently failed in its duty of protecting the interest of savings and loan depositors. It has been suggested, however, that the problem may have resulted from the board being inadequately funded and staffed and not from the fact that the board was made up of *ex officio* officials.

While differences may be cited between the *ex officio* bodies governing the savings and loan industry and the field of public education, the weight of the evidence seems to be that the Department of Education could be governed by a board with greater potential for providing more effective guidance to the Department. Calamity has struck the savings and loan business and the results are measurable. Unfortunately, issues are not usually black and white and the alternatives are not easily quantifiable. No one can tell, therefore, if our educational system has been as effective as it might have been without the *ex officio* type of governing board. It appears to be an extremely high risk to run, however, to continue to ignore the criticisms of the *ex officio* device as a method of providing guidance to state agencies. This is particularly true in light of recent savings and loan difficulties which tend to confirm the validity of the criticisms. In the case of the Department of Education the risk is magnified by the amount of resources involved, $452,000,000 per year, which is enough money to fund all but 5 of the 210 state agencies accounted for in Table 22. It might be concluded by some advocates of reorganization that continued reliance on the *ex officio* device to govern the State Department of Education is a problem of state government organization that deserves more attention than it has received in the past. As such, it is a problem that can be easily isolated from the overall discussions on state government reorganization. By focusing on this problem, the advocates of reorganization could concentrate their efforts on a very significant part of the state government organization question. This might make it easier to develop a strong case demonstrating the need for change along with a strategy for bringing about the desired change.

The preceding discussion of the Department of Education is included here to help illustrate that the broad question of state government reorganization is not one that readily reduces itself to "pat" answers or solutions. And, while political candidates and office holders alike have at various times found that they could gain a following by being critical of state government organization, seldom has the issue been explored in sufficient depth to provide a solid base for effecting improvements. As the brief discussion of the Department of Education suggests, an in-depth knowledge of the question (of state government reorganization) and an understanding of the complexities of the question might enable reform advocates to focus more clearly on specific aspects of the organization problem and in so doing increase their chances of bringing about significant changes.

One of the more serious deficiencies of past reorganization efforts has been that the need for reorganization has not been effectively presented to the public or to the legislature. For example, many persons have advocated sweeping reorganization as a plan to save money but have been unconvincing with explanations of just how savings could be achieved. Additionally, past efforts have not always taken note of the experiences in other states which indicate the disadvantages of trying to justify reorganization on a basis of savings.

In other states, the governor is often the most effective person in presenting the case for reorganization. The high visibility of the governor's office is one reason for this, but there is a more important factor; namely that the main concern of reorganization has been to improve the executive branch of state government. Since the governor is the head of the executive branch, his leadership is vital to a successful reorganization effort. The history of reorganization efforts in Mississippi, particularly those of 1950 and 1970, indicates that the best time to push for reorganization is during the governor's so called honeymoon period. Unfortunately, the governors in office in 1950 and 1970 had passed that period in their respective terms before the reorganization reports and the recommendations they requested were available.

As indicated by the studies of 1932, 1950 and 1970, reorganization is often discussed and usually proposed in Mississippi as a one-time major change in the structure of state government. Such proposals have been made about every 20 years beginning in 1932. More frequent analyses and adjustments, however, are needed in order to have an effectively managed organization. Many of the difficulties experienced in dealing with reorganization could be overcome if some mechanism were set up through a state agency or institution to make the effective organization and management of state government a matter of continuous concern. The purpose would be to gather, analyze, and dispense information bearing on the organization and or reorganization of state government and to stimulate, coordinate and perhaps assist with activities related to the change or improvement in the organization of state government.

The history of reorganization in Mississippi leaves little room to debate the need for such a mechanism or activity or to question the advisability of allocating state funds to support it. Reserving one penny out of every $100 budgeted for state government operations (or $1 out of every $10,000) would provide a modest amount of money with which to provide the necessary service. Relatively speaking the investment would be insignificant when compared to the total state budget. And, in terms of effectiveness, if it took the office 10 years to effect efficiencies or savings equivalent to only 1% of the total annual state budget, i.e., one-tenth of one percent a year for 10 years, this would be enough to support the office for 100 years.

While the operations of such an office would be strictly on a professional basis, the decision to allocate state resources to fund the work would be a political one. It is safe to conclude, however, that such an idea, as has practically every other proposal related to reorganization in the last 50 years, will generate opposition. The exceptions (proposals that do not generate opposition) seem to be on the occasions when the reform proposal is offered to remedy a situation that has developed into a crisis. Opposition to reform proposals in crisis situations is at a minimum because when a crisis occurs the goals and objectives of the reform proposal become clear. Advocates of change can more easily focus the necessary attention on the problem (crisis) and gain acceptance for the proposals offered to alleviate the problem. The public, opinion leaders, decision-makers and others concerned understand the problem and more readily express commitment to a plan to produce a speedy solution. A case in point is the reform produced by the Bankers Trust crisis.

Reform proposals advanced in the absence of crisis situations require the same amount of commitment. Unfortunately, in the absence of crisis, considerably more effort is required to adequately define the problem and to state with credibility the goals and objectives of the proposed reforms. This is not an easy task, but neither is it impossible. If we might venture a prediction based on the history of state government reorganization efforts over the past 50 years it would be that the degree of accomplishment of any person thrust into a leadership role based on his advocacy of reorganization will be correlated to his personal commitment to the issue. His greatest chance for success will come when he is able to assess his efforts as did Mike Conner in 1934. For the "truth of the record," Governor Conner said, "the responsibility for the disastrous results of indifference and delay will not rest upon my shoulders. I have done all that is within my province and power to do. My conscience is clear."

The issue of state government reorganization is a multifaceted and complicated one, however, and, as indicated in the case of Mike Conner, an individual leader committed to reform provides no assurance that reform will result from his efforts. Adverse public reaction has killed reorganization proposals that were inappropriate along with proposals that had merit. Another important dimension to the issue, therefore, is the involvement of the public. Public support, including press support, does not just happen; rather, much effort must go into its planning and development. Meritorious reform proposals advanced by dedicated leaders will have better chances for success as public awareness and understanding of the problem and possible solutions increases. Similarly, greater awareness will provide the basis not only for rejecting inappropriate solutions but for developing the attitude which says that "if a legitimate need for reform does in fact exist then we should modify that (unacceptable) proposal in this way in order to accomplish the desired objective."

Hopefully this book will make a small contribution toward heightening public awareness of the 50-year-old issue of state government reorganization.

Appendices

Appendix A

Appendix A

**Chi Square Tables Constructed From the Occurrence of the
Political Variables in the States With Successful
and With Unsuccessful Reorganizations Between 1917 and 1937**

Political Variable	Occurrence in States Where Reorganization Was	
	Successful	Unsuccessful
Executive Initiative	14 (14.6)	16 (15.4)
No Executive Initiative	5 (4.4)	4 (4.6)
Legislative Initiative	3 (3.9)	5 (4.1)
No Legislative Initiative	16 (15.1)	15 (15.9)
Follow-up by Governor	16 (10.2)	5 (10.8)
No Follow-up by Governor	3 (8.8)	15 (9.2)
Campaign Issue	6 (2.9)	0 (3.1)
No Campaign Issue	13 (16.1)	20 (16.9)
Executive Opposition	0 (1.5)	3 (1.5)
No Executive Opposition	19 (17.5)	17 (18.5)
Persistence of the Issue	8 (6.3)	5 (6.7)
No Persistence of the Issue	11 (12.7)	15 (13.3)
Private Support	5 (4.4)	4 (4.6)
No Private Support	14 (14.6)	16 (15.4)
Special Session	3 (2.9)	3 (3.1)
No Special Session	16 (16.1)	17 (16.9)

SOURCE: Adapted from Buck, *The Reorganization of State Governments*. Numbers in parentheses are expected frequencies.

Appendix B

The Seventy State Statutory Agencies Identified in the Brookings Study of 1932 Divided Into Functional Areas

FINANCE

State Tax Collector
State Tax Commission
State Bond Commission
State Depository Commission
State's Bond Attorney
Motor Vehicle License Tag Commission
State Board of Public Contracts
State Land Commissioner
Mississippi Rehabilitation Commission

EDUCATION

State Board of Vocational Education
State Board of Examiners
State Board of Music Examiners
Board of Trustees, State Library
State Library Commission
Board of Trustees, University of Mississippi
Board of Trustees, Mississippi Delta State Teachers' College
Board of Trustees, State Teachers' College
Board of Trustees, Mississippi School for the Blind
Board of Trustees, School for Deaf and Dumb
Board of Trustees, Department of Archives and History
Textbook Commission
High School Textbook Commission
Illiteracy Commission
Commission of Junior Colleges

AGRICULTURE

Commissioner of Agriculture and Commerce
State Plant Board
State Livestock Sanitary Board
Agricultural Service Department
State Chemist

WELFARE

Board of Trustees, Mississippi Industrial and Training School
Board of Trustees, Ellisville State School

Board of Trustees, East Mississippi State Hospital
Board of Trustees, Mississippi State Insane Hospital
Board of Trustees, Mississippi State Charity Hospital
Board of Trustees, South Mississippi Charity Hospital
Board of Trustees, Natchez Charity Hospital
Board of Trustees, Mississippi State Charity Hospital (Vicksburg)
Board of Trustees, Mattee Hersee Hospital
Jefferson Davis Memorial Home
Board of Trustees (three members) State Penitentiary
Appraising Board, State Penitentiary
State Blind Commission

CONSERVATION
State Geological Survey
State Forestry Commission
Sea Food Commission

BUSINESS REGULATION
Railroad Commission (three members)
Superintendent of Banks
Commissioner of Insurance
Insurance Commission

HEALTH
State Board of Health

PUBLIC WORKS
State Highway Commission (three members)
Capitol Commission
State Hospital Removal and Land Sale Commission
Mississippi Building Commission
Committee on Monumental Parks

PROFESSIONAL EXAMINING BOARDS
State Board of Pharmacy
State Board of Dental Examiners
State Board of Law Examiners
State Board of Public Accountancy
State Board of Embalmers
Optometry Board
Nurses Examining Board
Veterinary Examining Board
State Board of Engineers

State Board of Architecture
Board of Barber Examiners

MISCELLANEOUS
State Service Commissioner
State Board of Election Commissioners
Mississippi Athletic Commission
Mississippi Research Commission

SOURCE: Brookings Report, 443–44.

Appendix C

The Agencies of Mississippi Government Identified and Grouped into Nine Functional Fields by the 1950 Reorganization Committee

GENERAL GOVERNMENT
Attorney General
Auditor of Public Accounts
Budget Commission
Capitol Commission
Governor
Lieutenant Governor
Office of Motor Vehicle Comptroller
Secretary of State
State Board of Election Commissioners
State Board of Public Contracts
State Bond Attorney
State Bond Commission
State Bond Retirement Commission
State Building Commission
State Department of Audit and Investigation
State Depository Commission
State Land Office
State Motor Vehicle License Tag Commission
State Tax Collector
State Tax Commission
State Treasurer
Surplus Property Procurement Commission

PROTECTION TO PERSONS AND PROPERTY
Adjutant General
Board of Bar Admissions
Board of Cosmetology
Commissioner of Public Safety
Department of Bank Supervision
Department of Insurance
Factory Inspector
Public Service Commission
State Board of Architecture
State Board of Public Accountancy
State Board of Registration for Professional Engineers
State Insurance Commission
State Veterans' Affairs Board

Mississippi Employment Security Commission
Veterans' Farm and Home Board
Workmen's Compensation Commission

HIGHWAYS AND TRANSPORTATION
Mississippi Aeronautics Commission
Natchez Trace Parkway Right-of-Way Commission
State Highway Commission

CONSERVATION AND RECREATION
Board of Veterinary Examiners
Brice's Cross Roads–Tupelo Battlefield Commission
Lieu Land Commission
Lime Plant Board
Mineral Lease Commission
Mississippi Agricultural and Industrial Board
Mississippi Agricultural and Industrial Exposition Commission
Mississippi Athletic Commission
Mississippi Central Market Board
Mississippi Geological Survey
Mississippi Rural Electrification Authority
Monumental Park Commission
Sea Food Commission
State Board of Park Supervisors
State Chemist
State Department of Agriculture and Commerce
State Egg Advisory Board
State Forestry Commission
State Game and Fish Commission
State Livestock Sanitary Board
State Marketing Commission
State Oil and Gas Board
State Plant Board
State Soil Conservation Committee
War Veterans Memorial Commission

HEALTH AND SANITATION
Board of Nurses' Examiners
Mississippi Department of Public Health
State Board of Barber Examiners
State Board of Dental Examiners
State Board of Embalming
State Board of Optometry

State Board of Pharmacy
State Board of Health

HOSPITALS AND INSTITUTIONS
Beauvoir Soldiers' Home
Board of Trustees for the Deaf and Blind Institutes
Board of Trustees of Mental Institutions
Board of Trustees for State Eleemosynary Institutions
Mississippi Commission on Hospital Care
State Hospital Commission
Tuberculosis Sanitorium of Mississippi

CHARITIES AND CORRECTION
Board of Commissioners of the State Penitentiary
Board of Trustees of Mississippi Training Schools
Children's Code Commission
State Department of Public Welfare
State Parole Board

EDUCATION
Board of Trustees of State Institutions of Higher Learning
Board of Trustees of the Teachers' Retirement System
Junior College Commission
Mississippi Illiteracy Commission
Mississippi State Textbook Purchasing Board
State Board of Education
State Committee for Certifying In-Institution Training for Veterans
State Department of Education
State Historical Commission
State Medical Education Board
State Temperance Commission

LIBRARIES
Department of Archives and History
State Library Board
Mississippi Library Commission

SOURCE: Legislative Fact-Finding Committee, *Report on State Reorganization*, 2–4.

Appendix D

**The Twenty-Seven Agencies
Proposed by the 1950 Reorganization Committee
Showing the Existing Agencies Absorbed by Each**

EXECUTIVE OFFICE OF THE GOVERNOR
   Adjutant General
   Budget Commission
   Capitol Commission
   State Board of Public Contracts
   State Bond Commission
   State Bond Retirement Commission
   State Building Commission
   State Department of Audit and Investigation
   State Motor Vehicle License Tag Commission
   State Veterans Affairs Board
   Surplus Property Procurement Commission
   Veterans' Farm and Home Board

DEPARTMENT OF REVENUE
   Office of Motor Vehicle Comptroller
   State Tax Collector
   State Tax Commission

DEPARTMENT OF COMMERCE
   Department of Bank Supervision
   Department of Insurance
   Mississippi Aeronautics Commission
   Public Service Commission
   State Insurance Commission

SECRETARY OF STATE
   Board of Bar Admissions
   Mississippi Athletic Commission
   State Board of Architecture
   State Board of Public Accountancy
   State Board of Registration for Professional Engineers

DEPARTMENT OF AGRICULTURE
   Lime Plant Board
   Mississippi Agricultural and Industrial Exposition Commission
   Mississippi Central Market Board

State Chemist
State Department of Agriculture and Commerce
State Livestock Sanitary Board
State Marketing Commission
State Plant Board

DEPARTMENT OF CONSERVATION
Mississippi Geological Survey
Sea Food Commission
State Board of Park Supervisors
State Forestry Commission
State Game and Fish Commission
State Oil and Gas Board

DEPARTMENT OF HEALTH
Board of Nurses' Examiners
Board of Cosmetology
Board of Veterinary Examiners
Factory Inspector
State Board of Barber Examiners
State Board of Dental Examiners
State Board of Embalming
State Board of Health
State Board of Optometry
State Board of Pharmacy
Tuberculosis Sanitorium

DEPARTMENT OF HOSPITALS AND INSTITUTIONS
Beauvoir Soldiers' Home
Board of Trustees for the Deaf and Blind Institutions
Board of Trustees of Mental Institutions
Board of Trustees for State Eleemosynary Institutions
Mississippi Commission on Hospital Care
State Hospital Commission

DEPARTMENT OF PUBLIC WELFARE
Children's Code Commission
State Department of Public Welfare

DEPARTMENT OF CORRECTION
Board of Commissioners of the State Penitentiary
Board of Trustees of Mississippi Training Schools

174   Appendices

DEPARTMENT OF EDUCATION
  Junior College Commission
  Mississippi State Textbook Purchasing Board
  State Board of Education
  State Department of Education
  State Temperance Commission

DEPARTMENT OF LIBRARIES
  Brice's Cross Roads–Tupelo Battlefield Commission
  Department of Archives and History
  Monumental Park Commission
  State Historical Commission
  State Library Board
  Mississippi Library Commission

ATTORNEY GENERAL*
  State Bond Attorney

STATE TREASURER*
  State Depository Commission

DEPARTMENT OF PUBLIC SAFETY
  Commissioner of Public Safety*

DEPARTMENT OF HIGHWAYS
  Natchez Trace Parkway Right-of-Way Commission
  State Highway Commission*

STATE LAND OFFICE*
  Lieu Land Commission
  Mineral Lease Commission

AUDITOR OF PUBLIC ACCOUNTS*

BOARD OF TRUSTEES OF STATE INSTITUTIONS OF HIGHER LEARNING*

EMPLOYMENT SECURITY COMMISSION*

GOVERNOR*

LIEUTENANT GOVERNOR*

MISSISSIPPI AGRICULTURAL AND INDUSTRIAL BOARD*

STATE BOARD OF ELECTION COMMISSIONERS*

STATE PAROLE BOARD*

STATE SOIL CONSERVATION COMMITTEE*

WORKMEN'S COMPENSATION COMMISSION*

*Indicates agencies for which little or no change was proposed.

SOURCE: Legislative Fact-Finding Committee, *Report on State Reorganization,* 21–92.

Appendix E

List of Agencies of the Executive Branch of Government, by Category, Mississippi, January 1976

AGENCIES HEADED BY ELECTED OFFICIALS
Commissioner of Agriculture
Attorney General
State Auditor
Highway Commission
Insurance Commissioner
Land Commissioner
Lieutenant Governor
Public Service Commissioner
Secretary of State
Superintendent of Education
Supreme Court Clerk
State Treasurer

AGENCIES CONTROLLED BY THE LEGISLATURE
Budget and Accounting Commission
Building Commission[a]
Capitol Commission
Classification Commission[a]
Central Data Processing Authority
State Librarian[b]
Performance Evaluation and Expenditure Review Committees
Medicaid Commission
Tourism Study Commission
Wildlife Heritage Committee

STATE AGENCIES WITH ONE OR MORE MEMBERS APPOINTED BY THE GOVERNOR
Board of Public Accountancy
Examiner of Public Accounts
Adjutant General
Aeronautics Commission
Council on Aging
A & I Board
Board of Agricultural Aviation
Air and Water Pollution Control Commission
American Revolution Bicentennial Commission

Animal Health Board
Board of Architecture
Arts Commission
Athletic Commission
Department of Bank Supervision
Banking Board
Bar Admissions Board
Board of Barber Examiners
Blind and Deaf Schools Board
Boat and Water Safety Commission
Boiler and Pressure Vessel Safety Advisory Committee
Board of Chiropractic Examiners
Public Contractors Board
Board of Cosmetology
Crippled Children's Treatment and Training Center
Board of Dental Examiners
Economic Development Corporation
Post-Secondary Education Financial Assistance Board
Educational Finance Commission
Authority for Educational Television
Egg Marketing Board
Eleemosynary Institutions Board of Trustees
Embalming Board
Emergency Medical Services Advisory Council
Employment Security Commission
State Aid Engineer
Engineers and Land Surveyors Board of Registration
State Executioner
Forestry Commission
Game and Fish Commission
Geological, Economic, and Topographic Survey
Gettysburg Memorial Commission
Board of Health
Council of Advisors on Hearing Aid Dealers/Dispensers
Hospital Care Commission
Hospital Commission
Board of Trustees for Institutions of Higher Learning
Insurance Commission
Junior College Commission
Landscape Architecture Advisory Committee
Library Commission
Marine Conservation Commission

Marine Resources Council
Central Market Board
Marketing Council
Medical Examiner
Memorial Stadium Commission
Mental Health Board
Motor Vehicle Commission
Motor Vehicle Comptroller
Bureau of Narcotics
Advisory Committee on Nuclear Energy
Board of Nursing
Board of Nursing Home Administrators
Oil and Gas Board
Board of Optometry
Park Commission
Penitentiary Board
Pharmacy Board
Physical Therapy Board
Polygraph Examiners Board
Gulfport State Port Authority
Yellow Creek Port Authority
Probation and Parole Board
Board of Psychological Examiners
Public Employees Retirement System Board
Public Safety Commissioner
Real Estate Commission
Research and Development Center
Rural Electrification Authority
Board of Registration for Sanitarians
Small Businessman's Loan Committee
Sovereignty Commission
Soybean Promotion Board
Speech Pathology and Audiology Advisory Council
Tax Commission
Textbook Purchasing Board
Veterans' Affairs Board
Veterans' Farm and Home Board
Board of Veterinary Examiners
War Veterans Memorial Commission
Board of Water Commissioners
Board of Public Welfare
Commission on Status of Women

Workmen's Compensation Commission
Department of Youth Services

AGENCIES WITH LOCAL OR REGIONAL JURISDICTION TO WHICH THE
GOVERNOR APPOINTS ONE OR MORE MEMBERS
Air Ambulance Service Boards
Bienville Recreation District
Big Black River Basin District
Coast Coliseum Commission
Grand Gulf Military Monument Commission
Gulf Regional District
Harrison County Development Commission
Harrison County Parkway Commission
Horn Island Commission
Local Boards of Trustees for Hospitals
Advisory Committee for International Gardens
Jefferson Military Academy Historical Committee
Lower Mississippi River Basin Development District
Lower Yazoo River Basin District
Mississippi River Parkway Commission
Pat Harrison Waterway Commission
Pat Harrison Waterway District
Pearl River Basin Development District
Pearl River Industrial Commission
Pearl River Valley Water Supply District
Pine Belt Regional Airport Authority
Local Port Commissions
   Biloxi Port Commission
   Claiborne County Port Commission
   Greenville Port Commission
   Hancock County Port and Harbor Commission
   Jackson County Port Commission
   Natchez–Adams County Port Commission
   Pascagoula Port Commission
   Vicksburg Harbor and Port Commission
   Vicksburg–Warren County Port Commission
   Wilkinson County Port Commission
   Yazoo County Port Commission
Tombigbee River Valley Water Management District
Tombigbee Valley Authority
West Central Mississippi Waterway Commission
Yellow Creek Watershed Authority

INTERSTATE COMPACT AGENCIES ON WHICH THE GOVERNOR SERVES OR
TO WHICH HE MAKES APPOINTMENTS
  Southern Regional Education Board
  South Central Interstate Forest Fire Protection Compact
  Southern Growth Policies Board
  Interstate Compact on Juveniles
  Commission on Interstate Cooperation
  Gulf States Marine Fisheries Compact
  Southern Interstate Nuclear Compact
  Resources Advisory Board
  Gulf Coast Superport Development Authority
  Tennessee River Basin Water Pollution Control Compact
  Tennessee–Tombigbee Waterway Development Authority Compact

AGENCIES ESTABLISHED BY EXECUTIVE ORDER
  Mississippi Council on Children
  Governor's Committee on Children and Youth
  Coordinator of Federal–State Programs
    Criminal Justice Planning Division
    Division of Housing Coordination
    Executive Director of Education and Training
    Governor's Science and Technology Advisory Council
    Health Planning Advisory Council
    Office of Highway Safety
    Office of Human Resources
    Office of Science and Technology
  Governor's Natural Disaster Preparedness Plans and Programs Council
  Film Commission
  Executive Mansion Fine Arts Commission
  Fuel and Energy Management Commission
  Council for State Goals and Policies
  Entertainment Hall of Fame Commission
  Information and Statistics System Policy Board
  Ancillary Manpower Planning Boards
  Manpower Planning Council
  Merit System Council
  Offshore Terminal Advisory Council
  Commission on Preparation of Personnel to Serve Handicapped Citizens
  State Telecommunications Division
  Governor's Traffic Safety Advisory Committee
  Officials Traffic Safety Coordinating Commission
  Water Resources Council

EX-OFFICIO AGENCIES
Council of State Agencies on Agriculture
Bond Commission
Bond Retirement Commission
Civil Defense Council
Commission on College Accreditation
Confederate Monumental Park Commission
Credit Union Board
Depository Commission
Disability and Relief Appeals Board
State Board of Education
Election Commissioners
Fair Commission
Fire Fighters Academy Board
Hospital Reimbursement Commission
Library Board
Lieu Land Commission
Manpower Development and Training Advisory Board
Marketing Commission
Mineral Lease Commission
Plant Industry Advisory Board
Recreational Advisory Council
Savings and Loan Associations Board
Soil and Water Conservation Committee
Stonewall Jackson Memorial Board
Surplus Property Procurement Commission
Temperance Commission

OTHER AGENCIES
Department of Archives and History
Board of Bar Commissioners
State Bond Attorney
Drivers License Compact
Interstate Environmental Compact
Highway Arbitration Board
Interstate Library Compact
Mississippi Levee District Board
Interstate Oil Compact Commission
Yazoo–Mississippi Delta Board of Levee Commissioners

[a]Legislators are in the majority on these agencies by virtue of discretionary appointments made by the governor.

[b]Elected by the legislature.

Appendix F

List of Persons Interviewed

Allred, Sam S.—former member, Mississippi House of Representatives; member of the Reorganization Committee of 1950.

Arrington, Robert E.—member, Mississippi House of Representatives.

Barefield, Stone D.—member, Mississippi House of Representatives; chairman, Apportionment and Elections Committee; vice-chairman, Judiciary En Banc Committee.

Barnett, Ross R.—governor of Mississippi, 1960–64.

Bennett, Otis B.—member, Mississippi House of Representatives.

Biggs, Rachel—daughter of Governor Mike Conner. (by telephone)

Bivins, Walter—deputy executive director, Mississippi Employment Security Commission.

Black, Maurice—assistant attorney general, former member, Mississippi House of Representatives.

Bodron, Ellis—member, Mississippi Senate; vice-chairman, Highways and Highway Financing Committee.

Buckley, Wilburn—Mississippi staff assistant for United States Senator James O. Eastland.

Bullock, Charles L.—member, Mississippi House of Representatives.

Carty, Wyndell—member, Mississippi House of Representatives.

Case, George Milton—member, Mississippi House of Representatives; chairman, Pensions, Social Welfare and Public Health Committee. (by telephone)

Colmer, Donald—former member, Mississippi House of Representatives.

Conner, Dudley—relative of Governor Mike Conner.

Conner, Alma—wife of Governor Mike Conner.

Copeland, Forrest D.—former member, Mississippi Senate.

Cork, J. A.—former member, Mississippi House of Representatives.

Cossar, George Payne—member, Mississippi House of Representatives; chairman, Rules Committee.

Cox, James D., Jr.—former acting director, Mississippi Classification Commission; merit system supervisor, Mississippi Employment Security Commission.

Crook, Robert L.—member, Mississippi Senate; member, Committee on Salaries and Expenses in State Government, 1964–65; chairman, Fees and Salaries Committee. (by telephone)

Ethridge, Thomas R.—former member, Mississippi Senate; member of the Reorganization Committee of 1950. (by telephone)

Evans, Earl—former executive assistant to Governor William Waller; former member, Mississippi Senate; former director, Budget and Accounting Commission.

Ewing, Jack—former member, Mississippi House of Representatives.

Ferguson, George Robert—member, Mississippi House of Representatives.

Fleming, David—executive assistant to Governor William Waller.

Glazier, Herman—executive Assistant to Governor William Waller; former executive assistant to Governor John Bell Williams; former member, Mississippi Senate.

Graham, Mack—member, Mississippi House of Representatives; vice-chairman, Pensions, Social Welfare and Public Health Committee. (by telephone)

Hall, Stanton—former member, Mississippi Senate.

Harned, Horace, Jr.—member, Mississippi House of Representatives; chairman, Universities and Colleges Committee.

Hicks, Hervey O.—member, Mississippi House of Representatives; vice-chairman, Public Utilities Committee.

Howell, George, Jr.—former member, Mississippi House of Representatives; member of the Reorganization Committee of 1950.

Jacks, Phil—representative of International Business Machines Corporation on the Mississippi Commission on Efficiency and Economy in State Government.

Johnson, Paul B., Jr.—governor of Mississippi, 1964-68.

Jones, Rex K.—former member, Mississippi House of Representatives.

Junkin, John R.—speaker of the Mississippi House of Representatives.

Kelly, Roman—clerk of the Mississippi House of Representatives.

Kennedy, Carroll H.—member, Mississippi House of Representatives; member of the Committee on Salaries and Expenses in State Government, 1964-65.

Knight, Thomas—secretary-treasurer, Mississippi AFL-CIO Labor Council.

Ladner, Heber—secretary of state.

Livingston, Elwin B.—former member, Mississippi House of Representatives.

Livingston, Richard L.—member, Mississippi House of Representatives.

Long, Betty Jane—member, Mississippi House of Representatives; chairman, Public Buildings, Grounds and Lands Committee. (by telephone)

McCain, William D.—president, University of Southern Mississippi; former director, State Department of Archives and History.

McLemore, Richard A.—director, State Department of Archives and History.

McLeod, Clyde A.—research director, Mississippi Economic Council.

Meadows, R. B.—former member, Mississippi Senate, member of the Reorganization Committee of 1950.

Minor, W. F.—*New Orleans Times-Picayune* staff correspondent.

Mitchell, Charles B.—member, Mississippi House of Representatives.

Moss, Joe G.—member, Mississippi House of Representatives; chairman, Public Utilities Committee.

Newman, C. B.—member, Mississippi House of Representatives; chairman, Ways and Means Committee.

Pittman, Bob W.—manager, Mississippi Economic Council.

Pittman, Edwin L.—gubernatorial candidate, 1971; former member, Mississippi Senate; member of the Committee on Salaries and Expenses in State Government, 1964-65.

Pittman, James—chairman, Governmental Affairs Committee of the Mississippi Economic Council

Ramsey, Claude—president, Mississippi AFL-CIO Labor Council.

Robertson, James A., Jr.—former member, Mississippi House of Representatives.

Roebuck, Sidney T.—former member, Mississippi House of Representatives; former state highway commissioner.

Rogers, George W., Jr.—member, Mississippi House of Representatives; chairman, Education Committee.

Sewell, Charles—representative of Deposit Guaranty National Bank on the Mississippi Commission on Efficiency and Economy in State Government.

Simpson, James C.—member, Mississippi House of Representatives.

Smith, Lonnie—member, Mississippi House of Representatives; vice-chairman, Judiciary A Committee.

Smith, Lemuel A., Jr.—associate justice, Mississippi Supreme Court; former member, Mississippi House of Representatives.

Smith, Theodore—member, Mississippi Senate; chairman, Public Health and Welfare Committee.

Stephens, Edgar J., Jr.—member, Mississippi House of Representatives; chairman, Appropriations Committee.

Thigpen, J. A., Jr.—former member, Mississippi House of Representatives.

Thompson, Robert H.—former member, Mississippi Senate.

Thompson, William C.—former member, Mississippi House of Representatives.

Walley, Ben H.—former member, Mississippi House of Representatives; member of the Reorganization Committee of 1950.

White, Jesse L., Jr.—secretary of Mississippi Senate.

White, Martha—member, Mississippi House of Representatives.

Williams, John Bell—governor of Mississippi, 1968–72.

Williams, Kenneth—member, Mississippi House of Representatives; vice-chairman, Rules Committee.

Winter, William F.—lieutenant governor of Mississippi, 1972–76; former member, Mississippi House of Representatives.

Womack, David, Jr.—former member, Mississippi House of Representatives; member of the Reorganization Committee of 1950. (by letter)

Yarbrough, George M.—member, Mississippi Senate; chairman, Military Affairs Committee.

Selected Bibliography

PUBLIC REPORTS AND DOCUMENTS

Arkansas History Commission. *Annals of Arkansas*. Little Rock, Ark., 1947.
Biennial Report of the Attorney General of the State of Mississippi from July 1, 1931 to June 30, 1933.
Brookings Institution. *Report on a Survey of the Organization and Administration of State and County Government in Mississippi*. Washington, D.C.: The Institute for Government Research, 1932.
————. *Summary of the Facts, Findings and Recommendations of a Report on a Survey of the Organization and Administration of State and County Government in Mississippi*. Washington, D.C.: Brookings Institution, 1932.
Commission on Efficiency and Economy in State Government. *Report to the Governor, 1970*. Jackson, Miss.
Committee on Salaries and Expenses in State Government. *Report of the Committee on Salaries and Expenses in State Government*. (Hooker Report). Jackson, Miss., 1964–65.
General Laws of Mississippi, 1930, 1932, 1934, 1950, 1955, 1964, 1966, 1968, 1970, 1976.
General Legislative Investigating Committee. *A Report to the Mississippi State Legislature by the General Legislative Investigating Committee*. Jackson, Miss., 1950 and 1958.
Joint Committee on Salaries and Expenses. *Report of the Joint Committee on Salaries and Expenses in State Government*. Jackson, Miss., 1965.
Journal of the House of Representatives of the State of Mississippi. Jackson, Miss.: Hederman Brothers Printers, 1930, 1932, 1934, 1936, 1938, 1946, 1948, 1950, 1952, 1954, 1956, 1964, 1966, 1968, 1970, 1971, 1972, 1973.
Journal of the Senate of the State of Mississippi. Jackson, Miss.: Hederman Brothers Printers, 1930, 1932, 1934, 1936, 1938, 1946, 1948, 1950, 1952, 1954, 1956, 1964, 1966, 1968, 1970, 1971, 1972.
Legislative Fact-Finding Committee on Reorganization of State Government. *Mississippi: A Report on State Reorganization*. Jackson, Miss., 1950.
Message from President Taft to the Senate and House of Representatives on Economy and Efficiency in the Government Service. 62d Congress, 2nd Session, January 23, 1912. *Congressional Record*, XLVII, Part I, 1026.
Mississippi Code of 1972. (Annotated).
Mississippi Constitution (1890).
Mississippi Constitutional Convention, 1890. *Journal of the Proceedings of the Constitutional Convention of 1890*. Jackson, Miss.: E. L. Martin, 1890.
Mississippi Executive Department. *Executive Order No. 52*. Jackson, Miss., December 1, 1969.
Mississippi Historical Commission. *Administrative Report to the Governor*. University, Miss., 1901.
Mississippi Historical Records Survey. *State and County Boundaries of Mississippi*. Jackson, Miss., 1942.

Mississippi State Planning Commission. *Executive and Administrative Officers, Boards and Commissions in Mississippi.* Jackson, Miss., Release No. 14, August, 1937.

Ogle, David B. *Strengthening the Mississippi Legislature.* New Brunswick, New Jersey: Center for State Legislative Research and Services, Eagleton Institute for Politics, Rutgers University, 1969.

Paxton, John, ed. *Statesman's Yearbook.* London: The Macmillan Company, St. Martin's Press, 1952, 1971–72.

President's Commission on Economy and Efficiency. *Report of the Investigation of the U.S. Patent Office.* 62d Congress, 3rd Session, Document 1110, 1912.

Reorganization Committee of 1934. *Bills Prepared by Subcommittees of Reorganization Committee.*

A Report of Governor Bill Waller's First Year in Office. Jackson, Miss., 1973.

Secretary of State. *Directory of Mississippi Commissions & Boards, 1972–1976.*

———. *Official and Statistical Register,* 1949–51, 1956–60, 1968–72.

Study Committee on Constitutional Revision and Governmental Reorganization. *Report to the National Governors' Conference,* October, 1967.

U.S. Office of Government Reports. *Directory of Federal and State Departments and Agencies in Mississippi.* Little Rock, Ark., 1939.

U.S. Advisory Commission on Intergovernmental Relations. *Factors Affecting Voter Reactions to Governmental Reorganization in Metropolitan Areas.* Washington, D.C.: U.S. Government Printing Office, September, 1965.

U.S. Bureau of the Budget. *Measuring Productivity of Federal Government Organizations.* Washington, D.C.: Superintendent of Documents, 1964.

U.S. Department of Commerce, Bureau of the Census. *Fifteenth Census of the United States, 1930: Population.* Vol. III, Part 1. Washington, D.C.: U.S. Government Printing Office, 1274-80.

———. *Historical Statistics on Governmental Finances and Employment.* Washington, D.C.: U.S. Government Printing Office, 1969.

Williams, John Bell. "Message of Governor John Bell Williams to The Joint Assembly of the Mississippi State Legislature." Jackson, Miss., January 12, 1972. (mimeograph).

BOOKS

Abney, F. Glenn. *Mississippi Election Statistics, 1900–1967.* State Administration Series, No. XXV. University, Miss.: Bureau of Governmental Research, 1968.

Adrian, Charles. *State and Local Governments.* New York: McGraw-Hill, 1960.

Agger, Robert E.; Goldrich, Daniel; and Swanson, Bert E. *The Rulers and the Ruled.* New York: John Wiley and Sons, Inc., 1964.

Allen, William H. *Efficient Democracy.* New York: Dodd Mead and Company, 1912.

Almond, Gabriel, and Verba, Sidney. *The Civic Culture.* Princeton, New Jersey: Princeton University Press, 1963.

Anderson, William, and Weidner, Edward W. *State and Local Government in the United States*. New York: Henry Holt and Company, 1951.

Beckhard, Richard. *Organization Development: Strategies and Models*. Reading, Mass.: Addision Wesley Publishing Company.

Bell, James R., and Darrah, Earl L. *State Executive Reorganization*. Berkeley: Bureau of Public Administration, 1961.

Bennis, Warren G. *Changing Organizations*. New York: McGraw-Hill Book Company, Inc., 1966.

Bollens, John C. *Administrative Reorganization in the States Since 1939*. Berkeley: Bureau of Public Administration, 1947.

Bromage, Arthur W. *State Government and Administration in the United States*. New York: Harper and Brothers, 1936.

Buck, Arthur E. *The Budget and Responsible Government*. New York: Macmillan Company, 1920.

————. *The Reorganization of State Governments in the United States*. New York: Columbia University Press, 1938.

Bureau of Public Administration, University of Mississippi. *A Handbook of Mississippi State Agencies*. University, Miss., 1948.

————. *Public Administration Survey*. University, Miss., 1953.

Cooke, Morris L. *Our Cities Awake*. New York: Doubleday, Doran and Company, 1918.

Corly, Herbert. *The Promise of American Life*. New York: Macmillan Company, 1909.

Council of State Governments. *The Book of the States, 1948-49*. Vol. VII. Chicago: Council of State Governments, 1948.

————. *The Book of the States, 1950-51*. Vol. VIII. Chicago: Council of State Governments, 1950.

————. *The Book of the States, 1970-71*. Vol XVIII. Lexington, Ky.: Council of State Governments, 1970.

————. *Reorganization in the States*. Lexington, Ky.: Council of State Governments, January, 1972.

————. *Reorganizing State Government*. Chicago: Council of State Governments, 1950.

Dahl, Robert A., and Lindblom, Charles E. *Politics, Economics and Welfare*. New York: Harper and Brothers, 1953.

Deutsch, Karl M. *The Nerves of Government: Models of Political Communication and Control*. New York: Free Press, 1966.

Dewitt, Benjamin P. *The Progressive Movement*. New York: Macmillan Company, 1915.

Dolan, Paul. *The Government and Administration of Delaware*. New York: Thomas Y. Crowell Company, 1956.

————. *The Organization of State Administration in Delaware*. Baltimore: Johns Hopkins Press, 1951.

Dye, Thomas R. *Politics, Economics and the Public*. Chicago: Rand McNally and Company, 1966.

Easton, David. *A Framework for Political Analysis*. Englewood Cliffs, New Jersey: Prentice-Hall, Inc., 1965.

————. *A Systems Analysis of Political Life*. New York: John Wiley and Sons, Inc., 1965.

————. *The Political System: An Inquiry into the State of Political Science*. New York: Alfred A. Knopf, 1953.

Emerson, Harrington. *The Twelve Principles of Efficiency*. New York: John R. Dunlap, 1911.

Ethridge, William N., Jr. *Modernizing Mississippi's Constitution*. State Administration Series No. XII. University, Miss.: Bureau of Public Administration, 1949.

Etzioni, Amitai. *Complex Organizations*. New York: Holt Rinehart and Winston, 1964.

————. *Modern Organizations*. Englewood Cliffs, New Jersey: Prentice-Hall, Inc., 1964.

Fayol, Henri. *General and Industrial Management*. Translated by Constance Storrs. London: Sir Isaac Pitman and Sons, 1959.

Ferguson, George A. *Statistical Analysis in Psychology and Education*. New York: McGraw-Hill Book Company, 1966.

Fiedler, Fred E. *A Theory of Leadership Effectiveness*. New York: McGraw-Hill Book Company, 1967.

Filipetti, George. *Industrial Management in Transition*. Homewood, Ill.: Richard D. Irwin, Inc., 1953.

Friedrich, Carl J. *Constitutional Government and Democracy*. Boston: Ginn and Company, 1950.

————. *Man and His Government*. New York: McGraw-Hill Book Company, 1963.

Gantt, Fred, Jr. *The Chief Executive in Texas: A Study in Gubernatorial Leadership*. Austin: University of Texas Press, 1964.

Garner, A. W. *Governor of Mississippi*. A Supplement to James W. Garner's *Governor in the United States*. New York: American Book Company, 1915. Rev. ed., 1922.

Gore, William J. *Administrative Decision-Making: A Heuristic Model*. New York: John Wiley and Sons, Inc., 1964.

Grant, Daniel R., and Nixon, H. C. *State and Local Government in America*. Boston: Allyn and Bacon, Inc., 1963.

Graves, William Brooke. *Basic Information on the Reorganization of the Executive Branch*. Public Affairs Bulletin No. 66. Washington, D.C.: Library of Congress, Legislative Reference Service, 1949.

————. *Some Current Problems in State and Local Government*. University, Miss.: Bureau of Public Administration, 1955.

Gross, Bertram M. *Organizations and their Managing*. New York: Free Press, 1968.

Grub, Phillip D., ed. *Executive Leadership*. Wayne, Pa.: MDI Publications, 1969.

Hamilton, Alexander; Madison, James; and Jay, John. *The Federalist Papers*. New York: New American Library, 1961.

Harris, Joseph P. *Congressional Control of Administration*. Washington, D.C.: Brookings Institution, 1964.

Hawley, Willis D., and Writ, Frederick M., eds. *The Search for Community Power*. Englewood Cliffs, New Jersey: Prentice-Hall, Inc., 1968.

Heady, Ferrel. *Public Administration: A Comparative Perspective*. Englewood Cliffs, New Jersey: Prentice-Hall, Inc., 1966.

Henry, Laurin L. *Presidential Transitions*. Washington, D.C.: The Brookings Institution, 1960.

Hicks, Herbert G. *The Management of Organizations*. New York: McGraw-Hill Book Company, 1967.

Highsaw, Robert B. *Administering Mississippi's Wealth*. State Administration Series, No. IX. University, Miss.: Bureau of Public Administration, 1949.

————. *A Handbook of Elective Offices in Mississippi*. State Administration Series, No. III. University, Miss.: Bureau of Public Administration, 1947.

————. *Mississippi Wealth: A Study of the Public Administration of Natural Resources*. State Administration Series, No. II. University, Miss.: Bureau of Public Administration, 1947.

————, and Fortenberry, Charles N. *The Governor and Administration of Mississippi*. New York: Thomas Y. Crowell Company, 1954.

————, and Johnson, Edward McKenna, Jr. *Aids for Governing: An Analysis of Technical Assistance in Mississippi*. State Administration Series, No. VI. University, Miss.: Bureau of Public Administration, 1948.

————. *A Handbook of Mississippi State Agencies*. State Administration Series, No. V. University, Miss.: Bureau of Public Administration, 1948.

————. *A Handbook of Technical Service Agencies*. State Administration Series, No. VII. University, Miss.: Bureau of Public Administration, 1948.

————, and Mullican, Carl D. *The Growth of State Administration in Mississippi*. State Administration Series, No. X. University, Miss.: Bureau of Public Administration, 1950.

————. *The Units of Government in Mississippi*. State Administration Series, No. VIII. University, Miss.: Bureau of Public Administration, 1949.

Hobbs, Edward H., ed. *Yesterday's Constitution Today*. University, Miss.: Bureau of Public Administration, 1960.

Hodge, Billy J., and Johnson, Herbert J. *Management and Organizational Behavior*. New York: John Wiley and Sons, Inc., 1970.

Hodges, Luther H. *Businessman in the Statehouse*. Chapel Hill: University of North Carolina Press, 1962.

Holloway, William V., and Smith, Charles W., Jr. *Government and Politics in Alabama*. Tuscaloosa, Ala.: Weatherford Printing Company, 1941.

Homans, George C. *The Human Group*. New York: Harcourt, Brace and World, Inc., 1950.

Karl, Barry Dean. *Executive Reorganization and Reform in the New Deal*. Cambridge, Mass.: Harvard University Press, 1963.

Kast, Fremont E., and Rosenzweig, James E. *Organization and Management: A Systems Approach*. New York: McGraw Hill Book Company, 1970.

Krupp, Sherman. *Pattern in Organization Analysis*. New York: Chilton Company, 1961.

Lasswell, Harold. *Politics: Who Gets What, When, How*. New York: McGraw-Hill Book Company, 1936.

Leavitt, Harold J., ed. *The Social Science of Organizations*. Englewood Cliffs, New Jersey: Prentice-Hall, Inc., 1963.

Lepawsky, Albert. *Administration: The Art and Science of Organization and Management*. New York: Alfred A. Knopf Company, 1952.

Lipson, Leslie. *The American Governor from Figurehead to Leader*. Chicago: University of Chicago Press, 1939.

Lockhard, Duane. *The Politics of State and Local Government*. New York: Macmillan Company, 1963.

McFarland, Andrew S. *Power and Leadership in Pluralist Systems*. Stanford, Calif.: Stanford University Press, 1969.

McGregor, Douglas. *The Human Side of Enterprise*. New York: McGraw-Hill Book Company, 1960.

McKeigney, Alexander Fraser. *Mississippi Government*. Austin, Texas: Steck Company, 1959.

McLemore, Richard Aubrey; McLemore, Nannie Pitts; and Gonzales, John E. *An Outline of Mississippi History*. Hattiesburg, Miss.: Mississippi Southern College, 1958.

Macy, Jesse. *Our Government, How it Grew, What it Does and How it Does it*. Boston: Ginn Company, 1890.

Maddox, Russell, and Fuguay, Robert. *State and Local Government*. Princeton: Van Norstrand Company, 1962.

Mayo, Elton. *The Human Problems of an Industrial Civilization*. Cambridge, Mass.: Harvard University Press, 1933.

Merton, Robert K. *Social Theory and Social Structure*. Glencoe, Ill.: Free Press, 1957.

Mississippi Economic Council. *What the Reorganization Committee Found and Recommended*. Jackson, Miss.: Miss. Economic Council, 1951.

Mooney, James D. *Principles of Organization*. New York: Harper and Brothers Publishers, 1947.

Mosher, Frederick C., ed. *Governmental Reorganizations: Cases and Commentary*. New York: Bobbs-Merrill Company, Inc., 1967.

National Emergency Council. *Directory of Federal and State Departments and Agencies in Mississippi*. Jackson, Miss.: National Emergency Council, 1938.

National Municipal League. *Model State Constitution*. 6th ed. New York: National Municipal League, 1963.

Odegard, Peter H. *Political Power and Social Change*. New Brunswick, N.J.: Rutger University Press, 1966.

Palumbo, Dennis J. *Statistics in Political and Behavioral Science*. New York: Appleton-Century Crofts, 1969.

Pareto, Vilfredo. *Mind and Society*. Translated and edited by Arthur Livingston. New York: Harcourt, Brace and Company, 1935.

Pfiffner, John M., and Sherwood, Frank P. *Administrative Organization*. Englewood Cliffs, New Jersey: Prentice-Hall, Inc., 1960.

Polsby, Nelson W. *Community Power and Political Theory*. New Haven: Yale University Press, 1963.

Public Administration Survey. University, Miss.: Bureau of Public Administration, 1953.

The Pursuit of Excellence, 1964–1968. A Summary of the Administration of Governor Paul B. Johnson. Jackson, Miss., 1968.

Ransone, Coleman B., Jr. *The Office of Governor in the South*. University, Ala.: Bureau of Public Administration, 1951. Rev. ed., 1956.

Riggs, Robert E. *The Movement for Administrative Reorganization in Arizona*. Arizona Government Studies, No. IV. Tucson: The University of Arizona Press, 1964.

Robson, William A. *The Governors and the Governed*. London: George Allen and Unwin Ltd., 1964.

Rothlisberger, F. J., and Dickson, W. J. *Management and the Worker*. Cambridge, Mass.: Harvard University Press, 1939.

Scott, William G. *Organization Concepts and Analysis*. Belmont, Calif.: Dickenson Publishing Company, Inc., 1969.

————. *Organization Theory: A Behavioral Analysis for Management*. Homewood, Ill.: Richard D. Irwin, Inc., 1967.

Selznick, Phillip. *Leadership in Administration*. New York: Row, Peterson and Company, 1957.

Simon, Herbert A. *Administrative Behavior: A Study of Decision Making Process in Administrative Organization*. New York: Macmillan Company, 1957.

————; Smithburg, Donald W.; and Thompson, Victor A. *Public Administration*. New York: Alfred A. Knopf Company, 1959.

Smith, Reed M. *State Government in Transition*. Philadelphia: University of Pennsylvania Press, 1963.

Snider, Clyde F. *American State and Local Government*. New York: Appleton-Century-Crofts, Inc., 1950.

Stanley, David. *Changing Administrations*. Washington, D.C.: Brookings Institution, 1966.

Tannenbaum, Arnold S. *Social Psychology of the Work Organization*. Belmont, Calif: Wadsworth Publishing Company, 1966.

Taylor, Fredrick Winslow. *Scientific Management*. New York: Harper and Row, 1947.

Taylor's Encyclopedia of Government Officials, Federal and State. Dallas: Taylor Publishing Company, 1968.

Thompson, James D. *Organizations in Action.* New York: McGraw-Hill Book Company, 1967.

Vaughan, Donald S. *Administrative Responsibility in Alabama.* University, Miss.: University of Mississippi, 1967.

Waldo, Dwight. *The Administrative State: A Study of the Political Theory of American Public Administration.* New York: The Ronald Press Company, 1948.

Warner, W. Lloyd; Van Riper, Paul P.; and Martin, Norman H. *The American Federal Executive: A Study of the Social and Personal Characteristics of the Civilian and Military Leaders of the United States Federal Government.* New Haven: Yale University Press, 1963.

Watson, Richard C. *The Politics of Urban Change.* Public Affairs Monograph Series, No. III. Kansas City, Mo.: Community Studies, Inc., 1963.

Weber, Max. *Essays in Sociology.* Translated and edited by H. H. Gerth and C. Wright Mills. New York: A Galaxy Book, 1958.

————. *The Theory of Social and Economic Organization.* Translated by A. M. Henderson and Talcott Parsons. Glencoe, Ill.: Free Press, 1964.

Weyl, Walter E. *The New Democracy: An Essay on Certain Political and Economic Tendencies in the United States.* New York: Harper and Row, 1912.

White, Leonard D. *Trends in Public Administration.* New York: McGraw-Hill Book Company, 1933.

Whyte, William Foote. *Organizational Behavior.* Homewood, Ill.: Richard D. Irwin, Inc., 1969.

Williams, Oliver P., and Adrian, Charles R. *Four Cities.* Philadelphia: University of Pennsylvania, 1963.

Willoughby, W. F. *Principles of Public Administration.* Washington, D.C.: Brookings Institute, 1927.

Wilson, Woodrow. *Congressional Government.* New York: Meridian Books, 1956.

Yanouzas, John N., and Carzo, Rocco, Jr. *Formal Organization.* Homewood, Ill.: Richard D. Irwin, Inc., 1967.

Zeller, Belle, ed. *American State Legislatures: Report of the Committee on American Legislatures of the American Political Science Association.* New York: Thomas Y. Crowell Company, 1954.

ARTICLES

Ashcraft, Richard. "Political Theory and Political Reform: John Locke's Essay on Virginia." *Western Political Quarterly* 22 (December, 1969), 742–58.

Barnes, James F., and Hobbs, Edward H. "A Merit System for Mississippi?" *Public Administration Survey* 3 (March, 1956), 1–6.

————. "State Employees and Personnel Management." *Public Administration Survey* 3 (May, 1956), 1–6.

Bell, James R. "A Coordinator for State Agencies." *Public Administration Review* 18 (Spring, 1958), 98–101.

————. "State Government Reorganization in California." *State Government* 35 (Spring, 1962), 130–35.

Berle, Thad L., and Wickman, John E. "Gubernatorial Transition in a One-Party Setting." *Public Administration Review* 30 (January/February, 1970), 10–16.

Bone, Hugh A. "State Constitutional Revision." *State Government* (Winter, 1969), 43–49.

Bosworth, Karl A. "The Politics of Management Improvement in the States." *American Political Science Review* 48 (March, 1953), 84–99.

Boulding, Kenneth E. "General Systems Theory: The Skeleton of Science." *Management Science* 3 (April, 1956), 197–208.

Boynton, G. R. et al. "The Missing Links in Legislative Politics: Attentive Constituents." *Journal of Politics* 31 (August, 1969), 700–21.

Brams, Steven J. "Measuring the Concentration of Power in Political Systems." *American Political Science Review* 62 (June, 1968), 461–75.

Brown, David S. "The President and the Bureaus: Time for a Renewal of Relationships?" *Public Administration Review* 36 (September, 1966), 174–82.

Bryan, Gordon K., and Magruder, Augustin. "Does Mississippi Need a Hoover Commission?: An Examination of the Reorganization Problem in Mississippi." *The Social Science Council* 3 (March, 1950), 6–8.

Carzo, Rocco, Jr., and Yanouzas, John N. "Effects of Flat and Tall Organization Structure." *Administrative Science Quarterly* 14 (June, 1969), 178–91.

Coker, F. W. "Dogmas of Administrative Reform." *American Political Science Review* 16 (August, 1922), 399–411.

Conner, James E., and Morgan, Richard E. "The Governor and the Executive Establishment." *Proceedings of the Academy of Political Science* 28 (January, 1967), 381–90.

Cooke, Morris L. "Scientific Management of the Public Business." *American Political Science Review* 19 (June 1913), 481–93.

Cooper, Joseph, and Bombardier, Gary. "Presidential Leadership and Party Success." *Journal of Politics* 30 (November, 1968), 1012–27.

Crittenden, John. "Dimensions of Modernization in the American States." *American Political Science Review* 61 (December, 1967), 989–1001.

Dahl, Robert A. "Business and Politics: A Critical Appraisal of Political Science." *American Political Science Review* 53 (March, 1959), 1–34.

————. "The Science of Public Administration: Three Problems." *Public Administration Review* 7 (Winter, 1947), 1–11.

Dennison, Henry S. "The Need for the Development of Political Science Engineering." *American Political Science Review* 26 (April, 1932), 241–55.

Dimock, Marshall E. "The Objectives of Governmental Reorganization." *Public Administration Review* 11 (Autumn, 1951), 233–41.

Dodd, W. F. "State Governmental Organization, Proposed Reforms In." *American Political Science Review* 4 (1910), 243–51.

Dye, Thomas R. "Executive Power and Public Policy in the States." *Western Political Quarterly* 22 (December, 1969), 926–39.

Edwards, William H. "A Factual Summary of State Administrative Reorganization." *Southwest Social Science Quarterly* 19 (June, 1938), 53–67.

Eisenhower, Dwight D. "State Government and Liberty in America." *State Government* 37 (Summer, 1964), 138–42.

"Excerpts from Governors' Messages—1950." *State Government* 23 (March, 1950), 53–55.

Eley, Lynn W. "Executive Reorganization in Michigan." *State Government* 32 (Winter, 1959), 33–37.

Fairlie, John. "Reports on State, Local and Metropolitan Government." *American Political Science Review* 28 (April, 1933), 317–29.

Fesler, James W. "Administrative Literature and the Second Commission Reports." *American Political Science Review* 51 (March, 1957), 135–57.

French, John R., and Snyder, Richard. "Leadership and Interpersonal Power." *Studies in Social Power*. Ann Arbor: University of Michigan, 1959.

Friedman, Robert S. et al. "Administrative Agencies and the Publics They Serve." *Public Administration Review* 36 (September, 1966), 192–204.

Friedrich, Carl J. "Political Leadership and the Problem of the Charismatic Power." *Journal of Politics* 23 (February, 1961), 3–24.

Froman, Lewis A., Jr. "Some Effects of Interest Group Strength in State Politics." *American Political Science Review* 60 (December, 1966), 952–62.

Gallagher, Hubert A. "State Reorganization Surveys." *Public Administration Review* 9 (Autumn, 1949), 252–56.

Gibson, James L. "Organization Theory and the Nature of Man." *Academy of Management Journal* 9 (1966), 233–45.

Gore, Samuel K. "Why Strong Governors?" *National Municipal Review* 53 (March, 1964), 131–36.

Gulick, Luther. "Science, Values and Public Administration." *Papers on the Science of Administration*. New York: Institute of Public Administration, 1937.

Highsaw, Robert B. "Government Units in Mississippi Decline." *Public Administration Survey* 2 (November, 1954), 1–4.

———. "Southern Governor—Challenge to the Strong Executive Theme." *Public Administration Review* 19 (Winter, 1959), 7–11.

Holden, Matthew, Jr. "Imperialism in Bureaucracy." *American Political Science Review* 60 (December, 1966), 943–51.

House, Robert J. "A Path Goal Theory of Leadership Effectiveness." *Administrative Science Quarterly* 16 (September, 1971), 321–39.

Howell, George W. "Yesterday's Constitution Today—Still." *Public Administration Survey* 18 (May, 1971), 1–8.

Huckshorn, Robert J. "Decision-Making Stimuli in the State Legislative Process." *Western Political Quarterly* 18 (March, 1965), 164–85.

Hyneman, Charles S. "Administrative Reorganization: An Adventure into Science and Theology." *The Journal of Politics* 1 (February, 1939), 62–75.

Kammerer, Herbert. "Organization Theory and Political Theory." *American Political Science Review* 58 (March, 1964), 5–14.

Kaplan, Morton A. "Systems Theory and Political Science." *Social Research* 35 (Spring, 1968), 30–47.

Kaufman, Herbert. "Politics and Policies." *State and Local Governments.* Englewood Cliffs, N.J.: Prentice-Hall, Inc., 1963.

Klepak, Daniel. "Organizing for Effective Centralized Purchasing." *State Government* 35 (Summer, 1962), 176–81.

Levy, Frank, and Truman, Edwin M. "Toward a Rational Theory of Decentralization: Another View." *American Political Science Review* 65 (March, 1971), 172–79.

Lineberry, Robert L., and Fowler, Edmund P. "Reformism and Public Policies in American Cities." *American Political Science Review* 61 (September, 1967), 701–16.

Longley, Lawrence D. "Interest Group Interaction in a Legislative System." *Journal of Politics* 29 (August, 1967), 637–58.

McKinley, Charles. "Some Principles of Organization." *Public Administration Review* 12 (Summer, 1952), 157–65.

Mann, Dean E. "The Selection of Federal Political Executives." *American Political Science Review* 58 (March, 1964), 81–99.

Martin, Roscoe C. "Alabama's Administrative Reorganization of 1939." *Journal of Politics* 2 (November, 1940), 436–47.

Meyer, Marshall W. "The Two Authority Structures of Bureaucratic Organization." *Administrative Science Quarterly* 13 (September, 1968), 211–28.

Mohr, Lawrence B. "Determinants of Innovation in Organizations." *American Political Science Review* 63 (March, 1969), 111–26.

Moneypenny, Phillip. "The Changing Position of the Department Head in State Government." *State Government* 24 (April, 1951), 112–14.

Moore, Frank C. "New York State's New Office for Local Government." *State Government* 33 (Autumn, 1960), 227–32.

Monrey, Roy D. "The Executive Veto in Arizona: Its Use and Limitations." *Western Political Quarterly* 19 (September, 1966), 504–15.

Musicus, Milton. "Reappraising Reorganization." *Public Administration Review* 24 (June, 1964), 107–12.

Nedd, Albert N. B. "The Simultaneous Effect of Several Variables on Attitudes Toward Change." *Administrative Science Quarterly* 16 (September, 1971), 258–70.

Nusbaum, Joe E. "State Departments of Administration." *State Government* 35 (Spring, 1962), 124–29.

Olson, David J. "Citizen Grievance Letters as a Gubernatorial Control Device in Wisconsin." *Journal of Politics* 31 (August, 1969), 741–55.

"Organization and Operation of State Government." *State Government* 42 (Winter, 1969), 75–77.

"Organization and Reorganization of State Governments." *State Government* 23 (August, 1950), 178–79.

Ostrum, Vincent et al. "The Organization of Government in Metropolitan Areas: A Theoretical Inquiry." *American Political Science Review* 55 (December, 1961), 831–42.

Pearson, Norman M. "Fayolism as a Necessary Complement of Taylorism." *American Political Science Review* 39 (February, 1945), 68–80.

Presthus, Robert V. "Authority in Organizations." *Public Administration Review* 20 (Spring, 1960), 86–91.

Ransome, Coleman B. "Political Leadership in the Governor's Office." *Journal of Politics* 26 (November, 1964), 197–220.

Rich, Bennett M. "Administrative Reorganization in New Jersey." *Public Administration Review* 13 (Summer, 1952), 251–57.

Rourke, Francis E. "The Politics of Administrative Organization: A Case History." *Journal of Politics* 19 (August, 1957), 461–78.

Saxberg, Knowles, and Saxberg, Borje O. "Human Relations and the Nature of Man." *Harvard Business Review* (March–April, 1967), 22–48.

Schultz, Fred. "Legislative Modernization—The Florida Experiment." *State Government* 42 (Autumn, 1969), 256–59.

Scott, Thomas M. "Metropolitan Governmental Reorganization Proposals." *Western Political Quarterly* 21 (June, 1968), 252–61.

Sharkansky, Ira. "Regional Patterns in the Expenditures of American States." *Western Political Quarterly* 20 (December, 1967), 955–71.

Shipman, George A. "The Policy Process." *Western Political Quarterly* 12 (June, 1959), 535–47.

Simmons, Robert H. "American State Executive Studies: A Suggested New Departure." *Western Political Quarterly,* 18 (December, 1964), 777–83.

———. "American State Executive Systems: An Heuristic Model." *Western Political Quarterly* 18 (March, 1965), 19–26.

———. "The Washington State Plural Executive: An Initial Effort in Interaction Analysis." *Western Political Quarterly* 18 (June, 1965), 363–81.

Simon, Herbert A. "The Proverbs of Administration." *Public Administration Review* 6 (Winter, 1946), 53–67.

Somers, Herman Miles. "The Federal Bureaucracy and the Change of Administration." *American Political Science Review* 48 (March, 1954), 131–51.

Spicer, George W. "The Short Ballot Safe in Virginia." *National Municipal Review* 21 (September, 1932), 550–53.

"State Reorganization Studies." *State Government* 23 (September, 1950), 200–203.

Stein, Harold, ed. "The Transfer of the Children's Bureau." *Public Administration and Policy Development.* New York, 1952.

Stevenson, Adlai. "Reorganization from the State Point of View." *Public Administration Review* 10 (Winter, 1950), 1–6.

Storing, Herbert J. "Leonard D. White and the Study of Public Administration." *Public Administration Review* 25 (March, 1965), 38–51.

Suojanen, Waino W. "The Span of Control—Fact or Fable?" *Advanced Management* 20 (November, 1955), 5–13.

"The Impossible Job that has to be Done." *Public Administration Survey* 8 (July, 1961), 1–8.

Urwick, L. F. "Organization and Theories about the Nature of Man." *Academy of Management Journal* 10 (1967), 9–15.

Urwick, Luther. "Organization as a Technical Problem." *Papers on the Science of Administration.* New York: Institute of Public Administration, 1937.

———. "Public Administration and Business Management." *Public Administration Review* 17 (Spring, 1957), 77–82.

———. "The Manager's Span-of-Control." *Harvard Business Review* 34 (May–June, 1956), 39.

———. "The Span-of-Control—Some Facts About Fables." *Advanced Management* 21 (November, 1956), 5.

Vaughan, Donald S. "Administrative Reorganization Procedures." *Public Administration Survey* 18 (January, 1971), 1–4.

———. "Departmental Developments in Mississippi Government." *Public Administration Survey* 7 (March, 1960), 1–4.

Walker, Harvey. "The Role of the Legislature in Government." *State Government* 32 (Spring, 1960), 96–102.

Walker, Jack L. "The Diffusion of Innovations Among the American States." *American Political Science Review* 43 (March, 1969), 880–99.

Washington, George. Letter to Catherine Graham, January 9, 1790. *The Writings of George Washington.* Edited by John C. Fitzpatrick. Vol. XXX. Washington, D.C.: U.S. Government Printing Office, 1931–44.

Wiggins, Charles W. "The Politics of County Government Reform: A Case Study." *Western Political Quarterly* 21 (March, 1968), 78–85.

Wilber, Leon A. "Mississippi Governmental Development, 1945–63." *Southern Quarterly* 2 (October, 1963), 1–17; 2 (January, 1964), 91–110.

———. "The Governmental Structure of Mississippi: Its Strengths and Weaknesses." *Southern Quarterly* 6 (October, 1967), 65–94.

Wildavsky, Aaron. "The Political Economy of Efficiency: Cost Benefit Analysis, Systems Analysis and Program Budgeting." *Public Administration Review* 26 (December, 1966), 292–310.

Willbern, York. "Administration in State Governments." *The Forty-eight States: Their Tasks as Policy Makers and Administrators.* New York: The American Assembly, 1955.

Woodruff, Clinton Rogers. "The Complexity of American Governmental Methods."
    Political Science Quarterly 15 (1900), 26–272.
Wright, Deil S. "Executive Leadership in State Administration." *Midwest Journal of
    Political Science* 11 (February, 1967), 1–26.
Wyner, Alan J. "Gubernatorial Relations with Legislators and Administrators." *State
    Government* 41 (Summer, 1968), 199–203.
————. "Staffing the Governor's Office. *Public Administration Review* 30
    (January–February, 1970), 17–24.
Young, J. S. "Administrative Reorganization in Minnesota." *American Political
    Science Review* 9 (1915), 273–86.

NEWSPAPERS

Biloxi Daily Herald (Biloxi, Mississippi), January 28, 1976
Bolivar Commercial (Cleveland, Mississippi), February 6, 1976
Clarion-Ledger (Jackson, Mississippi), 1950, 1951, 1957, 1971, 1972, 1973, 1974,
    1975, 1976, 1977.
Commercial Appeal (Memphis, Tennessee), 1934, 1935, 1951, 1971, 1972, 1974,
    1975, 1976.
Commercial Dispatch (Columbus, Mississippi), 1975, 1976.
Commonwealth (Greenwood, Mississippi), 1975, 1976.
Daily Clarion-Ledger (Jackson, Mississippi), 1930, 1931, 1932, 1933, 1934.
Daily Herald (Gulfport, Mississippi), July 1, 1975.
Daily Journal (Tupelo, Mississippi), 1972, 1976.
Daily Leader (Brookhaven, Mississippi), July 14, 1976.
Delta Democrat Times (Greenville, Mississippi), December 12, 1976.
The Hattiesburg American (Hattiesburg, Mississippi), 1933, 1971, 1975, 1976.
Jackson Daily News (Jackson, Mississippi), 1932, 1933, 1934, 1950, 1971, 1972,
    1973, 1974, 1975, 1976.
Kosciusko Star Herald (Kosciusko, Mississippi), September 21, 1950.
Laurel Leader Call (Laurel, Mississippi), 1976.
Meridian Star (Meridian, Mississippi), October 24, 1976.
Mississippi Press (Pascagoula, Mississippi), 1974, 1975.
Natchez Democrat (Natchez, Mississippi), 1976.
The New Orleans Times-Picayune (New Orleans, Louisiana), 1950, 1971, 1972,
    1973, 1974, 1975.
Pascagoula Chronicle Star (Pascagoula, Mississippi), March 18, 1932.
Reporter (Jackson, Mississippi), 1976.
Simpson County News (Mendenhall, Mississippi), February 12, 1976
South Mississippi Sun (Biloxi, Mississippi), 1973, 1975, 1976.
Treaster, Joseph B. "States Widen Governor's Role in Effort to Benefit Taxpayers."
    New York Times, January 25, 1970, p. 49.

UNPUBLISHED MATERIALS

Batson, Robert J. ''Measuring the Effectiveness of Personnel Management in State and Local Government.'' Ph.D. dissertation, University of Chicago, 1963.

Council of State Governments. ''Summary: Conference on State Government Reorganization, 1949.'' Chicago, 1949.

Ethridge, Thomas Ramage. ''State Administrative Reorganization in Mississippi.'' Masters thesis, University of Mississippi, 1951.

Herson, Lawrence J. R. ''Administrative Reorganization and the 1917 Reform in Illinois: A Study in Scientific Demonstration.'' Ph.D. dissertation, Yale University, 1955.

Klingaman, Murray O. ''Administrative Reorganization in New York State Government: A Study of the Temporary State Commission on Coordination of State Activities.'' Ph.D. dissertation, New York University, 1967.

Mattos, Alexandre Morgado. ''The Patterns of Public Administrative Reorganization in the United States, 1945–55.'' Ph.D. dissertation, University of Southern California, 1962.

Sprengel, Donald P. ''Legislative Perceptions of Gubernatorial Power in North Carolina.'' Ph.D. dissertation, University of North Carolina, 1966.

Thomas, William C., Jr. ''The Politics of Bureaucracy: Ninety-one New York City Bureau Chiefs.'' Ph.D. dissertation, Colorado University, 1962.

Wallace, Frank. ''A History of the Conner Administration.'' Masters thesis, Mississippi College, 1959.

Index

Department, 55, 57, 60; opposition to by Lt.
  Gov. Murphree, 50–52
—Constitutional revision, 5, 6, 9, 16
—Continuing process, 162
—County government: 42, 52, 54, 55; role of
  in, 51
—Economy motive in, 16, 21, 24, 54, 85, 89,
  109, 128, 129, 150, 151
—Election year, 82, 83, 111, 112
—Executive order, 22
—Face Finding Committee, 64–68, 70–73,
  75, 77, 78, 80–88, 90, 92, 100
—Federal government's, 3, 4, 15, 62
—First successful, 45
—Georgia's, 6, 22, 37, 122, 123
—Highway Department, 45–47, 131, 132
—Idaho's, 6
—Illinois', 5
—Importance of, 27, 28, 119, 122
—Importance of expert advice in, 129
—Issue, persistence of, 6, 9, 11, 15
—Job security of employees in, 84–85, 125,
  130, 131, 150
—Leadership as Element of, 145–47, 149,
  151, 152, 163
—Legislature's: 98, 99; opposition to, 7; role
  in, 5, 6, 16, 27, 60, 98, 111, 112
—Massachusetts', 6, 22
—Maryland's, 6
—Media, role of in, 26, 41, 60, 77, 80, 110,
  148
—Minnesota's, 6
—Movement: 3, 4, 21; Phase I, 4, 15; Phase
  II, 15–20; Phase III, 20–23
—New York's, 7–9, 37
—Opposition to: in 1930, pp. 55–57, 60; in
  1950, pp. 85–87
—Oregon's, 8, 9
—Piecemeal, 37, 44–49, 88, 127, 128
—Plan's: Mike Conner's, 36–38, 44, 49–54;
  Fielding Wright's, 63, 64; John Bell
  Williams', 109; William Waller's, 114–17
—Planning in, 149, 150
—Principles of, 4, 30, 31, 72, 105, 106, 120
—Proposals: in 1932, pp. 31–35; in 1950, pp.
  73–77; in 1970, pp. 100–107
—Public interest in, 10, 122, 124
—Public Safety, Department of, 90, 114, 115
—Public support, role of in, 7, 9, 11, 15, 37,
  88, 114, 134, 146, 150
—Reports: of 1970, pp. 107, 111; of 1930, pp.
  27–35; of 1950, pp. 80–83, 86, 89, 90, 93,
  159

—Revenue system, 27, 28, 35
—Savings from, 30, 37, 55, 81, 93, 94, 95,
  115, 116, 120, 121, 126, 128, 129, 131,
  132, 151, 161
—Strategy, 6, 10, 15, 18–20, 23, 109, 149,
  150
—Studies: in 1932, pp. 24–36; in 1950, pp.
  64–72; proposed in 1956, pp. 92; in 1964–
  65, pp. 96–97; in 1970, pp. 99–112; pro-
  posed in 1972, p. 117; proposed in 1976,
  pp. 126, 127
—Study groups, composition of, 16, 17, 42,
  65, 84, 99, 100
—Success of: 5–8, 11, 15, 16, 18, 122; factors
  contributing to, 10, 11, 18, 19, 145, 147
—Sweeping, 64, 114, 128
—Tennessee's, 7
—Umbrella method, 109–110, 133, 148
—Unsuccessful, 8–11, 15, 16, 18
—Virginia's, 8, 37
Research Commission, 24, 25, 27
Research and Development Center, 126
Revenue, Department of, proposed, 114–16
Riggs, Robert E., 18
Roads, Ferries & Bridges Committee, 47, 48
Rules Committee, House, 117
Russell, Richard, 7

Sales tax, 39–43, 48, 49
Savings and Loan Associations Board, 159,
  160
Separation of powers, 135–39, 141, 144
Sillers, Walter, 47, 56, 57, 142
Sixteenth-section lands, 152–54
Smith, Al, 7
Smith, Theodore, 135–39, 142, 143
State Employees Association of Mississippi
  (SEAM), 131
Sullivan, Charles, 113
Supervisors, county, 38, 51, 55, 60

Taxes: increase of, 36, 39, 54; sales, 39–43,
  48, 49
Temperance Committee, 46
Treaster, Joseph B., 21

University of Mississippi Bureau of Public
  Administration, 62, 63, 65

Vaughan, Donald S., 10

Waller, William, 113–22, 124, 128, 142–44,
  150–52
Ways and Means Committee, House, 39, 115